GATHERING FOR WORSHIP

GATHERING FOR WORSHIP

PATTERNS AND PRAYERS
FOR THE
COMMUNITY OF DISCIPLES

edited by
Christopher J Ellis
and
Myra Blyth
for
The Baptist Union of Great Britain

CANTERBURY
PRESS
Norwich

Published by the Canterbury Press Norwich
(a publishing imprint of Hymns Ancient & Modern Limited,
a registered charity)
St Mary's Works, St Mary's Plain,
Norwich, Norfolk, NR3 3BH

www.scm-canterburypress.co.uk

First published June 2005
Reprinted with corrections January 2007

British Library Cataloguing in Publication data

A catalogue record for this book is available
from the British Library

ISBN I 85311 625 4

Illustrations and cover design by Leigh Hurlock
Illustrations on pages 102, 103 by Mark Westbrook

Designed and typeset in Spectrum and Lithos
by Simon Kershaw at crucix www.crucix.com

Printed and bound in Great Britain by
William Clowes Ltd, Beccles, Suffolk

CONTENTS

PART ONE:
WORSHIP IN
THE COMMUNITY OF DISCIPLES

GATHERING AND SENDING

Foreword   xiii

Preface   xiv

From the Editors   xxi

Using this Book   xxii

Planning for
Dynamic Worship   4

Gathering for
Celebration:
The Lord's Supper

A Simple Pattern   14

A Story-Telling Pattern   18

An Ecumenical Pattern   22

Hungering for Justice   30

Covenant-Making   36

Re-membering and
    Reconciling   40

Table Fellowship   43

Additional Prayers   46

WALKING TOGETHER

Presenting Infants and Children

Welcoming Disciples

Covenanting Together

*Presenting, Blessing
and Dedicating*   52
Presenting and Blessing   57
Additional Material   61

Baptizing Disciples   67
*Laying on Hands
and Receiving
into the Church*   74
*Receiving Those
Recently Baptized*   78
*Receiving Members
Through Transfer*   81
Nurturing New Faith   84
*Reaffirming
Baptismal Vows*   86
*Recognizing and
Giving Thanks for
Faithful Service*   91
et

92

*Making and
Renewing Covenant*   96
*A Pattern for a Congregation
including People with
Learning Disabilities*   100
*Covenanting to Form
a New Church*   107
Affirming Fellowship   111

CALLING AND SERVING

Ministry in the
Community of Disciples

Commissioning Within
the Local Church
Commissioning Deacons, Elders
and other Workers 117

Ordaining for Ministry
Ordaining for
Accredited Ministry 121
Additional Material 131

Inducting into Ministry
Inducting a Minister 135
A Covenant Pattern
of Induction 140
Inducting During
an Ordination Service 144
Inducting
a Youth Specialist 147

Commissioning
for Wider Ministry
Commissioning for
Sector Ministry 151

Inducting a Chaplain into
a Chaplaincy Team 152
Additional Material 155
Inducting
a Regional Minister 156
Inducting a College Tutor
or Principal 160

Forming Ministers
Inducting a
Minister in Training 163

Commissioning for
Locally Recognized
Ministry
Ordaining and Inducting
a Locally Recognized
Minister 170

Commissioning for
Ministry Overseas
Commissioning
a Missionary 179

LIVING AND CARING

Entering and Celebrating
Christian Marriage

Pastoral and Legal Notes 184
First Pattern for
Christian Marriage 188
Second Pattern for
Christian Marriage 201
Blessing a Civil Marriage 210
Thanksgiving for Marriage
with the Renewal of
Marriage Vows 214
Additional Material 220

Confronting Death –
Celebrating Resurrection

Gathering and Praying
for Healing

Visiting the Sick and
Praying with Those
Near Death

First Funeral Pattern
    for a Service followed by
    an Act of Committal   *230*
Second Funeral Pattern
    for a Service of Committal
    followed by a Service
    of Thanksgiving   *240*
Pattern for the Burial or
    Scattering of Ashes   *249*
Additional Material
    For the Funeral of
        a Still-Born or
        Newly-Born Child *252*
    On the Death
        of a Child   *254*
    After Suicide   *256*
    After Sudden or
        Violent Death   *259*

A Pattern
    for a Healing Service *264*
A Pattern of Prayer
    for Healing
    in People and Places,
    in Church and World   *271*
Additional Material   *278*

Prayers at Home or
    in Hospital   *282*

PART TWO:
PRAYERS IN
THE COMMUNITY OF DISCIPLES

COMMUNITY
IN PRAYER

DISCIPLES ON THE WAY:
WORSHIP THROUGH THE YEAR

Openings: Declarations
   and Invitations   291
Openings: Prayers   297
Adoration and Praise   302
Confession   308
Assurance of Pardon   316
Lament   318
Thanksgiving   323
Intercession   327
Petition   339
Dedication and
   Commitment   341
Offering   344
Responses   345
Blessing   347

Advent 1:
   The God who Comes   351
Advent 2:
   The God who Speaks   353
Advent 3: The Forerunner   354
Advent 4: Mary's Faith   356

Baptism of Jesus: Solidarity
   and Commissioning   367
The Week of Prayer
   for Christian Unity   369

Lent: Following Jesus   371
Mothering Sunday:
   Family Life   375
Passion Sunday:
   Suffering Love   377

Christmas: Incarnation   359

New Year: New Beginnings   362

Palm Sunday: Greeting
   Jesus on the Way   380

Epiphany: Christ for
   All the Nations   363

DEVOTIONAL
PRAYERS FOR
DISCIPLES

Good Friday: The Cross   382   Trinity: The Riches of God 394   Devotional Prayers   408

ACKNOWLEDGE-
MENTS

414

Easter Day: Resurrection 384   Harvest: The Generosity
Easter: Eternal Life   387   of God   398

Ascension: The Exaltation   One World Week:
    of Christ   389   Common Humanity   401

Pentecost: Remembrance: The Healing
    The Gift of the Spirit 391   of the Nations   403

FOREWORD

Christian worship is the most momentous, the most urgent, and the most
glorious action that can take place in human life.

These words of Karl Barth encourage us to see worship as an action which is
at the heart of the Christian community. Through Christian worship we are
summoned to meet the God who gives us life, sets us free from sin, transforms us into the likeness of Christ, calls us to witness in a broken world, and
empowers us to look for the coming of the King.

In worship we gather as disciples of Jesus, we open ourselves to the
power of the Holy Spirit and we offer all that we are and might be to the God
of all hope. When we leave the place of communal worship, our eyes are
refreshed to see where God is working in the world and we are strengthened
with a new obedience to walk in the words and ways of Jesus.

Worship is the primary means of opening our lives to the presence of
God and of being renewed in the life-challenging business of following Jesus
in the world; therefore it deserves the best that we can bring as worshippers
and worship leaders. This book offers many resources to those called to such
leadership and I commend it for use in Baptist churches in the United Kingdom and indeed wherever Christians gather to worship God.

Baptists have their roots deep within the Free Church tradition and
the freedom of the Holy Spirit is a significant factor in their worship. Increasingly, many are discovering the value of written resources which can either
be read in worship for its enrichment, or used as the basis for extempore, or
locally composed, prayers. This book's predecessor, *Patterns and Prayers for Chris-*
tian Worship, introduced the concept of *patterns* of worship which can suggest
helpful ways of shaping worship without seeming to squeeze it into a rigid
structure. *Gathering for Worship* builds on these *patterns* and provides a wealth of
ideas and resources for local churches in many different situations.

We are deeply indebted to the editors of *Gathering for Worship* for their
creative partnership in producing this worship resource. Myra Blyth and
Chris Ellis are gifted worship leaders and musicians who have experienced
the renewing power of worship in local congregations and I am confident
this book will be a treasured resource for many years to come.

Gathering for Worship is published at a time when Baptists around the
world are celebrating the centenary of the Baptist World Alliance. The
apostle John in the book of Revelation was swept up in his vision to see an
international city of worshippers. He sees a multitude from every nation,
tribe, people and language group that no one could number and they are
expressing extravagant praise to God (Revelation 7.9–10).

I pray that like the apostle John, we will be 'in the Spirit on the Lord's
Day', and open to the possibility of our imaginations being refurbished as we
worship the Living Lord. May we be empowered for witness in God's mission
among all peoples everywhere – to God be all glory!

DAVID COFFEY
General Secretary of the Baptist Union of Great Britain
President of the Baptist World Alliance

WORSHIP IN THE COMMUNITY OF DISCIPLES

A PREFACE

Worship is an event and this book cannot tell you how a service should happen. It cannot dictate what prayers should be offered or even what components should be present. Free church worship is just that – free. Not in the sense that each has the liberty to do what they like, but in the sense that each has the freedom to be open to the leading of God's Spirit, both in preparing and in leading worship.

This book can, however, offer you signposts to guide you in planning and preparing. We can explain why we believe certain concerns lead us to propose various guidelines as examples of good practice. We can offer you outlines and resources to help you prepare different kinds of worship event. In turn, you can use these as printed, you can adapt them for your local situation, or you can use them as examples to help you produce your own material.

During the last century, the Baptist Union of Great Britain published a number of books with the intention of helping those who lead worship in Baptist churches. They included material for special services and those occasions when rather more formality and structure might be helpful, as well as prayers for a variety of occasions.

Now this book also seeks to support the Baptist community, and others who wish to use its resources, in leading worship in the twenty-first century. Here you will find reflections on worship and guidance in its planning, sample patterns of worship, and prayer material which has been either especially composed or drawn from the resources of the wider Christian Church. There is also an accompanying CD, which includes the text of this book, in order to assist local use.

There is already a wealth of material available to those entrusted with leading worship. Many of the sources used here will be easily recognizable to some. But this book sets out both to serve the particular needs of the Baptist community and to offer a Baptist contribution to the worshipping life of the wider Church. We believe that embodied in these worship resources you will find evidence of the distinctive characteristics of the Baptist way of being Church.

THE WORSHIP OF GOD

The gathering of a church for worship is very difficult to define because it is such a rich and multi-faceted event, but here is an attempt from a Baptist perspective:

> Christian worship is a gathering of the church in the name of Jesus
> Christ and in the power of the Holy Spirit in order to meet God,

through scripture, prayer, proclamation and sacraments and to seek God's kingdom.

This reminds us of some important truths:

- Worship is communal and its most usual form is in the gathering of a local fellowship of believers.
- In worship, Christians meet God, though the nature of that meeting will vary and include various activities.
- This encounter will be mediated through various means, such as prayer, the sacraments, the reading of scripture, preaching and singing.
- Therefore, regularly in worship, God's word will be proclaimed, the Lord's Supper celebrated and new Christians baptized.
- However, the purpose of worship is not only to meet God but to seek God's kingdom. It is not primarily for the benefit of the participants but for the sake of God's future for all creation.
- Worship is in the power of the Spirit. As we worship we participate in the Triune life of God, for the Spirit draws us through the work of Jesus Christ towards the Father. God prompts and inspires, calling and filling us, as well as receiving our worship.
- The whole event is 'in the name of Jesus' which means not only that our approach to God is made possible by his mediation but that the whole event should have the character of Christ and those worshipping will seek to be formed increasingly into his likeness.

What the statement doesn't explain is that the event of worship will include the various dynamic ways in which we relate to God. As we are gathered by God and sent into God's world, there will be praise and adoration, confession and lament, intercession and petition, dedication and blessing. Nor does it communicate that personal commitment which each worshipper is called to bring to the communal activity of the church, for outward action must be accompanied by inward intent and devotion. Worship must also be a focus of that which is always true in the life of the Church and of its members, so a way of life which lives out what is expressed in worship, rather than underlines it, will be vital. Worship is the focus of Christian lives spent in witness and service, the dedication of discipleship at work and the consecration of all we are and do to God.

WORSHIP AND THE CHURCH

The Church is most truly itself when it is assembled to worship God, and in worship it expresses something fundamental about its own nature. It demonstrates that it is a community which owns God as supreme in all things, a community which listens expectantly for God's word and which prays for and dedicates itself to serving the kingdom. It is what the New Testament calls *ecclesia* – an assembly called by God to be his people – and in worship our covenant relationship with God and with one another is most evident. This worship will be *doxological*, as we praise God, and *pastoral*, as the people of God are fed by God's word. It will be *inspired*, as the supreme expression of life lived 'in the Spirit', and it will be *missionary*, as the good news is shared, as we pray for God's world and as we dedicate ourselves to his service.

The *way* in which we are called to be church will also express itself in the worship distinctives of each community or tradition. Those concerns which are important to Baptists should therefore be evident as they gather for worship and should be rightly expressed there. Worship in Baptist churches is both ordered and free. There are recurring patterns and concerns which both link Baptists to the wider church and also demonstrate something of the nature of the Baptist community, such as its evangelical identity. At the same time, there is a freedom which enables local congregations and their leaders to plan and lead worship in ways which are best suited to their local circumstances – an appreciation of spontaneity which can enable an openness to the leading of the Holy Spirit.

CORE WORSHIP VALUES IN THE COMMUNITY OF DISCIPLES

There are no clear instructions in scripture for the leading of worship, nor is there an agreed formula for Baptist churches! However, there are a number of concerns which have always been important for Baptists in worship and the spirituality which these values represents can guide us as we seek to be both imaginative and responsive in our leading of worship. A few years ago the Baptist Union affirmed a mission statement called *Five Core Values for a Gospel People,* which stated that Christian churches were called to be prophetic, inclusive, sacrificial, missionary and worshipping communities. Similarly, we can claim that this worshipping community has five core worship values:

- attention to scripture
- a devotional relationship with God and an openness to the Holy Spirit
- an understanding of the church as community
- a concern for the kingdom of God
- the Lordship of Jesus Christ, which is an over-arching commitment that binds these other values together

Attention to scripture is evident in the important place given to preaching, as well as in the concern, early in our story, to order worship on the basis of our reading of the Bible. While the reading aloud of scripture has been important in worship, preaching has expressed a commitment to seeing the living word of God speak into people's situations and circumstances. Scripture also influences worship through theology, image and nuance, as many of the resources in this book demonstrate.

Today, we need to ask what it means for us to pay attention to scripture? How can we ensure that both preacher and congregation listen for the voice of God and how can the Bible come alive in our prayers and praises?

Devotion and an openness to the Spirit is a theme which reminds us of the concern that worship should be 'spiritual'. God seeks the worship of our hearts and, in addition, God's Spirit prompts and inspires that worship. Even the regular act of gathering into a worshipping assembly is a work of the Holy Spirit, and the Spirit continues to gather us into the life of God as we journey through the service of worship. This expresses itself in a concern for freedom, spontaneity and openness to the Spirit of God, with a widespread use of extempore prayer. It also involves the religious affections, which includes the engagement of our emotions, as we offer the whole of ourselves to God. Our response to the sacrificial and generous love of God in Jesus Christ, and our readiness to be confronted in the depth of our being by an invitation to repentance and faith, is the worship of our hearts and lives. All this places a value on our trust in and dependence upon God, as we open ourselves to the leading of the Holy Spirit.

There is a creative tension between our attending to scripture and our openness to the Spirit. This is what we might call 'worship in Spirit and in truth'. We need to worship God with our minds, but we also need to worship God with those parts of our humanity which are not purely intellectual. This concern raises challenges for those who lead worship. What is the difference between the engagement of the religious affections and emotionalism, and how can we avoid laziness or lack of order, while still being open to the Spirit? And how does God lead us through the use of written prayer and traditional worship patterns, as well as through experiment and spontaneity? These are continuing challenges.

The Church is called to be a community and the Baptist way of being church has long emphasized the importance of the local congregation and its life together. As we have seen, in one sense God is the one who gathers the congregation. Yet as that congregation assembles for worship, we also see the gathering of friends and a focus of the fellowship relationships which are expressed in witness, service and mutual care during the week. Church members' meetings should be an exploration in communal discipleship, and pastoral care should be something undertaken by the whole congregation not simply by one or two leaders.

But what does this mean in worship? It is ironic that a denomination which, from its beginnings, has espoused a belief in the 'priesthood of all believers' has tended to have worship that has been led by one person, with the outward contribution of the congregation limited to a muttered 'Amen' and some singing. How can we ensure that the congregation plays a larger part in worship together, and how can community be expressed in our worship?

Seeking the kingdom of God is a vital part of true worship because loving God involves wanting what God wants. Worship, therefore, is not only about the present but is also orientated towards God's future. However intimate our communion with God, we must seek God's will which has yet to be realized in its fullness. The church has been called 'an eschatological community', which means that it is a community with an orientation towards the future in which God will act in power. This future hope in the coming kingdom is both short-term and long-term. In the short-term, we pray that God will change things now, as we yearn for more of his saving help in a broken world. In the long-term, we celebrate that the world's destiny is to be found in Jesus Christ who was crucified for our salvation, raised in power and is now enthroned in glory.

This yearning and this hope will be expressed in a number of ways. We gather not only to meet God but to seek God's will, and the seeking of God's will is this future orientation. In our prayers we pray that *God* will act, and in doing so we place the future in God's hands. Even prayers about ourselves are prayers for God's will to be done. Indeed, our prayers should always be for God's will and God's kingdom. But God also calls *us* to act. One expression of this is the mission of the church – or rather, the mission of God in which the church participates. Just as the Spirit *gathers* the church for worship, so in that worship the community is commissioned and *sent* as we participate in the out-flowing of God's love for the world. Hunger for justice, which will result in prayers of intercession and consecrated acts of service and witness, will link worship and daily living. Evangelism, in worship, in the life of individual Christians and in the church as a whole, is a part of this concern that God's will be done – that all might come to know the love of God in Jesus Christ. The church which doesn't have this future orientation is a church without faith and without hope, living only in the present. Worship will then become a luxurious self indulgence rather than an offering to God.

So, how do we express our concern for the kingdom in our worship? How do we come to God offering our prayers in such a way that our prayers become a part of God's kingdom strategy?

GATHERING IN THE NAME OF JESUS

All these themes come together in the fundamental Christian confession, 'Jesus is Lord'. This is not only expressed in worship in the words of our prayers and our songs, not only in the substance of our readings and preaching, but in the sacraments of baptism and the Lord's Supper. For in the waters of baptism we proclaim the Lordship of Jesus Christ over our life and over the world. At the Lord's Supper we not only remember what God has done in Jesus through the cross and the resurrection, but we anticipate the coming kingdom and pray 'Come, Lord Jesus'.

The church is called to be the 'body of Christ', a community of the disciples of Jesus, and our attention to scripture, our openness in devotion, our celebration of community in the church and our future orientation towards the kingdom are all expressions of this lordship and our commitment to it. This is where the individual and the community come together. Jesus Christ is Lord of the Church, but he is also the Lord of each believer. This is why the Church is a community of disciples.

How can we find ways of expressing this Lordship? How can we do this through our reverence for scripture? How can we provide opportunities for people to offer the whole of themselves in worship and devotion to Jesus their Lord? How can we express the Lordship of Jesus Christ in our life together as local congregations and how can this be best expressed in worship? How can we have that steadfast hope, that Jesus Christ is the same yesterday, today and forever? And how can we, in a counter-cultural and faithful way, express the coming kingdom of Christ in our worship?

These questions will not be answered in a book such as this, but locally, as each congregation expresses the Lordship of Jesus Christ in its life, its witness and its worship. However, this book can help those who lead local worship to keep these concerns as important considerations in the planning and leading of worship.

SETTING WORSHIP FREE

Through the pages of this book, and the electronic resources which accompany it, the editors invite those who lead worship to enter into a partnership. This is a ministry partnership as together we seek to serve God by serving the people of God. For leadership is a service, as Jesus made clear.

Pray and plan that the words in this book might live. Whenever possible, do this in collaboration with others, so that the worship event may become a sign of community, for life in the Spirit is communal. The privilege of leading worship is a call to lead *this* people in *this* place on *this* day. Sensitivity to the needs and resources of the congregation is an important part of what the leader offers to God, and an important means through which God meets the people of God in their place and time of calling. Guidelines and patterns, examples of good practice and resources can help, but always remember that our worship is an event in time in which the eternal God is encountered. As Ezekiel saw, while bones are important, they need flesh and blood, and they are nothing without life. So adapt this material to your local context, with its needs and opportunities.

Finally, the Baptist character of this material has been clearly stated and should be evident to the reader. However, what should also be clear is that the Baptist community is part of God's wider Church and this book reflects the rich resources available from Christians of many traditions. In turn, we hope that this book will also be of service to them, an ecumenical gift as well as a Baptist resource. To God be all glory.

FROM THE EDITORS

This book is the fruit of much generosity. Many people have shared in its planning and many have contributed prayers and other worship material. Each stage has been surrounded by prayer, characterized by dialogue and marked by a sense of partnership in the gospel of Jesus Christ.

As editors, we acknowledge our responsibility for the final version of what, in some sections especially, has been a long process of creation and development. We would like, in particular, to thank the Revd Dr Paul Sheppy, who has acted as our editorial consultant; the Revd Dr Pat Took, who has chaired our consultative reference group; and Hilary Treavis, who, as Faith and Unity co-ordinator for the Baptist Union of Great Britain, has organized and enabled us through the several years of this project. Each has been a source of encouragement and support.

Our hope is that these resources will benefit all who choose to use them, whether within or beyond the Baptist community. Our prayer is that God will graciously bless all who seek to lead the community of disciples in the worship of God.

We also warmly thank those who have contributed draft material, insights and reflections:

Chris Andre Watson	Viv Lassetter
Louise Armitage	Paul Lavender
Ruth Bottoms	Paul Merton
Faith Bowers	Kathryn Morgan
David Coffey	Simon Perry
Sior Coleman	John Rackley
Mary Cotes	Wale Hudson Roberts
Michael Cleaves	Roy Searle
Jenny Few	Paul Sheppy
Derek Fraser	Hazel Sherman
Bill Gabb	John Tattersall
Paul Goodliff	Sue Thompson
Ruth Gouldbourne	Chris Voke
Bernard Green	Mark Westbrook
Jo Harding	Nigel Wright
Stephen Heap	

Acknowledgement and thanks of those who have granted permission for us to print previously published material may be found at the rear of the book.

CHRISTOPHER J ELLIS
MYRA BLYTH

USING THIS BOOK

We hope that you will find this book a helpful guide and a useful resource as you prepare for and lead worship. The CD Rom that accompanies it contains all the texts that are in the book and will enable you to adapt material, or easily print it, for local use. Please check in the acknowledgements section to see if the copyright of particular material is restricted. Where this is not the case you may freely reproduce the texts for local use.

Baptist worship is both free and structured and we recognize that many people will want to adapt and develop material for local circumstances. Indeed, some may only use this book for guidance or inspiration and will then produce their own material. That is fine. We hope the introductions will give you helpful clues to how new services may be developed, as well as guidance in the use of the patterns provided. Wherever prayers are printed, they may be used as set out or adapted. If you plan to pray in an extempore manner, then the written prayers may give you some pointers as to what might be included.

The contents pages are intentionally comprehensive. We hope they are helpful in finding particular patterns or prayers. We also hope they will help you find and adapt material from various parts of the book for use on particular occasions. For example, prayers in the Christian Year section will be relevant in various contexts, and blessings and prayers in each pattern may well have a usefulness elsewhere. Please use this book creatively, both to enrich your existing local forms of worship and to expand their horizons.

Bold type indicates that someone other than the leader may say the words. It will often be clear that this is to be the congregation and the words may be printed in a leaflet or projected on a screen. In other places, the context will make clear that the bold type refers to the response of a particular person, such as the bride or groom at a wedding or the candidate in a baptismal service. Many of the prayers which include bold type may be used in others ways. For example, more than one voice may lead a prayer, or in many cases the whole prayer may be said by one person. Again, the material is intended to help local congregations and we encourage you to make it relevant in the ways you believe best.

PART ONE

WORSHIP IN
THE COMMUNITY OF DISCIPLES

GATHERING AND SENDING

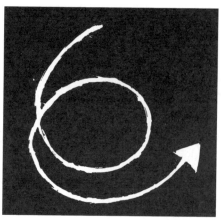

PLANNING FOR DYNAMIC WORSHIP
WORSHIP FOR EASTER PEOPLE

Christian worship has its origins in the death and resurrection of Jesus. Easter is what makes worship distinctively Christian. As followers of Jesus, we are Easter people; and our worship is always essentially an Easter celebration. This distinctive focus within Christian worship on Easter, or new life, has led Christians normally to worship on the Lord's Day, the first day of the week. The Church comes together to celebrate God's gracious activity in Christ through the cross and resurrection. In the scriptures, the first day of the week signifies the day of creation as well as the day of resurrection.

God's creating and redeeming work has been since the foundation of the world an unceasing activity. In the beginning God shaped order out of chaos and breathed life into creation. In worship God goes on graciously gathering us in, shaping order and breathing life into our lives, and sending us out as a new creation – his co-workers in the story of salvation.

GATHERING AND SENDING IN WORSHIP

Gathering and sending are not just the beginning and end of worship, any more than the north and south poles are the beginning and end of the earth. The circle of our planet is unbroken, and the circle of worship never ends.

Nor are gathering and sending separate and distinct from one another; together they express the continual movement of the Spirit in worship. As God gathers and sends us, our worship takes form and shape. It becomes a journeying into God and a journeying with God into the world. In the movement of gathering and sending worship can be seen as dynamic encounter with the Triune God. The Holy Spirit testifies to Christ as we gather around his word and sit at his table; Christ, in whom the fullness of God dwells, points us to the Father.

Baptists have always given particular attention to the idea that the church is a community which is both gathered and sent. In worship we are gathered to hear and receive the Word of God, testifying to *the Word-made-flesh* in Jesus Christ, and we are sent in mission to share him with others. This dynamic movement of God's Spirit *gathering and sending* which runs throughout the book signifies God's gracious engagement with the world always and everywhere creating and redeeming.

God gathering us

God sending us

THE FREEDOM OF THE SPIRIT

Freedom is also a key to a Baptist understanding of church and the worship of the church. In worship we listen to what the Spirit is saying (Revelation 2.7) and we taste and see that the Lord is good (Psalm 34.8). It is the risen Lord, by the indwelling and gifting of the Spirit, who gives life and freedom to the gathering people of God, enabling them to worship in Spirit and in truth (John 4.24). Where the Spirit is, there is freedom (2 Corinthians 3.16).

Our freedom is a freedom to live in God. As we are gathered, we thirst and drink from the well-spring, who is Christ; as we are sent by the Spirit, we share the living water with a thirsty world.

WORD AND TABLE

There are two places which have so influenced Christian worship that we cannot understand its shape without them: the Synagogue and the Upper Room. Word and table give distinctive shape and focus to Christian worship.

In Acts 2.42, we read that the earliest Christians *devoted themselves to the apostles' teaching and fellowship, to the breaking of bread and the prayers. Teaching, prayers* and *fellowship* characterized the worship of the Synagogue; the Upper Room was the place where *breaking bread* gained new meaning when Jesus said 'Remember me'.

Word

Table

SYNAGOGUE AND THE WORD

Synagogue worship was congregational in form with the reading and explanation of scripture, prayers and the singing of psalms. It included a responsive participation that we can know in our own worship. See, for example, Psalm 136, where the phrase *for his steadfast love endures forever* seems designed for congregational participation.

UPPER ROOM AND TABLE

Jesus, at table, blessed God for bread and wine and shared them with his friends, saying, *remember me*. The story of his actions and words became the basis of Christian worship. The story is retold many times in the New Testament (1 Corinthians 11.23–26; Mark 14.22–23; Matthew 26.26–28; Luke 2.17–20). Luke adds a second account in the story of the road to Emmaus (Luke 24.13–35), and in the Fourth Gospel the feeding of the five thousand leads into an extended meditation on being nourished by Christ (John 6.31–58).

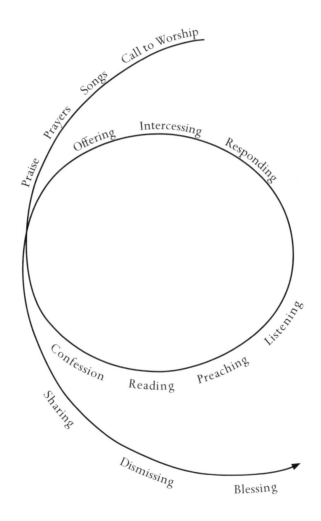

In most local congregations the pattern for weekly worship remains constant, gathering around the word or around the word and the table. This basic pattern has an inner dynamic of gathering and sending, and offers the possibility of endless variation.

In each local gathering, the shaping of worship becomes a matter of creative and prayerful preparation. As with care we weave moments of praise, intercession, confession, and proclamation around the word and at the table, we enable our worship to resonate with the traditions of the Church universal as, at the same time, we worship God in the freedom of the Spirit.

Given this potential for spontaneity and variation, this book seeks only to indicate the core shape and dynamic flow of worship from which planning may begin. As music, readings, prayers and other symbolic actions emerge in the process of preparation, so the shape will grow from a pattern on the page to the full expression of worship in the congregation. In the starter patterns suggested below, the central focus of word and table and the inner dynamic of gathering and sending are deliberately given prominence.

Historically, Baptists have not insisted on a set sequence of component parts in a service. Rather they have been concerned that the community is attentive to scripture; that is, gathers faithfully at the table and encounters Christ through the work of the Holy Spirit. They have been concerned within worship, whatever actions and media are used, that God is praised and the community is renewed, nourished and sent out in mission. The precise order in which prayers and songs and readings take place needs to serve the specific context and situation of the congregation. The diagram seeks to demonstrate that the actions/media used within worship (i.e., singing praying reading teaching) are secondary to the dynamic flow of God's Spirit gathering, transforming and sending.

PATTERN FOR WORSHIP AROUND THE WORD

WHAT ARE WE DOING?

GATHERING

As God gathers us to become the worshipping congregation, we are drawn into the presence of the holy. With Isaiah, we are lost in the vision of the greatness of God; with Isaiah's cherubim and seraphim we sing, 'Holy, holy, holy' (Isaiah 6.2–3). With Isaiah, we acknowledge our sense of being lost and our need to receive God's forgiveness and renewal. With the Psalmist, we say, 'Lord, have mercy' (Psalm 51.1). With the angels, we give thanks for the gift of Christ, 'Glory to God in the highest' (Luke 2.14), who is revealed to us in the word and at the table.

We gather around the word and we listen to the reading and proclaiming of scripture, which is a lamp for our feet (Psalm 119.105), pointing us to Christ in whom we have life (John 5.39–40). In the preaching we look for the connection of God's word with our world, so that we may discern the tasks to which God calls and sends us (cf. Isaiah 6.8).

SENDING

The call to mission begins as we affirm who God is and as we are reconciled to one another (2 Corinthians 5.20). It is the peace of Christ that drives us to seek the peace of the world. We bring the needs of the church and the world to God in prayer, and as we pray, the Spirit prays with us and through us (cf. Romans 8.26). So we are prompted to see how we must bear and do the will of God.

We pledge what we are, what we have and what we will be to God for the sake of one another and the world. We seek the blessing of God for ourselves and for all creation as we are sent out in the name of Christ.

HOW MIGHT WE DO IT?

GATHERING

With hymns and songs, reading, preaching, listening, looking and praying

we praise

we confess

we give thanks

we hear and tell the story

SENDING

In word (sung and spoken) and gesture (given and received)

we pray for peace

we offer ourselves and our lives

we go in the strength of the Spirit into God's world

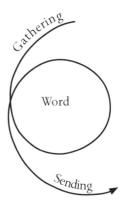

Together these elements enable us to prepare for mission. What is more important than the particular order in which hymns or songs and prayers and readings appear is that all have their place and all must work together (cf. 1 Corinthians 14.26)

PATTERN FOR WORSHIP AROUND THE TABLE

Worship around the Table always begins with worship around the Word (as outlined above). However, instead of moving to a dismissal after we have prayed for ourselves and others, we gather again — but this time around the Table. For this reason, a prayer of confession and the making of peace may call us to self-examination (1 Corinthians 11.28) as we approach the Table.

WHAT ARE WE DOING?

GATHERING

Gathering at the table is an act of remembrance; but remembrance is more than simply looking back. We remember that we are the body of Christ, divided and dismembered – yet to be re-membered as one. We remember the promised feast of the Lamb, when all those who hunger and thirst will be filled.

We gather to hear the story of Christ's death, resurrection and coming in glory. We gather to give thanks for the good work that Jesus began and that God will bring to completion (Philippians 1.6). We gather to seek the Spirit's indwelling and energy as we take our place on the road to the new heaven and earth.

SENDING

'As the Father has sent me, so I send you' (John 20.21). With these words Jesus breathes the Holy Spirit on his disciples and prepares them for mission. From the Table of the Risen Lord, we too are sent.

We remember the hungry to feed them, the oppressed to set them free, those we have forgotten but whom God never forgets.

HOW MIGHT WE DO IT?

GATHERING

With words (sung and spoken), in bread and wine (given and received)

we remember

we give thanks

we share bread and wine

In these actions we are nourished by the gifts of God for the people of God.

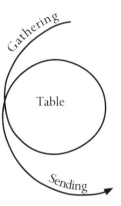

SENDING

In prayers and in hymns and songs:

we cry for justice – bread for all

we call for freedom – of mind and of heart

we seek the Spirit's presence

We have shared the feast of the Kingdom. Sent by the Spirit, we take that feast to the world.

GATHERING FOR CELEBRATION: THE LORD'S SUPPER

With bread and wine, the mystery of salvation is proclaimed through words and actions. These seven patterns offer a variety of approaches for celebrating the Lord's Supper appropriate to different settings and occasions.

Within the total flow of worship, the Lord's Supper forms the second 'act of gathering'. Having gathered around the Word, the congregation now gathers around the Table.

The first three patterns of the Lord's Supper are for general use

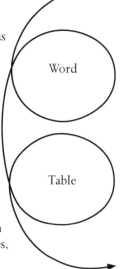

1   The **Simple Pattern** is an outline which, as well as for use in Sunday worship, can be easily adapted to various pastoral situations, such as home communions, hospital visits or retreats.

2   The **Story-Telling Pattern** follows the tradition of the early Baptists using the narrative structure of the Lord's Supper as told by Paul as the framework for the service. In this particular pattern there are opportunities for the congregation to share in the storytelling.

3   The **'Ecumenical' Pattern** draws freely upon prayers used by the Church throughout the ages, whilst maintaining a free church structure.

The next four patterns bring out more specific thematic emphases within the meal

4 **Hungering for Justice** highlights the Kingdom dimension of the Lord's Supper.

5 **Covenant-Making** celebrates the covenant between God and every believer and the covenant between believers within the community of disciples.

6 **Re-Membering and Reconciling** invites the worshippers to share in an act of dynamic re-membering:
   - re-membering the past — by recalling our liberation from Egypt;
   - re-membering the present — by bringing peace and reconciliation to broken and fragile relationships;
   - re-membering the future — by anticipating the coming Kingdom here and now.

7 **Table Fellowship** creates an intimate setting in which confession and reconciliation have a central place. True peace is costly and transformative.

THE LORD'S SUPPER: A SIMPLE PATTERN

This pattern is a short form of the Lord's Supper for use in Sunday worship, or on other occasions such as with those who are sick.

In the gathered worship of the church the Lord's Supper will be preceded by prayer, praise and the preaching of the word. On other occasions, the elements having been prepared, the minister may begin the service with an invitation, beginning with words of Scripture such as

GOSPEL WORDS

Jesus said to them, I am the bread of life.
Whoever comes to me will never be hungry,
and whoever believes in me will never be thirsty.   *John 6.35*

Listen! I am standing at the door, knocking;
if you hear my voice and open the door,
I will come in to you and eat with you, and you with me.   *Revelation 3.20*

God proves his love for us
in that while we still were sinners Christ died for us.   *Romans 5.8*

Come to me, all you that are weary and are carrying heavy burdens,
and I will give you rest.
Take my yoke upon you, and learn from me;
for I am gentle and humble in heart, and you will find rest for your souls.
For my yoke is easy, and my burden is light.
Matthew 11.28–30

INVITATION TO THE TABLE

Come to this table, not because you must but because you may,
not because you are strong, but because you are weak.
Come, not because any goodness of your own gives you a right to come,
but because you need mercy and help.
Come, because you love the Lord a little and would like to love him more.
Come, because he loved you and gave himself for you.
Come and meet the risen Christ, for we are his Body.

PRAYER

Almighty God,
to whom all hearts are open,
all desires known,
and from whom no secrets are hidden:
cleanse the thoughts of our hearts
by the inspiration of your Holy Spirit,

that we may perfectly love you,
and worthily magnify your holy name;
through Christ our Lord. **Amen.**

Fellowship news may now be shared, prayers for the church family offered and new members received.

INSTITUTION

The minister may lift, or point to, the bread and the wine when they are mentioned in the words of institution.

The apostle Paul tells us of the institution of the Lord's Supper:
For I received from the Lord
what I also handed on to you,
that the Lord Jesus on the night when he was betrayed
took a loaf of bread,
and when he had given thanks,
he broke it and said,
'This is my body that is for you. Do this in remembrance of me.'
In the same way he took the cup also, after supper, saying,
'This cup is the new covenant in my blood.
Do this, as often as you drink it, in remembrance of me.'
For as often as you eat this bread and drink the cup,
you proclaim the Lord's death until he comes.

1 Corinthians 11.23—26

THANKSGIVING

An extempore prayer of thanksgiving should be offered or a prayer such as

Loving God,
we praise and thank you
for your love shown to us in Jesus Christ.

We thank you for his life and ministry,
announcing the good news of your kingdom
and demonstrating its power
in the lifting of the downtrodden,
and the healing of the sick,
and the loving of the loveless.
We thank you for his sacrificial death upon the cross
for the redemption of the world,
and for your raising him to life again,
as a foretaste of the glory we shall share.

We give you thanks for this bread and wine,
symbols of our world
and signs of your transforming love.
Send your Holy Spirit, we pray,
that we may be renewed
into the likeness of Jesus Christ
and formed into his Body.
This we pray in his name and for his sake. **Amen.**

The Lord's Prayer may be said.

THE BREAKING OF BREAD

The bread may now be lifted and broken with the words

Jesus said, 'This is my body which is for you;
do this in memory of me'.

SHARING THE BREAD

When the minister has broken the bread and placed a portion on each plate, the bread shall be distributed with words such as

Take this in remembrance that Christ died for you and feed on him in your heart by faith with thanksgiving.

THE LIFTING OF THE CUP

The cup may now be raised in full view of the congregation with such words as

In the same way,
he took the cup after supper, and said:
'This cup is the new covenant sealed by my blood.
Whenever you drink it,
do this in memory of me.'   *1 Corinthians 11.25*

SHARING THE WINE

The wine is distributed. If individual glasses are used and the wine is retained to be drunk together, then the minister may say

Drink this and remember that Christ's blood was shed for you
and be thankful.

WORDS OF ACCLAMATION AND PRAYER

After all have received the wine and after a period of silence, sentences and prayers may be used, such as

Your death, O Lord, we commemorate.
Your resurrection we confess.
Your final coming we await.
Glory be to you, O Christ.

Father of all,
we give you thanks and praise,
that when we were still far off
you met us in your Son and brought us home.
Dying and living, he declared your love,
gave us grace, and opened the gate of glory.
May we who share Christ's body live his risen life;
we who drink his cup bring life to others;
we whom the Spirit lights give light to the world.
Keep us firm in the hope you have set before us,
so we and all your children shall be free,
and the whole earth live to praise your name;
through Christ our Lord. **Amen.**

Some may wish to include intercessions or a fellowship prayer at this point, and closing worship may follow.

THE GRACE

The grace of the Lord Jesus Christ,
the love of God
and the fellowship of the Holy Spirit
be with us all. **Amen.**

THE LORD'S SUPPER: A STORY-TELLING PATTERN

This pattern for the Lord's Supper uses the upper room narrative, as told by the Apostle Paul, as the framework for the entire meal. The opening words of Paul's narrative account remind us that this meal is not the dull repetition of a past event, but is a dynamic handing on or unfolding of a not yet completed story which is uniquely given and received in every time and place. The distinctive feature in this communion pattern which has been characteristic of the way the Lord's Supper has been celebrated by Baptists for centuries is that the meal is shared even as the story of the meal in the upper room unfolds. The sharing of bread is accompanied by a thanksgiving prayer and then later in the meal the sharing of the wine in the same way is accompanied by a prayer of thanksgiving. The words of thanksgiving and the calling upon the Holy Spirit to bless them are said by the congregation.

Following the service of the word the congregation is invited to gather around the table.

THE INVITATION

Here is the table of the Lord,
we are gathered to his supper,
a foretaste of things eternal.

Come, when you are fearful, to be made new in love.
Come, when you are doubtful, to be made strong in faith.
Come, when you are regretful, and be made whole.
Come, old and young,
there is room for all

THE PEACE

The kingdom of God is justice and peace.
Let us then pursue
the things that make for peace.

Where lies abound,
you call us to speak truth:
we will speak truth.

Where greed takes all,
you call us to act justly:
we will act justly.

Where violence consumes,
you call us to live peacefully:
we will live peacefully.

Where death mocks us,
you call us to live in Christ:
we will live in Christ.

We set aside our wisdom,
our will,
our words.
We empty our hearts
and bring nothing in our hands.
We yearn for the healing,
    the holding,
    the accepting,
    the forgiving,
which Christ alone can offer.

So may the peace of the Lord
rest within us
and remain with us
today and always. **Amen.**

The congregation may be invited to share the sign of the peace with one another, using this time for reconciling relationships and deepening fellowship.

THE STORY AND THE THANKSGIVING

The tradition
which I hand on to you,
comes from the Lord himself.

THE LOAF

For on the night of his arrest,
Jesus took bread,
gave God thanks
and then broke it,
saying,
This is my body that is for you.
Do this and remember me.

For the bread
we eat day by day:
God be blessed for ever.

For the bread of the great day
that feeds us for new life:
God be blessed for ever.

Jesus, true and living bread,
touch all our days
and fit us for your new day's dawning:
God be blessed for ever.

Nourish us with bread for the journey,
disciples in your way
this day and always.

**Come, Holy Spirit;
feed us with your love
and renew us with your life.**

We eat to remember.

As the bread is shared, prayer songs such as 'Jesus, remember me' (Taizé) may be sung.

THE CUP

In the same way,
Jesus took the cup after supper and said,
This is the cup of the new covenant in my blood.
Do this,
as often as you drink it,
and remember me.

For the wine
that makes hearts glad:
God be blessed for ever.

For the wine
that seals the covenant:
God be blessed for ever.

Jesus, true and living vine,
make hearts glad
and lives safe.
God be blessed for ever.

Enliven us with the wine of the kingdom,
this day and always.

**Come, Holy Spirit;
fill us with your love
and renew us with your life**

We drink to remember.

As the cup is shared, prayer songs such as 'Eat this bread, drink this cup' (Taizé) may be sung.

THE PROCLAMATION

As often as you eat this bread
and drink this cup,
you proclaim the Lord's death
until he comes.
**Dying you destroyed our death,
rising you restored our life:
Lord Jesus, come in glory.**

CONCLUDING PRAYERS

Loving God,
we thank you that you have nourished us at this table.
We pray for those who hunger and thirst –
may they be filled!
And may we, with them,
feast at the table of your eternal kingdom.
This we ask through Jesus Christ,
who was and is and is to come,
and who lives and reigns with you
in the unity of the Holy Spirit,
God for ever and ever. **Amen.**

Jesus said,
As the Father sent me,
So I send you:
**Come, Holy Spirit
Empower us with your love
inspire us with your life.**

THE LORD'S PRAYER

Our Father …

THE BLESSING

Go now and as you go
know this:
in grace you were created,
in mercy you have been sustained
in love you will be held for ever. **Amen.**

DISMISSAL TO SERVE

Our worship is ended:
our service begins.

THE LORD'S SUPPER: AN ECUMENICAL PATTERN

This pattern draws on prayers from the wider church, and follows a service of worship around the word – including singing, praying, the reading of scripture and the preaching of the Word. The minister may now be joined at the table by the deacons or whoever is appointed to share in the distribution of the bread and the wine.

INVITATION TO THE TABLE

Listen! I am standing at the door, knocking;
if you hear my voice and open the door,
I will come in to you and eat with you, and you with me.

Revelation 3.20

Come to this table, not because you must but because you may,
not because you are strong, but because you are weak.
Come, not because any goodness of your own gives you a right to come,
but because you need mercy and help.
Come, because you love the Lord a little and would like to love him more.
Come, because he loves you and gave himself for you.
Come and meet the risen Christ, for we are his Body.

A hymn or song may be sung.

PREPARATION

Scripture sentences such as the following may be read

'The LORD is my portion,' says my soul,
'therefore I will hope in him.'
The LORD is good to those who wait for him,
to the soul that seeks him.

Let us test and examine our ways,
and return to the LORD.
Let us lift up our hearts as well as our hands
to God in heaven.

Lamentations 3.24–25, 40–41

CONFESSION

There may follow a prayer of confession, if one has not been offered earlier, or a prayer of preparation, such as

Almighty God,
to whom all hearts are open,
all desires known,

and from whom no secrets are hidden:
cleanse the thoughts of our hearts
by the inspiration of your Holy Spirit,
that we may perfectly love you,
and worthily magnify your holy name;
through Christ our Lord. **Amen.**

THE PEACE

If not received earlier, new members may now be welcomed and received with the hand of fellowship and prayer.

At this point a pastoral prayer may be offered for the needs of the fellowship.

The minister may then invite the members of the congregation to greet one another with a sign of peace and with words such as

Either

Christ is our peace.
He has reconciled us to God in one body by the cross.

We meet in his name and share his peace.

Or

We are the Body of Christ.
In the one Spirit we were baptized into one body.

**Let us then pursue all that makes for peace
and builds up our common life.**

INSTITUTION

The minister may lift, or point to, the bread and the wine when they are mentioned in the words of institution

The apostle Paul tells us of the institution of the Lord's Supper:

For I received from the Lord
what I also handed on to you,
that the Lord Jesus on the night when he was betrayed
took a loaf of bread,
and when he had given thanks,
he broke it and said,
This is my body that is for you. Do this in remembrance of me.

In the same way he took the cup also, after supper, saying,
This cup is the new covenant in my blood.
Do this, as often as you drink it, in remembrance of me.
For as often as you eat this bread and drink the cup,
you proclaim the Lord's death until he comes.   *1 Corinthians 11.23—26*

THANKSGIVING

One of the following prayers may be offered, or extempore prayer which should include
THANKSGIVING for all God has done in creation and redemption and for bread and wine
which focus this redemption in the death and resurrection of Jesus Christ 'until he comes'. The
prayer should end with an INVOCATION, calling on the Spirit to transform and empower
God's people, as they gather and receive bread and wine, equipping them for service.

Eternal God,
we praise you
for your creation of the world
in all its richness and glory;
for your great work of redemption
in liberating the oppressed,
renewing the weary and forgiving the sinful;
for your calling of men and women to share in the work of salvation
in the story of Israel and our story.

And now we give you thanks
for Jesus Christ our Lord,
your word of love made flesh,
who shared our humanity
and revealed your grace.

Therefore with angels and archangels,
and with all the company of heaven,
we proclaim your great and glorious name,
for ever praising you and saying:

Holy, holy, holy Lord,
God of power and might,
heaven and earth are full of your glory.
Hosanna in the highest.
Blessed is he who comes in the name of the Lord.
Hosanna in the highest.

We thank you
for his lifting up of the lowly,
his healing of the broken
and his death on the cross
for the redemption of the world,
of which this bread and cup are sign and symbol.

We thank you for raising him to life
and exalting him
so that we might call him 'Lord',
and follow in his way.

We thank you for the gift of your Holy Spirit,
for the fellowship of your church,
and for all the means of grace and hope of glory.

Living God, fill us with your Spirit,
that, as we share this bread and wine,
we might feed on the body and blood of Christ
and be empowered for witness and service in your world.

Accept our prayers and thanksgiving
in the name of Jesus Christ,
the light of the world
and the life of your people. **Amen.**

Or

The Lord be with you.
And also with you.

Lift up your hearts.
We lift them to the Lord.

Let us give thanks to the Lord our God.
It is right to give our thanks and praise.

We give you thanks, God of peace and justice,
that you have made all things
to find their unity with you and in you.
For you are the life and energy of all that is
and you are making all things new.
Without you,
meaning is lost and we are estranged.
The stars and galaxies,
the waters and ocean-depths,
sing your praise.
Forest and mountain,
yes, even the desert —
all proclaim your splendour.
With all creation we join
the hymn of angels and archangels,
and all your people of every time and place
as we sing:

Holy, holy, holy Lord,
God of power and might,
heaven and earth are full of your glory.
Hosanna in the highest.
Blessed is he who comes in the name of the Lord.
Hosanna in the highest.

In you is our health and our wholeness,
the gift of the one who emptied himself.
We give you thanks for Jesus,
the wounded healer,
who by his words and deeds
brings new life to all creation.
We praise you
for his obedience even to the cross,
where he made death the gateway to glory.
We praise you that you raised him to new life
and set him on high to pray for us
and to bring all things into union with you.
At table with his friends,
he took bread and gave thanks,
he broke it and shared it with them.
'Take, eat,' he said, 'to remember me.'
And after supper,
he took the cup of wine,
he gave thanks and shared it with them.
'Drink it, all of you,' he said, 'to remember me.'
So we take these gifts of bread and wine,
give thanks, and share them.
Come, Holy Spirit;
take the things and people of earth
and make of them
signs of the peace Christ brings
by his body and blood.
So that we, feeding on him
and trusting in him alone,
may be led from death to that life
where strife and envy,
falsehood and pride are ended
in the holy communion
of your eternal kingdom.
These things we ask,
in and with and through our Saviour Jesus, the Christ,
who lives and reigns with you
in the unity of the Holy Spirit,
one God for ever and ever. **Amen.**

Holy things for holy people:
the gift and salvation of God.

The Lord's Prayer may be said here.

THE BREAKING OF BREAD

The bread may now be lifted and broken with the words

When we break the bread,
is it not a means of sharing in the body of Christ?
Because there is one loaf,
we, though many, are one body;
for it is one loaf of which we all partake.

1 Corinthians 10.16f.

Or

Jesus said, 'This is my body which is for you;
do this in memory of me.'

SHARING THE BREAD

*When the minister has broken the bread and placed a portion on each plate, the bread shall be
distributed with words such as*

Take this in remembrance that Christ died for you
and feed on him in your heart by faith with thanksgiving.

THE LIFTING OF THE CUP

The cup may now be raised in full view of the congregation with such words as

In the same way
he took the cup after supper, and said:
'This cup is the new covenant sealed by my blood.
Whenever you drink it,
do this in memory of me.'

1 Corinthians 11.25

Or

How can I repay the Lord for all his benefits to me?
I shall lift up the cup of salvation
and call on the Lord by name.
I shall pay my vows to the Lord
in the presence of all his people.

Psalm 116.12—14

SHARING THE WINE

If individual glasses are used and the wine is retained to be drunk together, then the minister, when all are ready to drink, may use one of the sentences above or

Drink this cup;
remember that Christ's blood was shed for you and be thankful.

If bread and wine are distributed together, with no words said in between, the following words may be used

Jesus is the Lamb of God
who takes away the sin of the world.
Blessed are those who are called to his supper:

Lord, I am not worthy to receive you,
but only say the word, and I shall be healed.

ACCLAMATION

After all have received the wine and after a period of silence, sentences and prayers may be used, such as

Your death, O Lord, we commemorate.
Your resurrection we confess.
Your final coming we await.
Glory be to you, O Christ.

Christ has died.
Christ is risen.
Christ will come again.

PRAYER AFTER THE COMMUNION

One of the following prayers may be used

As this bread, once scattered over the hills, was brought together and became one loaf, so, Lord, may your Church be united and brought together from the ends of the earth into your Kingdom.

Or

God of grace,
you have called us to be your disciple people
and gathered us to your table.
Here we have tasted the bread of heaven
and shared the new wine of your kingdom.

Empower us by your Spirit
that we may be a gospel people:

good news for all the world,
through Jesus Christ our Lord. **Amen.**

Or

Almighty God,
we thank you for feeding us
with the body and blood of your Son Jesus Christ.
Through him we offer you our souls and bodies
to be a living sacrifice.
Send us out
in the power of your Spirit
to live and work
to your praise and glory. **Amen.**

Intercessions or a fellowship prayer may be offered at this point.

A hymn or worship songs may be sung.

WORDS OF COMMISSIONING, DISMISSAL AND BLESSING

Love with all sincerity;
hate what is evil;
cling to what is good;
be joyful in hope,
patient in affliction,
faithful in prayer.
Bless those who persecute you;
bless and do not curse.
Rejoice with those who rejoice
and mourn with those who mourn.
Live in harmony with one another.

Do not repay anyone evil for evil.
And the blessing of God,
Father, Son, and Holy Spirit,
be with you all.   *from Romans 12.9–11*

Or

Let us go into God's world
as disciples of Jesus Christ
and messengers of the gospel.

**The grace of the Lord Jesus Christ,
the love of God
and the fellowship of the Holy Spirit
be with us all. Amen**

THE LORD'S SUPPER: HUNGERING FOR JUSTICE

This pattern highlights the Kingdom dimension to the Lord's Supper — hungering and thirsting for justice.

GATHERING SENTENCES

Gather us in,
the lost and the lonely, the broken and breaking,
the tired and the aching
who long for the nourishment found at your feast.

Gather us in,

the done and the doubting, the wishing and wondering,
the puzzled and pondering
who long for the company found at your feast.

Gather us in,

the proud and pretentious, the sure and superior,
the never inferior,
who long for the levelling found at your feast.

Gather us in,

the bright and the bustling,
the stirrers, the shakers,
the kind laughter makers
who long for the deeper joys found at your feast.

Gather us in,

from corner or limelight, from mansion or campsite,
from fears and obsession, from tears and depression,
from untold excesses, from treasured successes,
to meet, to eat, be given a seat,
be joined to the vine, be offered new wine,
become like the least, be found at the feast.

Gather us in!

INVITATION

This is the table,
not of the Church,
but of the Lord.
It is to be made ready
for those who love him and who want to love him more.

So, come,
If you have much faith
and if you have little,
if you have been here often
and if you have not been for a long time,
if you have tried to follow
and if you have failed.

Come,
not because it is I who invite you:
it is our Lord.
It is his will
that those who want him should meet him here.

A communion song may be sung here.

THE STORY

On the night on which Jesus was betrayed, he sat at supper with his disciples. While they were eating, he took a piece of bread, said a blessing, broke it, and gave it to them with the words, 'This is my body. It is for you. Do this to remember me.' Later, he took a cup of wine, saying, 'This cup is God's new covenant, sealed with my blood. Drink from it, all of you, to remember me'.

So now, following Jesus' example and command, we take this bread and this wine, the ordinary things of the world which Christ will make special. And as he said a prayer before sharing, let us do so too.

PRAYER OF THANKSGIVING

This may be said extempore or using a written prayer such as the following

Gratitude, praise, hearts lifted high,
voices full and joyful:
these you deserve.

For when we were nothing, you made us something.
When we had no name and no faith and no future,
you called us your children.
When we lost our way or turned away, you did not abandon us.
When we came back to you, your arms opened wide in welcome.

And look, you prepare a table for us
offering not just bread, not just wine, but your very self
so that we may be filled, forgiven, healed, blessed and made new again.
You are worth all our pain and all our praise.

So now, in gratitude, we join our voices
to those of the Church on earth and in heaven:

The Sanctus may be spoken or sung

**Holy, holy, holy Lord,
God of power and might.
Heaven and earth are full of your glory.
Hosanna in the highest.**

**Blessed is he who comes
in the name of the Lord.
Hosanna in the highest.**

The prayer continues

Lord God,
as we come to share the richness of your table,
we cannot forget the rawness of the earth.

We cannot take bread and forget those who are hungry.
Your world is one world and we are stewards of its nourishment.
Lord, put our prosperity
at the service of the poor.

We cannot take wine and forget those who are thirsty.
The ground and the rootless,
the earth and its weary people cry out for justice.
Lord, put our fullness
at the service of the empty.

We cannot hear your words of peace and forget the world at war
or, if not at war, then preparing for it.
Show us quickly, Lord,
how to turn weapons
into welcome signs
and the lust for power
into a desire for peace.

We cannot celebrate the feast of your family and forget our divisions.
We are one in spirit, but not in fact. History and hurt still dismember us.
Lord, heal our church
in every brokenness. **Amen.**

THE SHARING

Taking and breaking the bread

Among friends, gathered round a table, Jesus took bread, broke it and said,
'This is my body, it is for you'.

Taking the cup of wine

And later he took the cup of wine and said,
'This is the new relationship with God, made possible because of my death.
Take this – all of you – to remember me'.

Look,
here is your Lord coming to you
in bread and wine.

These are the gifts of God
for the people of God.

The bread and wine are shared according to the appropriate custom. A quiet prayer song may be sung as the elements are distributed.

THE PEACE

Christ who has nourished us, is our peace.
Strangers and friends, male and female, old and young,
he has broken down the barriers to bind us to him and to each other.

Having tasted his goodness,
let us share his peace.

The peace of the Lord be always with you.
And also with you.

The peace may be shared, giving time for participants to greet each other.

CONCLUDING PRAYER

Lord Jesus Christ,
you have put your life into our hands;
now we put our lives into yours.
Take us,
renew and remake us.
What we have been is past
what we shall be, through you,
still awaits us.

Lead us on.
Take us with you. **Amen.**

Or

Loving God,
we thank you that you have nourished us at this table.
We pray for those who hunger and thirst –
may they be filled!
And may we, with them, feast
at the table of your eternal kingdom.
This we ask through Jesus Christ,
who was and is and is to come,
and who lives and reigns with you
in the unity of the Holy Spirit,
God for ever and ever. **Amen.**

A closing song may be sung

CLOSING RESPONSES

The cross,
we shall take it;
the bread,
we shall break it;
the pain,
we shall bear it;
the joy,
we shall share it;
the gospel,
we shall live it;
the love,
we shall give it;
the light,
we shall cherish it;
the darkness,
God shall perish it.

Or

From where we are
to where you need us
Jesus now lead on.

From the security of what we know
to the adventure of what you will reveal
Jesus now lead on.

To refashion the fabric of the world
until it resembles the shape of your Kingdom
Jesus now lead on.

Because good things have been prepared
for those who love God
Jesus now lead on.

THE LORD'S SUPPER: COVENANT-MAKING

This pattern for covenant-making celebrates the eternal covenant of grace between God and humanity and also the covenant between believers within the community of disciples.

WE GATHER

God has made us a people:
we have been shaped by God's will.

Jesus calls us together:
we meet in Jesus' name.

The Spirit binds us together:
and leads us into truth.

WORDS OF INVITATION

Look, here is the Lord's Table spread as for a feast.
Bread for breaking, wine poured for drinking:
signs of his love and hospitality,
symbols of his life broken, his blood poured out.

He is not dead!
He is risen and present among us,
evidence of God's covenant grace and promise.

So we come in faith to the table, you and I,
companions on the journey.
Some of us fresh and eager,
others weary, in need of nourishment.
All of us conscious of our failings.

Words of confession and forgiveness may be offered here extempore or using prayers from Part Two of this book. At the conclusion of the prayer the words of invitation may be concluded

Come now, don't hesitate,
the feast is ready
and the Lord himself invites you.

WE COVENANT

Creating and redeeming God,
we give you thanks and praise.

Your covenant of grace
was made for our salvation
in Jesus Christ our Lord.

We come this day
to covenant with you
and with companion disciples:

to watch over each other
and to walk together before you
in ways known
and still to be made known.

Pour your Spirit upon us.
Help us so to walk in your ways
that the promises we make this day,
and the life that we live together,
may become an offering of love,
our duty and delight
truly glorifying to you –
Father Son and Holy Spirit. Amen.

This day,
we give ourselves again
to the Lord
and to each other

to be bound together in fellowship,
and to work together
in the unity of the Spirit
for the sake of God's mission.

The following may be named, as appropriate.

In our congregation,
in local partnerships,
in our association
and in the wider Union,
we commit all that we have and are
to fulfil God's purposes of love.

As a sign of covenant, we share the peace.

WE REMEMBER

It was the night of the Passover, and Jesus and his friends were sharing supper together.

While they eating he told them that one of them would betray him. They were appalled and protested saying, 'Not I Lord, I would never betray you.'

Jesus took some bread, gave thanks, broke it and gave it to them saying, 'Take this and eat. This is my body.'

He took the cup of wine and after giving thanks passed it among them, saying as they drank, 'This is my blood of the covenant. It is poured out for you and for many for the forgiveness of sins. I will not drink again until the day comes when I drink with you in my father's Kingdom.'

As the story is told (or immediately after) the person presiding breaks the bread and pours the wine.

PRAYER OF THANKSGIVING

Creating and redeeming God,
we give you thanks and praise
for your covenant of grace:
a covenant expressed
in sinful people who know forgiveness,
the weary who are refreshed,
the hungry who are nourished,
the captives who are set free
and the oppressed who experience liberation.
Thank you that you chose to make us a part of your story.

Thank you for Jesus Christ
who revealed your love in his death and resurrection
and who continues to share his life with us
through bread and wine.

Thank you for sending the Holy Spirit
who sustains us in our walk together,
helping us to watch over each other,
to pray for one another,
and to work together for justice and truth.

As we eat this bread
and drink from the cup,
(signs of hospitality and grace),
may we be empowered to serve boldly
wherever you may call.

Accept these prayers
and our heartfelt thanksgiving
in the name of Jesus Christ. **Amen.**

WE SHARE

The bread

One people, one loaf, a sign of our common faith
and testimony to the generosity of our Lord Jesus Christ.

Take this loaf, food for faith,
and feed on it with thanksgiving.

The wine

One people, one cup, a sign of the new covenant
poured out for you and for many.
It is a covenant sealed by his blood.
When we drink
we must be thankful
and agree together never to forget.

WE JOURNEY

Holy God,
we have been nourished and had our thirst quenched,
through bread broken and wine poured
in thanksgiving for your Son Jesus Christ.
Send us out to be as generous to those we meet this week,
that we might show through word and deed
that he is not dead,
but risen and present among us.

Hallelujah! Amen.

THE LORD'S SUPPER:
RE-MEMBERING AND RECONCILING

This pattern explores and celebrates the many meanings implicit in Jesus invitation: 'do this to remember me'. It highlights how the action of 're-membering' is a past, present and future tense experience. When we re-member: broken damaged and dismembered aspects of our past lives are put together again; mind and body and soul in the present tense enjoy wholeness; and helplessness in the face of the unknown future gives way to resurrection hope.

WORDS OF APPROACH

We gather at this table to celebrate Life:
the life of God in the world,

made flesh and blood in Jesus,
embodied in us.

We come to re-member
the body that was broken:

> the hands that touched the untouchable,
> healed the hurting and did no violence;

> the feet that got dusty along city streets
> and at the lake's shore;

> the arms that welcomed the stranger
> and embraced the outcast;

> the legs that entered homes and synagogues
> and danced at celebrations;

> the eyes that blazed against injustice,
> knew how to cry
> and saw the potential in everyone;

> the belly that shared table with unexpected people
> and shook with laughter;

> the lips that wove stories and painted pictures
> of a new community and a better world.

This blessèd body
that was broken, abused and rejected,
we come to re-member,
for we are called to be the body of Christ.

As you Risen Christ re-member our lives,
so we re-member you.

And not only at this table,
but in our life together
may we embody your kingdom
and re-member your life in the world.

WORDS OF THANKSGIVING

O God,
we give thanks for this bread and wine:

A timeless reminder
of the flesh-and-blood life of Jesus:
broken,
rejected,
yet unstoppable.

In Christ we see
– a life that could not be ended by death
– a purpose that could not be silenced by the forces of violence
– a desire deep within you for the transformation of the world.

As we eat the bread and drink the wine:

we thank you
for the acceptance and tenderness
with which you have transformed our shame into dignity
and loved us into life;

we thank you
for cherishing the potential in us
and for calling us to be partners
in your vision for this world.

As we eat the bread and drink the wine:

we call on your Spirit
to come alongside us, so that
together, in the company of your spirit
we may give ourselves afresh
to the task of re-membering you,
of being the body of Christ,
of living your life in this world. **Amen.**

THE SHARING

The bread is broken as these words are said

This broken bread we share
is the body of Christ.
It is a sign
of all that we live and risk together
as the community of Christ.

Let all who seek Christ take and eat.

The cup is lifted as these words are said

This cup we drink together is the wine of the kingdom of God,
the sign of God's undertaking for the life of the world.
Let all who seek Christ take and drink.

PRAYER AFTER COMMUNION

We have taken bread and wine into our bodies.
Now may these hands be the hands of Christ in the world,
may they do no violence.
May these eyes see those who are overlooked,
may these ears listen to those who are unheard,
may these voices be raised for the voiceless,
lest our songs of praise be empty.
May these feet take us where Christ leads,
and may these hearts and minds be open to your Spirit.

Christ has re-membered us,
may we re-member Christ. **Amen.**

THE LORD'S SUPPER: TABLE FELLOWSHIP

This pattern is well-suited in a domestic setting, or as part of a shared meal.

The words designated for the leader to speak may be spoken by whoever the gathering appoints. The leader's words are in ordinary type. The bold type signifies the whole company.

GREETING

Grace and peace to you from God our Father and the Lord Jesus Christ.

Selected scripture verses may be read here from Colossians 2.9–15, 3.1–4, 12–17; following which, reflections on the Scripture passage by those present may be shared.

INVITATION

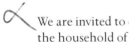 We are invited to come together around this table as those who belong to the household of Christ, brothers and sisters who in ~~our baptized~~ lives live out the death and resurrection of Jesus. The family of the reborn and the reconciled, who inhabit a universe of grace.

CONFESSION

Remembering the death and resurrection of the one who is our life and our meaning, we come first to die to all that is loveless and death dealing in our lives.

Jesus commands us to love God with all our heart and soul, mind and strength.

Silence to consider the reality of our living, after which the leader invites the company to say together these words of confession

**My brothers and sisters,
I have not kept this commandment;
forgive my godlessness and pray for me,
that God will light the fire of his love in my heart.**

Jesus commands us to love our neighbours in the same way that we love ourselves.

Silence, again to think about what we have been, after which the leader invites those present to say together the following words of confession

**I have been selfish, hard-hearted and mean spirited.
Forgive me, my friends,
and pray that God's grace
will melt and warm my heart.**

ASSURANCE OF FORGIVENESS

The Lord has promised that if we confess our sins
he is faithful and just to forgive our sins
and cleanse us from all unrighteousness.
Do you desire this grace and cleansing?
Without it there is no hope for me.

Our Lord has warned
that those who ask for forgiveness themselves
must also practise forgiveness.
Are you prepared to be generous and forgiving
to those who have hurt you and to let go of all bitterness?
I am but I will need God's help and yours.

Jesus is our peace.
He has reconciled those who were divided
through his body on the cross.
He came and preached peace to everyone, far and near,
because it is through him
that we all can come to the Father in the one Spirit.
Grace and peace to you
from God the Father and the Lord Jesus Christ.

Let us greet each other.

*A pause here allows for individual expressions of apology, conversations, prayer,
and thanksgiving.*

So as those committed to the life of grace,
we hear the story of the first Lord's supper:

Luke 22.14–27 is read.

PRAYER OF THANKSGIVING

Before Jesus broke the bread, before he poured the wine,
he gave thanks to you, Lord God, King of the universe,
giver of every good thing,
of food and drink, of companionship and love,
of all that gives us strength and delight.
Like him we bless you for your generosity.

Breaking the bread,
Jesus spoke about the destruction of his own body,
the result of human cruelty, indifference and envy.
Remembering his courage and integrity,
his willingness to die for the grace he proclaimed,
we bless you for our redemption, won at such cost.

Sharing the bread,
Jesus promises to be with us always,
and we acknowledge and delight in his presence here now.
We bless you for his Spirit binding us together
in a new and hope-filled humanity.
Fill us again, Lord, and empower us
to live together in the peace and truth of the gospel.

The bread is broken and shared, with everyone serving one another, and then the wine is shared with everyone serving one another.

POST COMMUNION

We turn to the days ahead and say together:

**Go with us Lord,
so that we can love in all sincerity,
loathing what is evil and clinging to what is good.
We will be devoted to one another as brothers and sisters,
honouring each other above ourselves;
we will be joyful in hope,
patient in affliction, faithful in prayer.
We will share with God's people who are in need
and practise hospitality.
With your help we will bless those who persecute us,
blessing and not cursing.
We will not repay evil for evil.
We will not be overcome by evil,
but by the power of your Spirit
we will overcome evil with good.
Go with us good Lord
and live in us the life of the Kingdom.**

GREETING

Grace and peace to you from God the Father and the Lord Jesus Christ.
Amen.

ADDITIONAL PRAYERS

OPENING SENTENCES

1   Among the poor,
       among the proud,
       among the persecuted,
       among the privileged,
       Christ is coming to make all things new.

       In the private house,
       in the public place,
       in the wedding feast,
       in the judgement hall,
       Christ is coming to make all things new.

       With a gentle touch,
       with an angry word,
       with a clear conscience,
       with burning love,
       Christ is coming to make all things new.

       That the kingdom might come,
       that the world might believe,
       that the powerful might stumble,
       that the hidden might be seen,
       Christ is coming to make all things new.

       Within us, without us,
       behind us, before us,
       in this place, in every place,
       for this time, for all time,
       Christ is coming to make all things new.

PRAYERS OF THANKSGIVING

2   Loving God,
       we give you thanks for all your gifts.

       In love you gave us Jesus your Son
       to rescue us from sin and death.

       To the darkness Jesus came as your light.
       With signs of faith and words of hope
       he touched untouchables with love
       and washed the guilty clean.

This is his story.

This is our song:
Hosanna in the highest.

On the night he was betrayed
he came to table with his friends
to celebrate the freedom of your people.

Therefore, with this bread and this cup,
we celebrate the cross
on which he died to set us free.
Defying death, he rose again
and is alive with you
to plead for us and all the world.

This is our story.

This is our song:
Hosanna in the highest.

Send your Spirit on us now
that by these gifts we may feed on Christ
with opened eyes and hearts on fire.

By your grace,
may we and all who share this food,
offer ourselves to live for you
and be welcomed at your feast in heaven
where all creation worships you,
Father, Son and Holy Spirit:
Blessing and honour and glory and power
be yours for ever and ever. **Amen.**

3   Remember God's people fleeing Egypt in terror,
eating the bread that had no time to rise,
sharing a feast of freedom and faith.

Picture how David outlawed and hungry,
goes to God's house and demands to be fed,
grabs a meal on the run of God's holy bread.

To the God who makes bread
and feeds the hungry
we give thanks.

Imagine Elijah tired of the journey,
longing for death given bread from God's hand,
rising to life with the strength to go on.

Come to the desert to hear Jesus teaching,
sit in the crowd as you watch him bless bread,
eat and be filled,
sense the kingdom is here

**To the God who blesses bread
and strengthens the weary
we give thanks.**

Join in the song as Mary rejoices,
pregnant with promise of life for the world,
good things for the hungry –
an end to the proud.

**To the God who breaks bread
and breaks the mighty
we give thanks.**

Hear Jesus calling to those on the edge,
'Come to my table, come eat with me.
The food is all ready, the banquet is spread.'

Sit at the table with Jesus and friends.
Remember his life and share in his name.
Bread broken, wine flowing –
a feast for the world.

**To the God who shares bread
and leaves no one out
we give thanks.**

Walk down the road with a stranger who listens
tell him your story, and hear him respond,
see the bread broken,
know the journey goes on.

WALKING TOGETHER

PRESENTING INFANTS AND CHILDREN

The opportunity to mark the birth of a child in worship, and to provide an opportunity for thanksgiving and commitment by parents and the local church community, is common among contemporary British Baptists. Moreover, there is some evidence that earlier generations also presented their children before God in worship.

THEOLOGY AND PRAYER

The provision of a service in which thanksgiving and dedication can be expressed, and in which God's blessing can be sought, is deeply pastoral. But that is not to say that it is 'purely pragmatic' or without theological or biblical justification. Jesus welcomed children and blessed them, and this gospel passage has been a warrant for Baptists over many years that they should follow his example. There are also holy instincts at work here which are not pragmatic but a trustful and intuitive response to God in the midst of human experience.

Here is joy over the gift of a child and the acknowledgement that all life comes from God. Here is a celebration of family life and an acknowledgement that children are not the property of parents, but children named before God, children with whose welfare and nurture we are entrusted. Here is concern about the dangerous world into which they are born, an honest recognition of the sinfulness which will soon mar their lives, and a hope and trust that God will bless and protect them. Here is a grateful celebration of the importance of community and the truth that parents and children need not be alone. Here is a confession that all hope rests in Jesus Christ and the best we can want for our children is that they become his true disciples.

Yet there is more. The emphasis of the gospels is not so much on what we adults can do, or promise to do, for children, as on what they can do for all of us. Jesus tells us that they are, for the church, a sign of the kingdom of God: a reminder that those who would seek to enter that kingdom must do so as little children. They are a gospel sign in the Christian community and their presentation before God provides an opportunity for this to be expressed and celebrated.

Finally, our God is a God who blesses. It is from God's gracious and saving love that blessing is poured out on us. Here the church engages in truth telling for, in the blessing of a child, we are proclaiming the heart of God as a heart of love and the hand of God as a power to save.

KEY ELEMENTS

As we present a child before God in the presence of the church community, we

- welcome people and explain the meaning of the rite,
- read scripture so that the church is addressed by God's word,
- give thanks.
- make promises as parents and church concerning the protection and nurture of the child,
- ask God's blessing on the child,
- surround the child and their family with prayer and love,
- welcome and introduce the child to the church community.

PRESENTATION AND PASTORAL VARIETY

The circumstance of the family involved can vary in many ways: the child may no longer be an infant; there may be sisters or brothers who need to be included; one parent may be absent from the service or indeed from the home; the parents may be unmarried; the child may be disabled; the service may be taking place after an adoption; there may be little or no church connection. These circumstances will have to be taken into account with pastoral sensitivity, consultation with the parent(s) and careful judgement in each case.

Two patterns are offered here, as well as additional material. Those leading these acts of presentation may mix material from across the patterns to suit the particular circumstances, so that human need may be met with welcome and integrity. For example, the language will need to fit the needs of each particular family, such as whether there are one or two parents, or whether the child is male of female. Sensitivity also needs to be shown towards those within the congregation who cannot have children.

Beyond these considerations, the main pastoral question has tended to focus on the relationship of the parents to the church and the level of commitment that can honestly be expressed in their promises. This is important, and careful preparation with parents who may be on the fringe of the church can be both an opportunity to embody gospel hospitality and gospel truthfulness. However, there is a greater truth and that is the importance of each child to God, irrespective of the faith, or lack of faith, of the parents. Consequently, whatever form of promise is chosen, the service is an act of presentation of the child before God and a request for God's blessing upon that child. Seen in this light, the service becomes a gospel celebration of God's love and a communal expression of divine grace through the welcome and caring of the local church.

PRESENTING, BLESSING AND DEDICATING

INTRODUCTION

In the name of Jesus Christ,
we welcome C and E
who come to give thanks with us for the gift of A.
Jesus was presented by his parents in the Temple.
In turn, he took young children in his arms and blessed them.
Celebrating the gift of life and the faithfulness of God,
we covenant together, as parents and as a church,
making promises before God for the sake of this child.

Here we share joy over the gift of A
and praise God, the giver of all life.
We celebrate family life,
acknowledging that children are not the property of parents
but, named before God,
they are persons
with whose welfare and nurture we are entrusted.
Concerned about the dangerous world into which they are born,
and honestly aware of the sinfulness which will soon mar their lives,
we here pray in trust
that God will bless and protect them.

Together we celebrate the importance of community
and the truth that parents and children need not be alone.
Here we confess and proclaim
that all our hope rests in Jesus Christ
and the best we can want for our children
is that they become his true disciples.

Scripture calls us to see in children a sign of the kingdom of God.
A is a living sign that God welcomes us without condition
lavishing love and grace
on all who come to him with empty hands and open hearts.

READINGS

Hear, O Israel: The Lord is our God, the Lord alone. You shall love the Lord
your God with all your heart, and with all your soul, and with all your
might. Keep these words that I am commanding you today in your heart.
Recite them to your children and talk about them when you are at home
and when you are away, when you lie down and when you rise. Bind them
as a sign on your hand, fix them as an emblem on your forehead, and write
them on the doorposts of your house and on your gates.

Deuteronomy 6.4—7

At that time the disciples came to Jesus and asked, 'Who is the greatest in the kingdom of heaven?' He called a child, whom he put among them, and said, 'Truly I tell you, unless you change and become like children, you will never enter the kingdom of heaven. Whoever becomes humble like this child is the greatest in the kingdom of heaven. Whoever welcomes one such child in my name welcomes me.'

Matthew 18.1—5

People were bringing little children to him in order that he might touch them; and the disciples spoke sternly to them. But when Jesus saw this, he was indignant and said to them, 'Let the little children come to me; do not stop them; for it is to such as these that the kingdom of God belongs. Truly I tell you, whoever does not receive the kingdom of God as a little child will never enter it.' And he took them up in his arms, laid his hands on them, and blessed them.

Mark 10.13—16

Other suitable readings include Matthew 18.10—14; Luke 2.22—32, 39—40; 18.15—17.

PRAYER OF THANKSGIVING

A prayer of praise and thanksgiving for God as creator of all life, and for the gift of this child's life in particular, extempore or as follows

Lord God, creator of all things,
giver of life, we praise you.
You are the loving parent of each person
and joyfully we thank you now
for the gift of new life in the birth of this child.
For all that you have given, and will give to us, through *her/him*,
and for the possibilities of *her/his* new life,
we thank you.
For the love which has beckoned *her/him* into existence,
for the love and hope *she/he* has awakened,
and for the care which surrounds *her/him*,
we give you our thanks and praise.
in the name of Jesus Christ our Lord. **Amen.**

PROMISES

C and *E*, do you thank God for the gift of your child,
and do you accept the joys and duties of parenthood?

Gladly, we do.

Do you promise to bring your *daughter/son* up
within the Christian community,
and, by God's grace, so to live
that *she/he* will be nurtured by Christian love
and surrounded by the life of Jesus?

As disciples of Jesus, we do.

The minister asks any brothers or sisters of the child being presented

Will you promise to love
and help care for your *brother/sister*?

Yes!

The minister then addresses the parents

What names have you given to your *daughter/son*?

The parents state the names of the child.

The minister receives the child from the parents.

AB we greet you in the name of the Lord Jesus
and welcome you into the community of God's people.

Addressing the congregation

Gathered here as members of this congregation
and as representatives of the wider church of God,
do you promise to offer *A* and *her/his* family
your love and support,
and, being faithful in prayer,
will you share your faith with *her/him*
by word and example?
If you will promise this, please stand.

BLESSING

The minister addresses the child

A, we rejoice, for you are God's gift to us.

Grow strong in the knowledge and love of God;
we pray that one day
you will be a disciple of Jesus Christ,
following him through the waters of baptism
and in a life of faithful witness;
bear the fruit of his Spirit
and live his great gift of love.

The minister may lay a hand upon the head of the child while saying

A, the Lord bless you and keep you;
the Lord make his face to shine upon you
and be gracious to you;
the Lord lift the light of his countenance upon you
and give you peace,
this day and always. **Amen.**

Or

A, the Lord bless you and guard you;
the Lord make his face shine on you
and be gracious to you;
the Lord look kindly on you
and give you peace. **Amen.**

MEETING THE CONGREGATION

The children of the church may be invited to come forward and greet the child who has been presented. They may bring gifts as a sign of welcome and later accompany the minister and child around the church.

A, these are your friends and family.
You are a gift to them and a sign from God
that we must all come as little children,
with empty hands and open hearts.
Come and meet them,
that they may thank God for you.

The minister, accompanied by the church children, walks around the church so that all may see and greet the child. Returning to the front of the church, the minister returns the child to the parents, and continues in prayer.

PRAYERS

A prayer may be offered for the child and their family, asking for God's help in the days ahead, extempore or as follows

Loving God, we thank you for the gift of this child
and now pray for *her/his* protection and flourishing.
We live in a difficult and dangerous world
and we ask that you will keep *her/him* safe from harm.
We pray for *C* and *E* and ask for your help in the care and nurture of *A*.
We pray *she/he* might know your love through their love,
discover your guidance through their guidance
and come to trust in you and become a disciple of Jesus.
This we ask in the name of our saviour Jesus Christ. **Amen.**

Or

Loving God, we pray for this child and *her/his* family.
We pray that they might know
the challenge and the comfort of your love,
and see its power.
Take all we offer to *A*,
our care, wisdom and our mistakes,
and through them reveal yourself.
Take the experiences which *A* will have,
and through them speak your gracious word.
As *A* grows in body, mind and spirit,
feed and guide *him/her* by your Spirit;
bring *her/him* safe through childhood and youth,
and lead *her/him* to make the good confession
that 'Jesus Christ is Lord';
through Christ your Son, our saviour. **Amen.**

A hymn of discipleship or thanksgiving may be sung, after which the service continues.

Further prayers and other material may be found in the section of additional material on page 61.

PRESENTING AND BLESSING

INTRODUCTION AND WELCOME

In the name of Jesus Christ,
we welcome today *CD* and *ED* and *A their* baby,
their friends and family.

C and *E* have come here
to thank God for the gift of *A*
and to seek God's help in the upbringing of their child.
Their sponsors will promise to help and support them
as their child grows older.
We as members of this church,
will promise that there will always be a place for children here.
Then we will ask God's blessing on *A*
and pray for *her/him,*
for the church's work with children,
and for children in need throughout the world.

PRAYER OF THANKSGIVING

Living Lord, you are the source of all life.
No one is born and no one dies
without your knowledge or outside your love.
We thank you for the birth of *A,*
for *her/his* new life
and all the potential which rests in *her/him.*
We also thank you for the love which brought *her/him* to life
and which continues to surround *her/him* today.
We know how much *she/he* depends
on those who care for *her/him,*
how frail and small *she/he* is.
But we believe that you will give *her/his* parents and family
all the wisdom, patience and skill which they need.
We thank you for all the gifts and talents
which will be revealed in *A* as *she/he* grows older
and present *her/him* to you now
with all our thanks and praise.
Through Jesus Christ our Lord. **Amen.**

SCRIPTURE READING

People were bringing little children to him in order that he might touch them; and the disciples spoke sternly to them. But when Jesus saw this, he was indignant and said to them, 'Let the little children come to me; do not stop them; for it is to such as these that the kingdom of God belongs. Truly I tell you, whoever does not receive the kingdom of God as a little child will never enter it.' And he took them up in his arms, laid his hands on them, and blessed them.

Mark 10.13—16

Also Deuteronomy 6.4—7; Matthew 18.1—5; 18.10—14; Luke 2.22—32, 39—40; 18.15—17.

CHURCH PROMISES

The members of the local church are invited to stand

Do you, the members and friends of this church,
promise that there will always
be a place for children here
and that you will play your part
in bringing our children to a knowledge of Jesus Christ
as their own Lord and Saviour?
If you do promise this, then please stand.

FAMILY PROMISES

The family are invited to stand. A selection or all of the following may be used

Do you thank God for the gift of *A*
and do you trust God
to help you as parents
as you care for *her/him*?

I/we do.

Will you try, with God's help,
to share with *A* your understanding of the Christian faith?

We will.

Will you bring *her/him* up within the community of the church?

We will.

Do you promise to surround *her/him*
with goodness, love and respect?

I/we do.

The minister asks any brothers or sisters of the child being presented

Will you promise to love
and help care for your *brother/sister*?

Yes!

The minister then addresses the wider family:

Will you, as members of *A*'s family,
help *C* and *E* as they bring up *A*,
and will you promise to surround *her/him*
with all that is good and true?

With God's help, we will.

BLESSING

The minister receives the child, may lay a hand on the child's head, and says

A, you are one of God's children
and your name is written in the palm of his hand.
The blessing of God,
who is Father, Son and Holy Spirit,
be with you today and always. **Amen.**

The congregation greets the child by clapping, or in some other way.

WELCOME

After the blessing of the child, the children of the church may offer a sign of welcome to the child. This may be the gift of a children's Bible or, as below, a candle.
A representative of the church, perhaps a child or a member of the junior church staff, may say

A, I give you this candle
to remind you that Jesus is the light of the world.
May you grow in his light and, one day,
shine for him.

PRAYERS

Prayers may be offered for the family, for the children of the church and for children in need everywhere, extempore or as follows

Faithful God, in faith and hope
we entrust to you this child's future life
as it stretches out before *her/him*.
Protect *her/him* in moments of danger.
Reassure *her/him* in moments of doubt.
Strengthen *her/him* as *she/he* passes from childhood to youth
and from youth to the life of an adult.
Surround *her/him* with your love
expressed in people who will care for *her/him*,
and give *her/him* those with whom that love can be shared.
And grant that when understanding comes
she/he may confess you as Lord and saviour
in the waters of baptism. **Amen.**

A hymn of discipleship or thanksgiving may be sung.

Further suitable prayers may be found in the section of additional material on the following pages.

ADDITIONAL MATERIAL

INTRODUCTION AND WELCOME

This introduction may be used with parents or a single parent or with others responsible for the child.

Today we welcome to our fellowship *A*.
Her/his family have brought *her/him*
to be presented before God.
C (and E) come*(s)* to give thanks to God
for this new life entrusted to *her/his/their* care,
and to dedicate *himself/herself/themselves*
to the joys and responsibilities of *parenthood/guardianship*.

With them, we thank God for the birth of this child.
With them, we make our solemn promise
to lead this child by our loving care and nurture
to the knowledge of Jesus as Saviour, Lord and Friend.

Jesus said:
'Truly I tell you, unless you change and become like children, you will never enter the kingdom of heaven. Whoever becomes humble like this child is the greatest in the kingdom of heaven. Whoever welcomes one such child in my name welcomes me.'   *Matthew 18.3–5*

PRAYER OF THANKSGIVING

Loving God,
we thank you for the gift of life,
and for life in families.
We thank your for the joy that a new child brings,
and we ask that you will accept our thanks
for this child,
in Jesus' name. **Amen.**

Or

Gracious God, we give thanks for this child
whom you have given to these parents:
for the love that has created *her/him*,
for the atmosphere of care and hope
into which *she/he* has come,
for the richness of life with which *she/he* is surrounded,
and for all the opportunities for joy and living
that await *her/him*,
we bless your holy name. **Amen.**

PRAYERS FOR THE CHILD AND FAMILY

Loving God, you are father and mother to us,
and we thank you for giving us this child
to nurture and protect.
Help us, as true disciples,
to set *her/him* a good example in all we think or say or do.
Keep *her/him* well in body and mind;
and grant that *she/he* may grow in grace
and in the knowledge and love of your Son,
our saviour Jesus Christ. **Amen.**

Or

Loving God,
we remember that Jesus
lived in the family home at Nazareth.
You entrusted your only Son
to the care of Joseph and Mary.
Grant your Spirit's wisdom, love and energy to C and E *[parents'/guardians' names]*,
so that the home in Nazareth
may be found once again in … *[name of town or village]*.
This we ask in Jesus' name. **Amen.**

Heavenly Father, bless the home of this child,
and help all the family to live together in your love.
Help them to serve you and each other,
and to be always ready
to show your love to those in need;
for the sake of Jesus Christ our Lord. **Amen.**

God of love, we rejoice in your faithfulness.
Guide and guard *A* all *her/his* days.
May your love hold *her/him*,
your truth guide *her/him*,
your joy delight *her/him*.
Bless *her/his* parents,
that *she/he* may grow up
in a secure and happy home.
Give to *her/his* family
wisdom and courage,
laughter and peace,
and the love that endures all things,
through Jesus Christ our Lord. **Amen.**

FOR A CHILD WITH A DISABILITY

For following prayer may be used or adapted

Loving God, your Son Jesus Christ
called on his friends to join with him
in giving honour to children,
not for what they might become
but for what they are:
those to whom your Kingdom belongs.

We greet this child today,
not only conscious of how *her/his* disability
may affect the future we want for *her/him*,
but also conscious of all that *she/he* already is.

Make your love known to *her/him*
through the presence of your Spirit
and through our love and care.

Help us to honour this child in *her/his* own right,
as an example to all who would enter your Kingdom;
and to welcome this child with love,
knowing that to receive *her/him* in your name
is to receive you.

As the family faces the challenges of the future,
we pray that all their happiness and sorrow
may be filled with the joy of finding in this child of yours
the gift of your own presence,
though Jesus Christ our Lord. **Amen.**

WELCOMING DISCIPLES

Baptism is an action instituted by Jesus Christ in which God, the believer and the Christian community are all involved. In baptism new believers confess faith and share what God has already done in their lives. Here, there is also a 'letting go' in which new Christians abandon themselves to the grace of God and the resurrection power of the one who overcomes the chaos of death and sets our feet on the new path of life. The waters of baptism are a meeting-place where human trust and the life-giving acts of God come together.

In baptism the Church celebrates the gospel of salvation through the cross and resurrection of Jesus Christ and the life-giving, new-world-creating power of the Holy Spirit. The local church is again invited to follow Jesus Christ, and is reminded that life in the Spirit, from which all fellowship and mission flows, is an immersion into the life of the triune God and a patterning after the likeness of Christ.

In baptism, God meets us and calls us to obedience and self-offering, as the forgiveness and grace of God are given tangible form. Here, the believer is incorporated into the Church, the body of Christ. Here, God commissions us for service and witness, and promises us the presence of the Holy Spirit – a promise made explicit in the laying on of hands.

FULLNESS OF MEANING AND FULLNESS OF PRACTICE

There are four dimensions which should find expression in our practice of baptism and the worship of which it is a part:

Repentance, faith and commitment
These features have often been seen as the heart of baptism, not only for the one being baptized but also for all who are present as they renew their own baptismal vows and reconsecrate themselves to God. As well as giving an account of their faith in their own words, structured questions may be asked of those presenting themselves for baptism. Such questions provide an

opportunity to expand their heart-felt response to the love of God to include acts of will and decision – to turn *from* evil and the value systems of this age, *towards* Christ and the tough, though joyful, road of discipleship.

Testimony, proclamation and evangelism
Candidates should also be given an opportunity to express their trust in God in their own words. God's work in their lives is a contemporary part of the gospel of Jesus Christ and will often challenge those in the congregation who are struggling with faith. Proclamation also happens through preaching and especially through the baptism itself. The church as a whole is reminded of its identity as a community which is immersed into Jesus Christ, and those individuals who may hesitate over the cost of commitment are presented again with the call and command of Christ. If baptism is celebrated in its richness of gift and call, the mystery of God's love in Christ and the promise of his Spirit will do their missionary work as the Spirit moves in hearts and lives.

Renewal of life, receiving the Spirit and commissioning for service
Baptism is a 'rendezvous of grace' in which God promises to meet us and change our lives. God also commissions for service and this has, both in the early church and, sometimes, within the Baptist community, been made explicit through the laying on of hands. This may occur either in the baptismal pool or later during reception into membership. In either case, it points to a life of discipleship which includes following the servant king and keeping in step with the Spirit.

Union with Christ and incorporation into the Church
To be 'in Christ', is to be incorporated into a fellowship which gains its identity from Jesus Christ and which provides the communal setting within which the new Christian will be nurtured and challenged. It is this communal dimension of baptism which leads to church membership and life in the fellowship of believers.

BAPTISM AND THE CHURCH

Belonging to Christ involves belonging to his people. Christ invites us to follow him in company with other disciples and reception into membership should follow immediately, or at least very soon after baptism. Reception will also occur, of course, when someone who moves to live in a new area covenants with a new local church in that new place. Christian discipleship is embodied living and needs to be continually embodied in the local body of Christ.

In all this, Jesus Christ is central. The saving work of cross and resurrection, the identity of Christian community under the Lordship of Christ, and the discipleship character of life in the Spirit should all feature in baptism. Here is a patterning of the believer and the Church into the image and likeness of God which is our human destiny and Christ's revelation. This pattern is focused in baptism, but is a continuing process of entry and re-entry into the way of Christ and the life of the Church.

The following elements should normally be included in the process of baptism and reception into the membership of a local church, whether these take place in the same service or in two closely related services:

- opening worship
- the reading of scripture
- preaching
- statement of faith though questions and testimony
- baptism in the name of the Triune God
- evangelistic invitation, possibly including an opportunity for the congregation to renew baptismal vows
- prayer for the candidates
- the laying on of hands for blessing and commissioning
- welcome into membership
- the Lord's Supper
- blessing and dismissal.

If reception into the church is to happen on a later date, then it should be at the next occasion when the fellowship gathers around the Lord's Table. The practice of not receiving people into membership following their baptism is to be discouraged as a privatizing of their faith and a reducing of the meaning of baptism to testimony and commitment alone. In what follows, material is offered which may be incorporated into a single service or distributed over more than one occasion.

More than one person may take part in the act of baptizing, either to give a fuller expression of the involvement of the whole church community or simply to provide physical assistance.

Candidates for baptism may be invited to choose a member of the church to sit with them before the baptism, and to be waiting for them as they leave the baptistery, with a towel to dry their faces, and to help them up the steps.

Baptism is normally by total immersion, but alternative forms may be preferred because of illness or disability. Water from the baptistery may be poured over the person's head, which may be done while the person is within the baptistery, perhaps having been lowered into the water in a chair. The most appropriate means for the person concerned should be used, and informed medical advice should be sought and followed where necessary. Whatever the mode of baptism, the fact that it is the baptism of believers must be clearly expressed and understood. In the case of a person with learning difficulties, care must be taken to find a means by which the candidate can appropriately make a declaration of faith.

BAPTIZING DISCIPLES

*After opening worship, including praise and confession, and the reading and preaching of
God's word, the service will continue with the act of baptism.*

One or more of the following scriptures may be read

And Jesus came and said to them, 'All authority in heaven and on earth
has been given to me. Go therefore and make disciples of all nations,
baptizing them in the name of the Father and of the Son and of the Holy
Spirit, and teaching them to obey everything that I have commanded you.
And remember, I am with you always, to the end of the age.'

Matthew 28.18–20

Now John was clothed with camel's hair, with a leather belt around his
waist, and he ate locusts and wild honey. He proclaimed, 'The one who is
more powerful than I is coming after me; I am not worthy to stoop down
and untie the thong of his sandals. I have baptized you with water; but he
will baptize you with the Holy Spirit.'
    In those days Jesus came from Nazareth of Galilee and was baptized
by John in the Jordan. And just as he was coming up out of the water, he
saw the heavens torn apart and the Spirit descending like a dove on him.
And a voice came from heaven, 'You are my Son, the Beloved; with you I
am well pleased.'

Mark 1.6–11

Peter said to them, 'Repent, and be baptized every one of you in the name
of Jesus Christ so that your sins may be forgiven; and you will receive the
gift of the Holy Spirit. So those who welcomed his message were baptized,
and that day about three thousand persons were added. They devoted
themselves to the apostles' teaching and fellowship, to the breaking of
bread and the prayers.

Acts 2.38, 41f.

Do you not know that all of us who have been baptized into Christ Jesus
were baptized into his death? Therefore we have been buried with him by
baptism into death, so that, just as Christ was raised from the dead by the
glory of the Father, so we too might walk in newness of life.

Romans 6.3f.

For in Christ Jesus you are all children of God through faith. As many
of you as were baptized into Christ have clothed yourselves with Christ.
There is no longer Jew or Greek, there is no longer slave or free, there is no
longer male and female; for all of you are one in Christ Jesus. And if you
belong to Christ, then you are Abraham's offspring, heirs according to the
promise.

Galatians 3.26–28

When you were buried with him in baptism, you were also raised with him through faith in the power of God, who raised him from the dead.

Colossians 2.12

Other suitable readings include: Isaiah 6.1–9a; Matthew 3.1–12; 3.13–17; Mark 1.1–13; Luke 3.21–22; John 3.1–8; Acts 2.38–47; 8.26–39; 9.1–19; 10.34–38; 16.11–15; 16.25–34; 19.1–7; 22.16; Romans 6.3–11; Ephesians 4.1–6; Colossians 3.1–17; 1 Timothy 6.12; Titus 3.3–7; Hebrews 10.19–25.

INTRODUCTION

Suitably adapted if only one person is to be baptized, the following statements may be used as an introduction to baptism, or as the basis for teaching or preaching.

Following his resurrection,
Jesus commanded his disciples
to go and make disciples of all the nations,
baptizing them
in the name of the Father, the Son
and the Holy Spirit.

In obedience to Christ
and in joyful thanks for God's redeeming love,
we gather to baptize those
whom the Spirit has led to repentance and faith.

Jesus was baptized in the river Jordan,
and still disciples are called to follow Jesus Christ
through the waters of baptism,
to be buried and raised in union with him.

Here is the grace of God:
washed free of sin,
disciples of Jesus are immersed
into all that God has done in Christ
and all that he promises to do through his Spirit.

By the one Spirit
we are baptized into one body,
patterned after the likeness of our Lord Jesus
and anointed for his service.

PRAYER

Extempore prayer may be offered, or the following

Almighty God,
we give you thanks for your Son, Jesus Christ,
who was baptized in the river Jordan
and passed through
the deep waters of death.
We praise you that you raised him to life and exalted him.

Send your Holy Spirit, we pray,
that this baptism may be for your servant(s)
a union with Christ in his death and resurrection,
so that, as Christ was raised from death
through the glory of the Father,
they also might be raised to newness of life.
Pour out your Spirit and anoint *them* for service
that they may grow
into the likeness of Jesus Christ,
in whose name we pray. **Amen.**

Or

Eternal God,
your Spirit hovered over the waters in creation,
you brought your people through the parting of the desert sea,
and your Son came to John to be baptized.
Pour out your Spirit on those
whom now you meet in these waters,
that they may enter Christ's tomb and be reborn,
that they may die to all that is death
and be born to a new and living hope.
This we ask through the same Jesus Christ,
who lives and reigns with you in unity with the Holy Spirit,
one God for ever and ever. **Amen.**

DECLARATION OF FAITH

The Apostles' Creed, or some other confession of faith, may be said by the congregation. Alternatively, members of the congregation may be invited to renew their own baptismal promises after the baptisms.

The minister then says

My friends, today we hear of the work of God
in the lives of those who are to be baptized.
They are here because Jesus Christ has found them
and through the work of the Holy Spirit
they have discovered new life in him.

The love of God has become real,
the call of Christ has beckoned them
and the life of the Spirit has renewed them.

The minister then addresses each of the candidates by name. They may reply as indicated, or more briefly with such words as 'I do' or 'I will'.

A do you believe in one God,
Father, Son and Holy Spirit?

I do. This is the God in whom I trust.

Do you confess Jesus Christ
as your Lord and Saviour?

I do. He has redeemed me and called me by name.

Do you turn from sin, renounce evil
and intend to follow Christ?

**I do. Christ is my way,
he is the truth and now he is my life.**

Will you live within the fellowship of the church
and will you serve Jesus Christ in the world?

With the Spirit's help, this will be my witness.

Or

Do you renounce all evil,
and the powers
which defy God's righteousness and love?

I renounce them.

Do you turn from the ways of sin
that separate you from the love of God?

**Trusting in the gracious mercy of God,
I renounce them.**

Who is your Lord and Saviour?

Jesus Christ is my Lord and Saviour.

Will you be Christ's faithful disciple,
obeying his word and showing his love.

**With the Spirit's help,
I will follow Jesus
in the church and in the world.**

After the candidate's have responded to these questions, each should be invited to tell, in their own words, the story of God's call upon their lives.

BAPTISM

A hymn or song may be sung as those about to be baptized prepare to enter the baptistery.

Children and others, with due regard to safety precautions, may be invited to gather near the baptistery.

Each candidate enters the pool in turn and the minister may greet each one by name and read aloud a scripture verse which has been especially chosen for them. The minister then says to each

A, we have heard of your repentance and faith.
I now baptize you, my *sister/brother*
in the name of God,
the Father, the Son and the Holy Spirit. **Amen.**

Or

Minister
Christ is risen!

All
He is risen indeed.

Candidate
Jesus is Lord!

All
Hallelujah!

Minister
A, you are called to be a disciple of Jesus Christ.
I now baptize you
in the name of God
the Father, the Son, and the Holy Spirit.

The challenge and witness of baptism may be followed by inviting others to respond to the Gospel, either by coming forward at this point or by presenting themselves for prayer at the close of the service.

Baptism may be followed by singing and, if there is more than one candidate, singing may continue between each baptism.

While the baptized and baptizer(s) are changing, the congregation may be led in praise, as well as prayers of intercession for the world, the church and the candidates.

Members of the congregation may also be invited to renew their own baptismal vows by means of the Apostles' Creed or the questions which have already been asked of the candidates before the baptisms, thus

Do you not know that all of us who have been baptized into Christ Jesus were baptized into his death? Therefore we have been buried with him by baptism into death, so that, just as Christ was raised from the dead by the glory of the Father, so we too might walk in newness of life.

Romans 6.3f.

As the people of God in this place,
do you believe in one God,
Father, Son and Holy Spirit?

We do. This is the God in whom we trust.

Do you confess Jesus Christ
as your Lord and Saviour?

We do. He has redeemed us and called us by name.

Do you turn from sin, renounce evil
and intend to follow Christ?

We do. Christ is our way.
With the Spirit's help,
we will follow this Jesus
in the church and in the world.

Or

I believe in God, the Father almighty,
creator of heaven and earth.

I believe in Jesus Christ, God's only Son, our Lord,
who was conceived by the Holy Spirit,
born of the Virgin Mary,
suffered under Pontius Pilate,
was crucified, died, and was buried;
he descended to the dead.
On the third day he rose again;
he ascended into heaven,
he is seated at the right hand of the Father,
and he will come to judge the living and the dead.

I believe in the Holy Spirit,
the holy catholic Church,
the communion of saints,
the forgiveness of sins,
the resurrection of the body,
and the life everlasting.

Prayers may conclude with the offering and, if the Lord's Supper is to be celebrated, the table may be put in place and laid as the gifts are brought forward. The candidates return and may bring the bread and wine before they receive the laying on of hands and are received into church membership.

LAYING ON HANDS
AND RECEIVING INTO THE CHURCH

This act should follow baptism, either as part of the baptismal service or as soon afterwards as is practical. It should be followed by the Lord's Supper.

Appropriate readings include Acts 8.14–17; 9.17–19; 13.1–3; 19.1–6; 1 Timothy 4.14; and Revelation 1.17.

COVENANT QUESTIONS

A, you have been baptized
into the Church of Jesus Christ.
Now we welcome you as a member of this fellowship,
asking God to bless and equip you for service and witness.

Do you believe that
as a follower of Jesus Christ
you are called to gather with other disciples
and that now you are now called
to covenant with this local church?

I do. This is my duty and my delight.

Will you accept the privileges and responsibilities
    of church membership?
Will you be faithful in worship and prayer,
        steadfast in service
        and witness to the love of God?
Will you share in its mission,
        encourage and support its leaders and members,
        and always represent Christ to those around you?

I will.
This is my calling as a disciple of Jesus
in company with his people
and in the fellowship of the Holy Spirit.

LAYING ON OF HANDS

The New Testament records
that those who were baptized
often received the laying on of hands, with prayer,
as a sign of commissioning and blessing.

We are now to lay hands on ...
who *have* been baptized,
commissioning *them* for service as disciples of Jesus Christ.
We shall pray for the Holy Spirit
to equip and empower *them*
for *their* calling in the church
and *their* witness in the world.

Or

Sisters and brothers,
we are now to pray for
those who have been baptized,
lay our hands upon *them*
and receive *them* into the membership of this church.

This rite, which was practiced by the apostles,
is an act of acceptance, commissioning and blessing.
We shall pray that,
being blessed and strengthened by the Holy Spirit,
they may be fully equipped for *their* calling and ministry
as disciples of Jesus Christ.

As we pray for *them*,
we welcome *them*
into the membership of this church,
promising to encourage and support *them*
as followers of Jesus Christ
and members together of his body.

Let us together
hear the words of scripture:

The candidate (s) may be addressed with words of scripture

You are a chosen race,
a royal priesthood,
a holy nation,
God's own people,
in order that you may proclaim the mighty acts of him
who called you out of darkness into his marvellous light. *1 Peter 2.9*

You are the light of the world.
Let your light shine before others,
so that they may see your good works
and give glory to your Father in heaven. *Matthew 5.14a, 16*

Each candidate kneels and the minister and another representative of the church lay hands on each, offering prayer such as

Living and gracious God,
you have called *A*
to be a disciple of Jesus Christ
and a citizen of your kingdom.
Pour out your Spirit,
that *she/he* may be empowered for service
and strengthened for witness.
Lavish your gifts of grace
and the fruit of your Spirit
upon *her/him,*
that *she/he* may live
to serve and praise you
and grow into the likeness of Jesus Christ,
in whose name we pray. **Amen.**

Or

Almighty and eternal God,
strengthen, we pray,
these your servant(s)
with your Holy Spirit:
the Spirit of wisdom and understanding,
the Spirit of counsel and might,
the Spirit of knowledge and the fear of the Lord
As disciple(s) of Jesus Christ,
and as priest(s) in your kingdom,
equip *them* for every good work
that *their lives* may reflect your glory
and witness to your grace,
through Jesus Christ our Lord. **Amen.**

The candidates stand as the leader says

You are no longer aliens in a foreign land,
but fellow citizens with God's people,
members of God's household.
You are built on the foundation of the apostles,
with Christ Jesus himself as the cornerstone.

Ephesians 2.19f.

COVENANT PROMISE

The congregation may say together

We promise to pray for you,
to encourage and support you,
for together we are disciples of Jesus Christ
and members of his body.

Let us walk together before the Lord,
in ways that are known
and yet to be made known,
gathering for worship,
seeking the mind of Christ,
praying for God's kingdom
and sharing in its life and witness.

We are sisters and brothers together;
praise be to God,
Father, Son and Holy Spirit.

RECEPTION INTO MEMBERSHIP

*Each candidate may be greeted and welcomed into membership of the local church with the
hand of fellowship and with words such as*

A, we welcome you in the name of the Lord Jesus Christ
into the membership of … Baptist Church.

Others may also greet the new members and prayer is offered, extempore or

Loving God,
we thank you for calling us to be disciples
in the fellowship of this church.
We thank you for one another
and especially today for *A.*
By the power of your Spirit
make us more like Jesus Christ
that together we may serve you
and witness to your redeeming love
in the world for which Christ died.
We ask this in his name. **Amen.**

*The service continues with the Lord's Supper, at which the new members may be served first as
a sign of hospitality and welcome.*

RECEIVING THOSE RECENTLY BAPTIZED

Those being received into membership following baptism earlier in the service, or very recently, will not need to profess their faith again before being received into the membership of the local church. However, they do need to commit themselves to the privileges and responsibilities of membership and the church members also need to share in that covenant commitment. The new members should be greeted and, if this is in a subsequent service, reintroduced.

In the name of God and this worshipping community,
we prepare to welcome *A* into membership
having witnessed *her/his* profession of faith in baptism.

As *A* has declared *her/his* commitment to God in Jesus Christ,
so we, the people of God in …
are about to declare our commitment to *her/him*
in our covenant relationship of faith.

COVENANT QUESTIONS

A, as a member of this church,
do you promise to share your life
and your journey of faith
with these people in this place?

I do.
Together we are called
to be disciples of Jesus Christ.

Will you keep listening for the call of God,
ready to serve others
and to witness to Jesus Christ
as a member of this church?

I will.
We are the body of Christ,
and the Spirit shares the gifts of grace
for service and witness.

Or

Together we are called
to be disciples of Jesus Christ.
A, as a member of this church,
do you promise to share your life
and your journey of faith
with these people in this place?

I do.

We are the body of Christ,
and the Spirit shares the gifts of grace for service and witness.
Will you use your gifts and talents to serve God
and to further the witness of Jesus Christ
as a member of this church?

With God's help, I will.

COVENANT PROMISE

The members of the church are invited to stand.

Will you, as members of ... Church,
promise to share your lives and journey of faith with *A*,
walking together in ways that are known
and yet to be made known?

We will.

Will you pray for *A*
and do all you can to help *her/him/them*
to witness to Jesus Christ?

**We will.
In our life together we celebrate
the grace of our Lord Jesus Christ,
the love of God
and the fellowship of the Holy Spirit.**

RECEPTION INTO MEMBERSHIP

The leader offers the hand of fellowship saying

We welcome you among us
as a member of this church of Jesus Christ.

*Prayer, which may be accompanied with the laying on of hands, should be offered, extempore
or as follows*

Loving God,
we thank you for bringing *A* to us.
We trust you for the future
as together we seek to serve you
in this fellowship and in your world.
Help us to be generous in time and gifts,
giving and receiving from each other with humility and patience,
encouraging and supporting one another
as we walk together in our shared journey of life and faith.
We pray with confidence
in the name of our saviour, Jesus Christ
who is Lord of this fellowship. **Amen.**

*Others may also greet the new members and/or the members may say together the words of
the Grace.*

*The service continues with the Lord's Supper, at which the new members may be served first as
a sign of hospitality and welcome.*

RECEIVING MEMBERS THROUGH TRANSFER

One of the other patterns for the reception of members may be adapted and used.

Those being welcomed into membership through transfer or on profession of faith, should be invited to declare their faith.

The covenant questions and promises may be used from the first pattern, in the baptismal service, or as follows

In the name of our loving God,
it is our joy to welcome …
into the membership of this church.
They are committed to serving God in this community,
and today we acknowledge and thank God
for that commitment.

They have been disciples of Jesus Christ for some years
and are transferring from … Church with its blessing.

DECLARATION OF FAITH AND COVENANT QUESTIONS

Do you believe in one God,
Father, Son and Holy Spirit:
your creator and redeemer
and the sustainer of all things?

I do. This is the God in whom I trust.

Do you believe that God has led you
to share in the worship, life and witness
of this local congregation?

I do, and I thank God for the gift of fellowship.

Will you share with us the gifts God has given you,
that together we may serve God
in our local community and in the wider world?

I will. All I have is given by God.

As Baptist Christians we covenant together
as a community of the disciples of Jesus Christ.
Baptized into his name,
we share the joys and responsibilities of fellowship:
we gather for worship and to discern the mind of Christ;
together we seek the kingdom of God
through prayer, witness and service;
and in the power of the Holy Spirit
we seek to build one another up in love.
Will you share with us in this common life and service,
and will you walk together with us before God,
in ways that are known and yet to be made known?

I will. Thanks be to God.

COVENANT PROMISE

The church members are invited to stand and are addressed with the following questions.

Do you welcome … into the fellowship
of this worshipping community?

We do. This is our joy and our calling.

God has given us the gift of …
and through them has given us gifts for ministry
in the life and witness of this congregation.
Will you support … in Christian service
and in the responsibilities of church membership?

We will. Thanks be to God.

Will you pray for … and encourage *them*
through hospitality, friendship and prayer?

**We will, in the fellowship of the Holy Spirit
and in the name of Jesus Christ.**

The new members are welcomed with the hand of fellowship and others may share in this greeting.

Prayer, which may be accompanied with the laying on of hands, may be offered, extempore or as follows

PRAYER

Loving God,
we believe you have guided ... to this church
and we rejoice in the covenant promises we have made together.
We pray that *they* may grow in grace.
Strengthen *their* faith and ours
and build up this community of your people,
that together we may be faithful followers of Jesus Christ.
Send your Holy Spirit upon ...
strengthen *them* for service,
and make *them* more like Jesus.
Through your grace empower us,
that our life together might glorify you
and witness to a needy world,
though Jesus Christ our Lord. **Amen.**

The service continues with the Lord's Supper. New members are usually served first as a sign of welcome.

NURTURING NEW FAITH

The Christian life was early called 'the way' and the image of journey has often been used to describe the life of discipleship. As people prepare for baptism, or begin a period of learning what it means to be a Christian and to practise the way of Christ, it may be helpful to recognize this within worship or in other, more informal, settings. Here is material suitable for such circumstances which may be lead by one or several people.

As we follow the Way of Christ,
we affirm the presence of God among us,
Father, Son and Holy Spirit.

God calls us to share in worship.
Jesus said, where two are three are gathered in my name,
I am there among them.
Jesus, you are the Way: guide us on our journey.

God calls us to share in prayer.
Jesus said, abide in me, and I will abide in you.
Jesus, you are the Way: guide us on our journey.

God calls us to share the scriptures.
Jesus met his disciples on the road
and opened the scriptures to them.
Jesus you are the Way: guide us on our journey.

God calls us to share in fellowship and the breaking of bread.
Jesus said, do this in remembrance of me.
Jesus you are the Way: guide us on our journey.

God calls us to share in service.
Jesus said, as you do it for the least of these, you do it for me.
Jesus you are the Way: guide us on our journey.

God calls us to share in witnessing to truth and justice.
Jesus said, seek first the kingdom of God and his righteousness.
Jesus you are the Way: guide us on our journey.

God calls us to share a life of sacrificial love.
Jesus said, to be my disciple you must deny yourself,
take up your cross and follow me.
Jesus you are the Way: guide us on our journey.

God calls us to share in a community open to all.
Jesus said, love your neighbour as yourself.
Jesus you are the Way: guide us on our journey.

God calls us to share the good news.
Jesus said go and make disciples of all nations.
Jesus you are the Way: guide us on our journey.

On the same, or another, occasion the words of the beatitudes (Matthew 5.3—10 or Luke 6.20—23) may be read.

Listen to the words of Jesus and take heed:

After the reading and a moment of silence, the leader may pray, extempore or as follows

Almighty God,
you search us and know us:
help us to rely on when we are strong
and to rest in you when we are weak,
now and always,
through Jesus Christ our Lord, **Amen.**

Alternatively, Jesus' summary of the law (Mark 12.28—34) may be read aloud with the introduction

Listen to the words of Jesus and take heed:

After the reading and a moment of silence, the leader may pray, extempore or as follows

Loving God,
help us to love you with all we are,
to keep your way of love
and to live in the way of Jesus Christ,
in whose name we pray.

Prayers from the section 'Devotional Prayers for Disciples', page 408f., may be used in place of those given above.

REAFFIRMING BAPTISMAL VOWS

There are various occasions when the reaffirmation of baptism vows may be an appropriate pastoral action for the church as a whole or for individual members, such as

- *church anniversary*
- *a baptismal service, after the baptisms*
- *a vigil on Easter eve*
- *a general opportunity for recommitment*
- *following personal failure or a falling away from faith*
- *the reception of members*
- *the reinstatement of a church member.*

Whatever the circumstances, the central truth proclaimed by this action should be the grace of God — through our redemption in Jesus Christ and through his constant welcoming of us into fellowship with him and with the people of God. While this may come at any point in a service, the most suitable place would be at the Lord's Supper.

Three versions of the declaration of faith are offered: one for personal use and two for corporate profession.

Scripture verses which are appropriate to the occasion may be read, such as

Do you not know that all of us who have been baptized into Christ Jesus were baptized into his death? Therefore we have been buried with him by baptism into death, so that, just as Christ was raised from the dead by the glory of the Father, so we too might walk in newness of life.

Romans 6.3f.

If you confess with your lips that Jesus is Lord and believe in your heart that God raised him from the dead, you will be saved. For one believes with the heart and so is justified, and one confesses with the mouth and so is saved. The scripture says, 'No one who believes in him will be put to shame.' For there is no distinction between Jew and Greek; the same Lord is Lord of all and is generous to all who call on him. For, 'Everyone who calls on the name of the Lord shall be saved.' *Romans 10.9–12*

For just as the body is one and has many members, and all the members of the body, though many, are one body, so it is with Christ. For in the one Spirit we were all baptized into one body — Jews or Greeks, slaves or free — and we were all made to drink of one Spirit.

1 Corinthians 12.12f.

In Christ Jesus you are all children of God through faith. As many of you as were baptized into Christ have clothed yourselves with Christ. There is no longer Jew or Greek, there is no longer slave or free, there is no longer male and female; for all of you are one in Christ Jesus. And if you belong to Christ, then you are Abraham's offspring, heirs according to the promise.

Galatians 3.26–28

DECLARATION OF FAITH

The responses may be as indicated below, or, more briefly, with such words as 'I/we do' or 'I/we will'.

A, do you believe in one God,
Father, Son and Holy Spirit?

I do. This is the God in whom I trust.

Do you confess Jesus Christ
as your Lord and Saviour?

I do. He has redeemed me and called me by name.

Do you turn from sin, renounce evil
and intend to follow Christ?

**I do. Christ is my way,
he is the truth and now he is my life.**

Will you live within the fellowship of the church
and will you serve Jesus Christ in the world?

With the Spirit's help, this will be my witness.

Or

As the people of God in this place,
do you believe in one God,
Father, Son and Holy Spirit?

We do. This is the God in whom we trust.

Do you confess Jesus Christ
as your Lord and Saviour?

We do. He has redeemed us and called us by name.

Do you turn from sin, renounce evil
and intend to follow Christ?

**We do. Christ is our way.
With the Spirit's help,
we will follow this Jesus
in the church and in the world.**

Or

As the people of God in this place,
we believe and trust in one God,
Father, Son and Holy Spirit?

We confess Jesus Christ
as our Lord and Saviour
for he has redeemed us and called us by name.

Here and now we turn from sin, renounce evil
and intend to follow Christ,
who is the way, the truth and life itself.
With the Spirit's help,
we will follow Jesus
in the church and in the world.

The Apostles' Creed may be said together

I believe in God, the Father almighty,
creator of heaven and earth.
I believe in Jesus Christ, God's only Son, our Lord,
who was conceived by the Holy Spirit,
born of the Virgin Mary,
suffered under Pontius Pilate,
was crucified, died, and was buried;
he descended to the dead.
On the third day he rose again;
he ascended into heaven,
he is seated at the right hand of the Father,
and he will come to judge the living and the dead.

I believe in the Holy Spirit,
the holy catholic Church,
the communion of saints,
the forgiveness of sins,
the resurrection of the body,
and the life everlasting.

Or this form of the Apostles' Creed may be used

Do you believe and trust in God the Father?

**I believe in God, the Father almighty,
creator of heaven and earth.**

Do you believe and trust in his Son Jesus Christ?

**I believe in Jesus Christ, his only Son, our Lord,
who was conceived by the Holy Spirit,
born of the virgin Mary,
suffered under Pontius Pilate,
was crucified, died, and was buried;
he descended to the dead.
On the third day he rose again;
he ascended into heaven,
he is seated at the right hand of the Father,
and he will come to judge the living and the dead.**

Do you believe and trust in the Holy Spirit?

**I believe in the Holy Spirit,
the holy catholic Church,
the communion of saints,
the forgiveness of sins,
the resurrection of the body,
and the life everlasting. Amen**

PRAYER

Loving God, we praise you.
Your love and grace are more than we can imagine.
For your word of love made flesh in Jesus Christ,
for his birth in Bethlehem, sharing our life,
for his baptism in the Jordan, sharing our way,
we thank you.
For his proclaiming of your rule in word and action,
for his death on the cross
and for your raising him to life again,
we praise you.

You have called us to follow Jesus
and, by your grace,
you have met us in the waters of baptism.
Here we have renewed our vows
and called upon your gracious help.
Anoint us by your Spirit
that we might live truly as those
who are baptized into your name,
Father, Son and Holy Spirit.
Empower us by your Spirit
that we may live to your praise and glory,
through Jesus Christ our Lord. Amen

The Lord's Prayer may be said by all, followed by the words of the grace, before the service continues.

RECOGNIZING AND GIVING THANKS FOR FAITHFUL SERVICE

There will be times when a local church will want to mark a special occasion, such as the completion of a term of service by a deacon, elder, youth leader or other person in the fellowship, or the anniversary of a minister's induction to that pastorate.

This act of recognition and thanksgiving may be included at an appropriate place in Sunday worship or a church meeting.

A is a disciple of Jesus Christ.
In baptism *she/he* was buried and raised with Christ
and commissioned for service.
We rejoice especially that
she/he was called by God
to serve this church in its life and witness
through the ministry of *an elder / a deacon / a teacher etc.*

We are disciples of Jesus Christ
and we celebrate God's call
to all who minister amongst us.

The service being recognized is outlined and a prayer is offered, extempore or as follows

God of grace,
we praise you for the call to follow Jesus Christ
as a company of his disciples.
We thank you for all the gifts of ministry
you have lavished upon us
and for the gift of one another.
Now we thank you for *A*
and for *her/his* faithful service.
Continue to guide and sustain *her/him*, we pray,
that *she/he* may glorify you
in a life of discipleship and grace.
These blessings we ask in the name of Jesus Christ,
our Lord and saviour. **Amen.**

BLESSING DEPARTING MEMBERS

This act of recognition, thanksgiving and farewell is an opportunity to celebrate the fellowship of the church and to pray for those who are leaving and will need to belong to another local church elsewhere. It may occur during the Lord's Supper, at another suitable point in a Sunday service, or at a church meeting.

Those who are leaving are mentioned by name, along with the reason for their departure and any other relevant personal information.

A and C, we rejoice in your having been a part of this fellowship
and we want to wish you farewell
and seek God's blessing as you move to ...

In baptism
you confessed your faith,
were buried with Christ
and raised with him to newness of life.
You were incorporated into the body of Christ
and commissioned for service and witness
in the church and in the world.

We have together sought
to follow Christ
and to be his church in this place.
Now you are called elsewhere.
We shall miss your companionship,
but rejoice that God will bless others through you
as we have been blessed.

The leader prays extempore, or as follows. Alternatively, the congregation may say together

Faithful God,
keep, preserve and protect A and C
all their days.
By the power of your Holy Spirit,
may they be salt of the earth
and light for the world.
Lead them to a new fellowship
and to new ministries,
secure in the faith
that binds us forever in the body of Christ. **Amen.**

Go in the peace of Christ.

The Lord bless you and keep you.
The Lord make his face to shine upon you
and be gracious to you.
The Lord lift up the light of his countenance upon you
and give you peace.

Those departing may say

Amen.

COVENANTING TOGETHER

At the time of the Reformation stress was laid upon the church being the community of the new covenant. Confident in the unconditional gracious gift of God's covenant in Christ, Baptists along with other radical separatists nevertheless believed themselves called to make covenant with God as an act of obedience. Alongside this 'vertical dimension' of covenant, between God and his people, early Baptists also found a horizontal dimension. Often under the pressure of persecution, members of a local church made a covenant between themselves in which they promised 'to walk with each other and watch over each other'.

Baptist understanding of church is deeply rooted in the belief that God makes covenant with each congregation. The local church lives its life under the rule of Christ, who is the covenant mediator. God takes the initiative in covenant making – believers are gathered together by Christ and have their being in Christ.

Being bound together in communion by the work of the Holy Spirit has radical implications for our commitment to each other and for the nature of our sharing today. Covenanting together is an opportunity for worshippers to express commitment to God and to express their commitment and care for each other through fellowship. The patterns within this section celebrate God's generous and costly love for us. They invite us, as an act of obedience, to acknowledge God's gift of covenant life by responding in generous costly love for one another and for his world. Covenant patterns are also to be found in the Lord's Supper and the Ministry sections within this book.

Three patterns for covenanting together are offered here. The first two both use the text produced by the Baptist Union of Great Britain in 2000. The first pattern is merely a shortened version of the original, while the second is a special adaptation of the original text for use in congregations where there are people with learning difficulties and has been written in partnership with BUild, the Baptist Union initiative with people with learning difficulties. The third pattern is to enable covenant-making to shape the beginnings of a new congregation.

Church anniversary occasions or fellowship renewal events are good opportunities to use the covenant-making pattern. Association and ecumenical gatherings also provide occasions for covenant making and these texts could be adapted for such purposes.

MAKING AND RENEWING COVENANT

A covenant service is an opportunity for believers to acknowledge God's covenant grace, and to express anew their commitment to covenant fellowship. This service celebrates God's generous and costly love for us and calls us to generous and costly love for one another and for God's world. The text is an adapted version of the Covenant 21 text published by the Baptist Union of Great Britain in 2000. It encourages congregations to covenant together not only amongst themselves but with other Baptists in other places and ecumenically.

WE GATHER AND ARE GATHERED

God has made us a people:
we have been shaped by God's will

Jesus calls us together:
we meet in Jesus' name

The Spirit binds us together:
and leads us into truth.

A time of praise, thanksgiving, and confession may follow.

WE BELIEVE

Together with all God's people,
we proclaim our faith
and celebrate the story of our salvation.

The Apostles' Creed, a simplified version of the same known as the 'Action Creed' (see pages 102, 103), or an alternative agreed statement may be recited here.

I believe in God, the Father Almighty,
creator of heaven and earth.

I believe in Jesus Christ
God's only Son, our Lord,
who was conceived by the Holy Spirit
born of the virgin Mary
suffered under Pontius Pilate
was crucified, died, and was buried;
he descended to the dead.
On the third day he rose again;
he ascended into heaven,
he is seated at the right hand of the Father,
and he will come to judge the living and the dead.

I believe in the Holy Spirit,
the holy universal Church,
the communion of saints,
the forgiveness of sins,
the resurrection of the body,
and the life everlasting. Amen

A Trinitarian song or hymn may be sung.

WE SERVE

We baptize
those who repent
and trust in Christ
as Lord and Saviour.

In baptism,
we are called to be disciples,
sharing in Christ's death and resurrection.

Through baptism,
we are received into the church,
the body of Christ,
immersed into the fellowship
of Father, Son and Holy Spirit.

To know Christ is to follow him;
to name him Lord is to obey him.

A song or hymn on the theme of service may be sung, followed by readings from the Old and New Testaments and a sermon.

RESPONSE TO THE WORD

We are called to be a worshipping community,
offering all to God in prayer.

We are called to be a missionary community,
making known the redeeming love of God.

We are called to be a sacrificial community,
generously giving from all that God has given us.

We are called to be an inclusive community,
sharing the hospitality of God's Kingdom with all.

We are called to be a prophetic community,
challenging powers that oppress and corrupt

As a Gospel people,
let us covenant together
before God and each other:

WE COVENANT

**Creating and redeeming God,
we give you thanks and praise.
Your covenant of grace
was made for our salvation
in Jesus Christ our Lord.**

**We come this day
to covenant with you
and with our companions in discipleship:**

**to watch over each other
and to walk together before you
in ways known and still to be made known.**

**Pour down your Spirit on us.
Help us so to walk in your ways
that the promises we make this day,
and the life that we live together,
may become an offering of love,
our duty and delight,
truly glorifying to you,
Father, Son and Holy Spirit. Amen.**

This day,
we give ourselves again
to the Lord
and to each other,

to be bound together in fellowship.
and to work together
in the unity of the Spirit
for the sake of God's mission.

The following may be named, as appropriate

In our congregation,
in local partnerships,
in our association
and in the wider Union,
we commit all that we have and all that we are
to fulfil God's purposes of love.

WE SEND AND ARE SENT

A time of intercession may follow here, highlighting the needs of the world and the community in which the congregation meets.

Now may the God of hope
fill us with all joy and peace in believing ,
that we may abound in hope
by the power of the Holy Spirit.

Now to him who,
by the power at work within us,
is able to accomplish abundantly
far more than we can ask or imagine:
to him be glory in the church
and in Christ Jesus
to all generations,
for ever and ever. **Amen.**

MAKING AND RENEWING COVENANT: A PATTERN FOR A CONGREGATION INCLUDING PEOPLE WITH LEARNING DISABILITIES

This approach to the covenant service has been prepared for use by and with people with learning disabilities. The ideas are only suggestions and it may be that group leaders who are used to working with particular groups or individuals will want to use more familiar material. Some of these suggestions may, where appropriate, be incorporated in a church's own covenant service.

The service follows closely the five parts of the covenant service

- *we gather*
- *we believe*
- *we serve*
- *we covenant*
- *we share*

WE GATHER

God made us:
Hallelujah!

Jesus calls us together:
Hallelujah!

The Holy Spirit leads us:
Hallelujah!

A worship song may be sung here. Local group leaders will know which songs would be appropriate.

PRAYER OF CONFESSION

Groups may prefer to make their own prayer of confession.

**Dear Lord,
we are sorry for the bad things we do.
Help us to be good and kind. Amen.**

THE LORD'S PRAYER

The BUild version of the Lord's Prayer has been reproduced here, but groups may choose to use a sung version.

Father God in heaven
you are very special.
We want you to be our King
and for everyone to do what you say
here in ... *[supply the name of your town]*
as in heaven.
Give us today the food we need.
We are sorry when we are nasty or unkind
and we forgive those who are unkind and hurt us.
Keep us safe from badness,
for you are the King of everything.
You are the strongest
and we worship you for always. Amen.

WE BELIEVE

This section includes the Action Creed from Angola which has a number of simple actions which are illustrated on pages 102, 103. The Action Creed is also very usable by children (and adults too!). For those who can, it ends with a jump of joy!

We believe in God the Father Almighty
who sent Jesus into the world.
He came as a baby, born of the Holy Spirit,
was crucified, died and was buried.
On the third day he rose again from the dead.
He ascended into heaven
where he prays for us continually.
Praise the Lord. Halleluia!

WE BELIEVE

We believe in God the Father Almighty
who sent Jesus into the world.
He came as a baby, born of the Holy Spirit,
was crucified, died and was buried.
On the third day he rose again from the dead.
He ascended into heaven
where he prays for us continually.
Praise the Lord. Halleluia!

We believe in

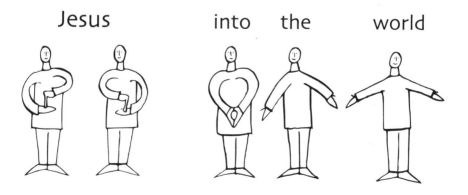

He came as a baby born of the Holy Spirit

was crucified

died

and was buried

On the third day he rose again from the dead

He ascended into heaven

where he prays for us continually

Praise the Lord

HALLELUIA!

WE SERVE

The statements that appear here are taken from the BUild version of the Five Core Values.

A talk, drama or meditation can take place at this point to illustrate and explore the Five Core Values of the church.

We are a prophetic community.

> This means
>> that God speaks to his people and God speaks through his people
>> about the wrongs and hurts in the world.

We are an inclusive community.

> This means
>> making everyone who comes to our church
>> feel welcome, wanted and needed.

We are a sacrificial community.

> This means
>> a church made up of people who want to be like Jesus
>> and give their lives for others.
>
> This means
>> thinking about the work we do for God
>> and thinking about how the way we live day by day
>> will make a difference to other people.

We are a missionary community.

> This means
>> if we follow Jesus and do what he asks,
>> others will see and hear about his love for them
>> and will want to follow Jesus too.

We are a worshipping community.

> This means
>> worship must not just be what we do on Sunday
>> but how we follow Jesus every day of the week.

WE COVENANT

Thanking our loving God is normal in teaching and worship with special groups. Caring friendship and mutual help are important parts of their experience. Often those with varying disabilities are alert to others' needs and difficulties and they feel for, help and enable one another: examples might be drawn out. They rely on people's promises, like the friends who provide transport to the church. They are disappointed if a promise fails. This covenant prayer is a special promise.

Illustrations to go with the Covenant Prayer are included in the accompanying CD and are also available on the Baptist Union of Great Britain website: www.baptist.org.uk.

It is helpful if those with a learning disability are able to look at the themes and reflect in advance on their own experiences. It is important that people with a learning disability are given the opportunity to share in the preparation process. The material might even be incorporated into the period of preparation of the whole fellowship.

Let us say together:

**God you are very special;
you made us,
and you go on loving us every day of our lives**

**There are so many reasons to say thank you, God;
you work hard to keep your friendship with us alive.**

**Your Son, Jesus, has set us free
from everything that can harm us.**

**Today we are going to make promises:
to you, God, and to our Christian friends.**

**We promise to take care of each other;
and to work together for you.
Please help us to keep these promises each new day. Amen.**

One sentence prayers for help can be added.

WE SHARE

Sharing the Peace may depend on what a group is used to. For example, the Living Stones Group from Harlow have a way of singing the repeated line, 'The Father himself loves you', sung to one person after another as they go round greeting the congregation.

BENEDICTION

The words of the Grace are often appropriate for people with a learning disability — the associations of these words (in terms of church life) are as important as the content!

**The grace of our Lord Jesus Christ,
the love of God
and the fellowship of the Holy Spirit
be with us all evermore. Amen**

COVENANTING TO FORM A NEW CHURCH

The forming of a new church should be marked by the presence of the wider Christian community. A regional minister, and other representatives of the local Baptist association, together with guests from other parts of the Christian Church and of the civic community should be invited. In an ecumenical situation, where there is a shared building or a Local Ecumenical Partnership, the service should be planned in co-operation with the other participants.

When the congregation is gathered together, it is appropriate that the believers who are to form the new church should sit together at the front.

After worship which includes praise, confession, scripture reading and preaching, a representative of the new church tells of the steps that led to the formation of this church, laying special emphasis on why the people believe it is the will of the Lord Jesus Christ to establish his Church in this place.

ACT OF COVENANTING

A regional minister, or another representative of the wider church, introduces the act of covenant

We have gathered today
in the name of our Lord Jesus Christ
so that you may covenant
with the Lord and with each other
and be fully constituted
as a fellowship of believers,
the body of Christ.

There are four things asked of those who enter this covenant:
> faith in the Lord Jesus Christ;
> mutual love within the fellowship;
> a willingness to obey Christ's great commission;
> a commitment to the wider fellowship of God's people,
> > and to working with others.

The members of the new church stand and respond to the following questions

As believers who are to form … Church,
do you believe in one God,
Father, Son and Holy Spirit?

We do. This is the God in whom we trust.

Do you confess Jesus Christ
as your Lord and Saviour?

We do. He has redeemed us and called us by name.

Do you turn from sin, renounce evil
and intend to follow Christ?

We do. Christ is our way.
With the Spirit's help,
we will follow this Jesus
in the church and in the world.

Jesus said: 'I give you a new commandment:
love one another; as I have loved you,
so you are to love one another.
If there is this love among you,
then everyone will know
that you are my disciples.'

I call on you to greet one another
in the name of the Lord Jesus Christ
and to share his peace.

The members of the new church may share the peace with one another and may also be joined
in this by the whole congregation. The leader then says

I invite you now to covenant together
before God and each other.

Creating and redeeming God,
we give you thanks and praise.
Your covenant of grace
was made for our salvation
in Jesus Christ our Lord.

We come this day
to covenant with you
and with our companions in discipleship
**   to watch over each other in love**
**   and to walk together**
**   in ways known and still to be made known.**

Pour down your Spirit upon us,
help us so to walk in your ways
that the promises we make this day,
and the life that we live together,
may be an offering of love,
our duty and delight,
glorifying to you,
Father, Son and Holy Spirit. Amen

This day we give ourselves to the Lord
and to each other
to be bound together in fellowship
and to work together in the unity of the Spirit
for the sake of God's mission:

in our local congregation,
in partnership with other Christians,
in our ... Baptist Association
and in the Baptist Union of Great Britain.

We commit all we have and all we are
to fulfilling God's purposes of love.

*Representatives of the Baptist community and the wider Church are invited to greet
representatives of the new church with the hand of fellowship.*

*As an act of unity, the entire congregation should be asked to stand, and a prayer be offered,
which may be extempore or as follows*

We dedicate this fellowship
to live to the glory of God,
Father, Son, and Holy Spirit.

Creator God, we praise you
that you made the whole earth
to shine with your glory.
Lord Jesus Christ, we praise you
that you lived among us,
and we have seen your glory;
that you were lifted up on the Cross for us,
raised from death, and exalted to heaven.
Holy Spirit, we praise you
that on the day of Pentecost you gave birth
to the Church of Jesus Christ,
and still you gather God's people
for worship, fellowship and mission.

Now we pray for this new community of your people,
that they may be rooted in the gospel of Jesus Christ:

a worshipping community
**living in your love
and seeking your will;**

a missionary community
**where Jesus Christ is proclaimed
as Saviour and Lord;**

an inclusive community
**where all are welcome
and the peace of Christ is shared;**

a sacrificial community
**where the servant way is honoured
and self is left behind;**

a prophetic community
**witnessing to God's kingdom
and seeking the Spirit's work in the world.**

As this church continues in fellowship
with the association, the Baptist Union,
and the whole Church of Christ,
we pray for the grace to support and encourage one another,
that we may all grow together in the unity of the Spirit;
through Jesus Christ our Lord.

The members of the new church may now come forward and sign the church roll.

The service continues with the Lord's Supper.

AFFIRMING FELLOWSHIP

There will be various occasions, such as church anniversaries or the new year, when a congregation may wish to affirm the joys and responsibilities of fellowship. Covenant material will often be appropriate for such purposes and covenant material from this and others sections may be helpfully adapted. Here is some additional material which may be of use.

As well as covenant-making, prayers may include thanksgiving for the past and the hope of faithfulness in the future; thankfulness for those who have passed on the faith to us; and prayers for the fellowship of the church and its responsiveness to God's will in its life and mission. Dedication and trust are also suitable themes.

Genesis 12.1; Deuteronomy 6.4–9; 30.11–15; Psalm 90.1f.; Isaiah 49.5f.; 51.1–3; Acts 2.42–47; 1 Corinthians 1.26–31; 10.16f.; 12.4–7; 14.26; 15.1f.; 2 Corinthians 4.5–9; 5.16–18; Ephesians 3.14–19; 4.1–6; Philippians 2.1–5; Hebrews 11.1f., 8–10; 12.1f.; 12.18a, 22–24a; 1 Peter 2.9f.; 1 John 1.5–7; Revelation 7.9–10.

DEDICATION

Lord, how strange it is
that you should call us to be your Church,
yet you have always worked through women and men
in the working out of your purpose.
Through prophets and disciples,
leaders and followers, preachers and listeners,
you have called your people,
that your redeeming love might work through them.
Above all, in Jesus your Word has become flesh
and a human being has lived your will.
He has died for us and you have raised him for us,
that he might be our foundation and our head.
Fill us with his love
that we might truly be his disciples.

We dedicate ourselves now
to being your people.
Accept our worship and our prayers,
our intentions and our gifts.
All has come from you and now, as we pray,
your Spirit prompts us and empowers us.
Grant us your grace
that we might be faithful to our calling as your Church.
Deepen our faith,
strengthen our love,
and increase our hope
that we might be an offering acceptable to you
and available for your will;
through Jesus Christ our Lord. **Amen.**

COLLECT

Covenant God,
you are always faithful
and your promises of grace are certain and sure.
Open our hearts by the influence of your Spirit
that we may delight in the fellowship of your people;
strengthen our wills by the work of your Spirit
that we may be faithful in the promises
we have made to you and to each other,
through Jesus Christ
in whose cross and resurrection
you have established a new covenant. **Amen.**

CALLING AND SERVING

MINISTRY IN
THE COMMUNITY OF DISCIPLES

The fundamental ministry in, and of, the Christian Church is exercised by God in Christ; and all Christians are called to share in the ministry of this missionary God, to serve God and to serve God's world. This section therefore begins with material for the **commissioning** of various forms of ministry within a local church.

However, the Church has always recognized that some are called to forms of leadership and service within the Church of Jesus Christ as ministers of word and sacrament, pastors of the flock and proclaimers of the good news, the gospel. The Baptist Union of Great Britain affirms those called to these ministries by accrediting them as Baptist ministers, and calling them into covenant relationship with the whole church. For many this calling will express itself in the pastoral leadership of a local Baptist church, for others this will be a calling to work primarily as an evangelist, or youth specialist. Others are called as chaplains and sector ministers, or to the oversight of an association as a regional minister. Others serve the church nationally as servants of the Union, or are called to teach and train within the context of a Baptist theological college. The calling of those recognized and affirmed by the Baptist Union is celebrated in services of **ordination** to Christian ministry, while each new stage on the journey of ministry is marked by a service of **induction.**

At the conclusion of appropriate training, and having received an affirmation of the call to ministry through the invitation to the ministry of a local church, or of another pastoral community, a service of ordination celebrates the beginning of a life of service as a minister. This often takes place in the church in which the minister first received a call to ministry, and from which he or she will have received much encouragement through the process of selection and training. Sometimes, however, the ordination is combined with the induction to ministry in the church to which they are initially called to serve. The materials in this section offer resources which may be adapted for both kinds of service, and for the various forms of ministry which are nationally accredited: pastoral, evangelistic and youth ministries, as well as the translocal ministries of association teams, sector ministries and college tutors. It is normally a regional minister who presides on such occasions, although other representatives of the wider Church may, on occasion, be invited to preside.

Not all who give pastoral leadership to local congregations are nationally accredited by the Baptist Union. A growing number of associations are recognizing the local ministry of those who are not nationally accredited but who have undergone a process of testing, formation and service within the association. This recognition of local ministry is increasing, though not universal, and a pattern of **ordination for locally recognized ministry** is offered below. In addition, a pattern of **induction and commissioning for a minister in training** is offered for the growing number of people who prepare for accredited ministry through a congregation-based process of formation.

There are others whose calling takes them from their home community to serve with the Baptist Missionary Society, or other missionary agencies. A local church sending someone to serve overseas in such a capacity will want to mark that significant step in worship and promise. This section also contains resources for such a service of **commissioning**.

Patterns for such acts will be offered, indicating the essential ingredients and participants. These will be followed by a series of resources, with a number of alternative acts of ordination and induction, and the section will conclude with a few additional resources. Each act of commissioning, ordination or induction should occur within an act of worship in which the worship of God, preaching and prayer will have due place.

COMMISSIONING
WITHIN THE LOCAL CHURCH

The commissioning of deacons, elders or other local church workers within the context of worship (preferably at the Lord's Supper) is appropriate when the church meeting has previously called a person to a position of leadership and responsibility.

The minister or leader introduces each worker by name, indicates the office or work to which he or she has been called, and expresses the welcome and prayerful support of the church. Then follow scripture readings and prayer, which may be accompanied with the laying on of hands

- Introduction and welcome
- Confession of faith
- Affirmation of call and vow of dedication
- Prayer of thanksgiving and invocation with the laying on of hands

COMMISSIONING DEACONS, ELDERS AND OTHER WORKERS

This pattern for the commissioning of elders and deacons may be adapted for other offices and forms of ministry, with the suggested scripture readings and extra prayers incorporated. If only one person is being commissioned, the words should be amended accordingly.

In the name of the Lord Jesus Christ
we are now to receive and welcome these friends
whom God has called,
and whose calling the church meeting has recognized,
to serve as *deacons/elders* in this fellowship.

The leader reads the names of the deacons or elders, making reference to any particular sphere of service, such as church secretary or treasurer.

As servants of Christ in this church,
they are called to share with the minister
in the tasks of pastoral care, leadership and stewardship
within the life and mission of this congregation.
Trust them and pray for them,
and at all times help them in the work of the Lord.

One or more of the following scripture passages is read: Mark 10.43–51; Acts 6.1–6; Romans 12.1–4, 6–7, 11; Ephesians 4.1–3; 4.11–13; 1 Peter 4.10–11.

The minister asks the deacons or elder to be commissioned the following questions and they respond with the words indicated in bold

My *brothers/sisters*,
do you believe in one God,
Father, Son and Holy Spirit,
and do you confess Jesus Christ
as your Saviour and Lord?

**This is the God in whom we trust,
as we follow Jesus Christ.**

Do you believe that God has called you
through his church to this office,
and do you promise,
in dependence upon his grace,
to exercise this ministry faithfully.

As disciples of Jesus Christ, we do.

The leader addresses the congregation

Do you, members of this church,
confirm the call of God
to our *brothers/sisters A* and *B*
as ... *[sphere of service]*
in the service of Jesus Christ?

We do.

Will you support and encourage *them* in this ministry?

Gladly, we will.

Those to be commissioned may stand or kneel for the laying on of hands in which others may join the leader. The leader then prays, extempore or as follows

Loving God,
we wonder at the way you call women and men
into partnership with you
for the sake of your saving purposes for the world.
You call us in Christ and empower us by your Spirit,
so that your church may be built up
and your gospel proclaimed and lived.

We thank you for these *brothers/sisters*
whom you have called to serve you within this fellowship.
We give you thanks for all you give us through them,
for their following of Jesus and their willingness,
by your grace, to serve together.

As we commission them for this ministry,
we ask your blessing on them.
Guide and equip them by your Spirit
that your church may grow in wisdom, love and unity,
and that your name may be glorified,
through Jesus Christ our Lord.

The leader shall then, on behalf of the church, give the right hand of fellowship to the deacons/ elders/others, saying

A and *B*, you are commissioned to serve
as ... in this congregation.
May God bless you as you share in the ministry of Jesus Christ.
In all your words and deeds,
do everything in the name of the Lord Jesus,
giving thanks to God through him.

The congregation says

The Lord bless you and keep you;
the Lord make his face to shine upon you,
and be gracious to you;
the Lord lift up his countenance upon you,
and give you peace.

SCRIPTURE PASSAGES FOR OTHER OFFICES

Children's leaders: Deuteronomy 6.4—9; 6.20—21, 23; Matthew 19.14; Mark 9.37; 1 Timothy 4.16.

Youth workers: Matthew 20.26—29; 23.11—12; Galatians 6.9; 2 Timothy 2.1—7.

Preachers: Isaiah 52.7; 1 Corinthians 1.17; 2.1—2; 2 Corinthians 4.5—6; 2 Timothy 2.15; 4.1—2, 5.

Music leaders: Psalms 96.1—2; 100.1; 150.1—2, 6; Ephesians 5.18b—19.

Housegroup leaders: Romans 12.1, 6, 11—12; Colossians 3.17; 1 Peter 4.10—11b; Hebrews 13.20—21.

ORDAINING FOR MINISTRY

The presiding minister is normally a regional minister or other minister with regional or national responsibility. Others, of course, may well lead the rest of the service or preach.

Ordination should only take place when the call of God has been tested and affirmed by the wider church and due formation and training have occurred. Consequently, the service should include commendations of the ordinand from the home church, the association which has commended them for ministry, the college where they have trained (or those responsible for their training) and the church, or other pastoral community, which has now invited them to minister.

The service should reflect the fact that ordained ministry is recognized nationally by the Baptist Union of Great Britain, and by the wider Church, for service and leadership within and beyond the local church and should include the following elements

- *Introduction* – on the meaning of ordination.
- *Telling the Story* – including testimony by the ordinand concerning his or her call to ministry and commendations by those who have tested and affirmed this call, including home church, association, college and calling church.
- *Confessing Faith and Promising Faithfulness: The Ordination Vows.*
- *Ordination Prayer with the laying on of hands.*
- *Presentation of an ordination Bible* or other symbol of ministry by the college representative and, perhaps, by others, the presentation of other symbols.
- *Declaration of Ordination and Blessing.*

ORDAINING FOR ACCREDITED MINISTRY

INTRODUCTION

After a welcome and opening worship, the presiding minister addresses the congregation

Sisters and brothers,
we meet together in the name of God,
Father, Son and Holy Spirit,
to ordain *AB*
to the office and work of a Christian minister.

We believe God has called *A* to serve as a *pastor/evangelist/youth specialist*
and today we acknowledge and celebrate that call,
setting *her/him* apart with prayer
for the service and purposes of God.

If an act of induction is to follow in the same service, then words referring to induction may be inserted here (see page 144). Otherwise, the introduction continues uninterrupted.

All God's people are called to ministry.
All who are baptized into Jesus Christ
and have received the Holy Spirit
are called to serve our Lord Jesus Christ,
and one another,
in the fellowship of the Church
and in all that they do.
God gives gifts to all, so that, like a body,
all may share in the purposes of Christ
for the world which God has made
and for which Jesus Christ has died.

All are called to be disciples.
All are called to be servants of God in Christ Jesus
through the power of the Holy Spirit.
Yet God calls some to servant leadership in the Church
and these are to be honoured among us.

None may take this office upon themselves.
Today we acknowledge
our dependence upon God
and seek to do his will.
We have sought God's guidance
and prayerfully tested the calling of *A*
within the local and the wider church
Now we gather in the name of Jesus Christ
to ordain *A* as a Christian minister
and to seek God's blessing
through the power and graces of the Holy Spirit.

TELLING THE STORY

Statements are made by the ordinand, a representative of the church which commended the ordinand for ministerial training, the association which tested and commended that call through its recognition processes, the college at which the ordinand trained for ministry (or those responsible for their training) and the church which has now called her or him to the office of pastor [associate pastor/youth specialist/evangelist]. If the ordination follows a recommendation from a national selection process, the association representative may adapt the section where the college commends the ordinand. Alternatively, the following questions and responses may be used or adapted.

The presiding minister first addresses the ordinand

Christian ministry is a sharing in the ministry of Jesus Christ,
through the power of the Holy Spirit
and in response to the call of God.
A, you are already a disciple of Jesus Christ,
do you now acknowledge this further call on your life?
Do you willingly and joyfully submit yourself
as God's servant and as a minister in God's Church?

I do, for God has called me.

A, come and tell us of the work of grace in your life
and of God's calling of you to ministry.

The one to be ordained testifies to the call of God upon his or her life.

The presiding minister then addresses a representative of the sending church

EF, you represent the church
of which A was a member
when *she/he* heard and responded to this call of Jesus Christ.
Can you confirm that the members of the church
recognized God at work in this?

Church representative

I can.
A was received into the membership of ... Church

A brief account of the ways in which that call was recognized may be given here.

As she/he played her/his part in the life and ministry of our church,
the members recognized the calling of God,
and commended A for preparation for ordination.

The presiding minister addresses a representative of the commending association

GH, you represent the … Baptist Association,
also charged with testing A's call to Christian ministry.
Do you believe God has set *her/him* apart
for the work of Christian ministry
amongst the churches of the Baptist Union of Great Britain?

We do.
Having tested this call to ministry
through question, commendation and prayer.
We gladly commend A for ordination today.

The presiding minister addresses a representative of the college at which the ordinand prepared
for ministry

JK, you represent … College,
where A was prepared for Christian ministry.
[or: you represent those who prepared A for ministry]
Do you now recommend *him/her*
for ordination to ministry in the Church of Jesus Christ?

A has prepared for Christian ministry
through a life of study, prayer and service.
***She/he* has studied the scriptures**
and the faith of the Christian Church,
and has applied *herself/himself*
to the practice of ministry.
Sharing in the Church's fellowship and witness,
***she/he* has been equipped for Christian ministry**
as a *pastor/evangelist/youth specialist*,
and we now commend *her/him* to the churches.

The presiding minister addresses a representative of the calling church

The call to be a minister of the Church of Christ is a call to service
and will be sealed through the invitation to serve
in the fellowship and witness of a local Christian community.
LM, you represent … *Church [or other pastoral community]*,
can you confirm that A is called to Christian ministry
and that you have invited *her/him* to exercise that ministry amongst you?

I can.
We the members of … Baptist Church have invited A
to be our *pastor/associate pastor/youth specialist/evangelist*.
We have worshipped together,
shared our hopes for the future,
and believe that God is calling us to journey together.

We have heard how the call to Christian ministry
has been heard by *A*
and confirmed by those charged with testing it.
A will now make promises
to exercise that ministry
with faithfulness and love.

CONFESSING FAITH AND PROMISING FAITHFULNESS: THE ORDINATION VOWS

Do you believe in one God,
Father, Son and Holy Spirit,
and do you confess Jesus Christ
as your Saviour and Lord?

I do.
This is the God in whom I trust

Do you believe that you are called by God
to a life of ministry
and the work of a *pastor/evangelist/youth specialist?*

I believe that God has called me.

Will you proclaim the good news of Jesus Christ
through word and deed,
making disciples
and seeking the coming kingdom of God

As a disciple of Jesus Christ,
I will call others to follow him.

Do you accept the scriptures
as revealing the salvation of God in Jesus Christ?
Will you live a life of holiness and prayer
and open yourself
to the ministry of the Holy Spirit
who will lead us into all truth?

As a disciple of Jesus Christ,
I will search the word of God
and be open to the Spirit's leading.

Will you serve and pastor the people of God
with gentle nurture and faithful teaching?
Will you set before them the whole counsel of God
as you proclaim Christ, the living Word?
Will you be faithful in worship and prayer,
and, through word and sacrament,
will you celebrate the grace of God,
seeking to pattern yourself and those you serve
after the likeness of Jesus Christ?

**As a disciple of Jesus Christ,
I will minister in his way.**

Will you 'make every effort
to maintain the unity of the Spirit in the bond of peace'?
Will you represent the wider Church of Jesus Christ
in the places where you serve,
and watching over them in humility and patience,
will you care for the people of God,
serving, and not lording it over them?
Will you welcome the stranger
and build up the body of Christ
until we all come 'to maturity,
measured by nothing less than the full stature of Christ?' — reply overleaf.

For youth specialists

Will you serve, nurture and protect
those young people entrusted to your care
and will you share in oversight, leadership and support
of those who serve with you?
Will you seek to reach others
with the good news of Jesus Christ,
making disciples and living the love of God?

For evangelists

Will you witness to the gospel of Jesus Christ
in a needy world
and amongst those who do not know his name?
Will you seek to be a minister of peace,
a sharer of love
and a sign of hope?

The ordinand replies and the service continues

Abiding in the love of God,
and relying on his grace, I will.

Will you pray for the coming kingdom of God?
Will you, under God, build up the body of Christ,
seek peace, work for justice,
minister forgiveness
and always walk in the way of love?

**As a disciple of Jesus Christ
and with the help of God's Spirit, I will.**

Jesus challenged his disciples to leave self behind,
take up a cross and follow him.
Will you follow Christ wherever he leads you,
remaining faithful to your Lord
until he comes or calls you to your heavenly rest?

With the Lord's help, I will.

May the God of grace
keep you steadfast
in the vows you have made,
living and serving
in the power of the Holy Spirit
as a faithful disciple of Jesus Christ.

The Declaration of Principle may be read aloud by another

As members of the Baptist Union of Great Britain,
we make this Declaration of Principle.

The basis of this Union is:

1 That our Lord and Saviour Jesus Christ,
God manifest in the flesh,
is the sole and absolute authority
in all matters pertaining to faith and practice,
as revealed in the Holy Scriptures,
and that each church has liberty,
under the guidance of the Holy Spirit,
to interpret and administer his laws.

2   That Christian baptism is the immersion in water
into the name of the Father, the Son, and the Holy Ghost,
of those who have professed repentance towards God
and faith in our Lord Jesus Christ
who 'died for our sins according to the Scriptures;
was buried, and rose again on the third day'.

3   That it is the duty of every disciple
to bear personal witness to the gospel of Jesus Christ,
and to take part in the evangelization of the world.

Are you in whole-hearted agreement with this statement?

 I am.

Alternatively, the Declaration of Principle may be printed and the ordinand asked

Are you in whole-hearted agreement
with the Declaration of Principle
of the Baptist Union of Great Britain?

I am.

ORDINATION PRAYER WITH THE LAYING ON OF HANDS

Following the practice of the early Church, we formally set *A* apart with
the laying on of hands. In this act of ordination, representatives of the wider
Church will share with those representing local congregations, for we are
ordaining *A* to Christian ministry in the whole Church of Jesus Christ.

*The ordinand kneels or stands and representatives of those who are sharing in the service,
ministerial and lay, gather around. The presiding minister prays extempore, or as follows,
adapting words as necessary for particular forms of ministry.*

Gracious and eternal God,
with joy we give you thanks and praise
for you are a faithful God.

By your word, you called creation into being
and made us in your image
to love and serve you.
By your saving love
you sent Jesus Christ to live among us,
to redeem your people and establish your peace.
By your Holy Spirit,
you shower gifts on your children,
opening hearts and lives to your grace,
empowering us to live holy and joyful lives.

We praise you, eternal God,
for the church throughout the world,
born of your love,
saved by your grace,
and sustained by your Holy Spirit.
Make us the community you have called us to be:
a chosen race, a royal priesthood,
a holy nation, your very own people,
gifted to proclaim your marvellous love.

Those gathered around the ordinand lay hands on her/him and the presiding minister and congregation say together

Gracious God,
pour out your Spirit upon your servant A,
whom you have called.
Grant *her/him* the same mind
that was in Christ Jesus.

Using the appropriate section, the presiding minister continues

For pastors

Give *her/him* a spirit of wisdom
rightly to proclaim your word in Christ
through preaching and through sacrament,
and in the words and actions of daily living.
Give *her/him* the gifts of your Holy Spirit
to build up the church,
to strengthen the common life of your people,
and to lead with compassion and vision.

For youth specialists

Give *her/him* a spirit of wisdom
rightly to proclaim your word in Christ
to young people,
in friendship, service and witness,
and in the words and actions of daily living.
Give *her/him* the gifts of your Holy Spirit
to make disciples,
to care for the vulnerable,
to share in the pastoral care
of those who work with young people,
to inspire the hopeful
and embody the love of Jesus Christ.

Give *her/him* a spirit of wisdom
rightly to proclaim your word in Christ
with courage and love, word and action.
Give *her/him* the gifts of your Holy Spirit
to make disciples and to bring
hope to the despairing,
meaning to the lost
and the love of Christ to all.

Then the congregation may say

**In the walk of faith and for the work of ministry,
give to your servant A,
and to all who serve among your people,
gladness and strength,
discipline and hope,
humility, humour and courage,
and an abiding sense of your presence.**

The laying on of hands is completed and the presiding minister continues

Generous God,
pour out your Holy Spirit upon your church and all its people,
that, baptized into your service and united in Christ's love,
we may serve you with joy and faithfulness
until all things are made new.
Let the word we proclaim
be your word of truth.
Let the compassion we show to the world
be your love in Christ.

Show us the transforming power of your grace
in our life together,
that we may be effective servants of the gospel
and offer a compelling witness in the world
to the good news of Christ Jesus our Lord. **Amen.**

Alternative ordination prayers may be found in the section of additional ordination material below.

If the prayer is extempore, it should contain
- *an invocation of the Spirit of God*
- *a setting aside for the work of ministry*
- *prayer for God's blessing and an enduing with wisdom, authority and spiritual power*

Further prayers may be offered by those sharing in the laying on of hands, and by others.

DECLARATION AND BLESSING

In the name of the Father, the Son and the Holy Spirit,
we declare you, *A*, to be ordained
a pastor/youth specialist/evangelist
in the church of Jesus Christ
and commissioned for ministry
within the Baptist Union of Great Britain.
Seek the kingdom of God,
be faithful and true in your ministry
so that your whole life may bear witness
to the crucified and risen Christ.

PRESENTATION OF THE ORDINATION BIBLE

College representative

Here is the living word of God:
words to encourage the weak,
restore the lost,
and build up the body of Christ.
Read them and teach them,
proclaim the gospel of Christ
that the people of God
may be a gospel people.

Others may at this point present other symbols of ministry, with suitable accompanying words. For example, a towel may be presented with the words, 'Jesus washed his disciples' feet and gave us an example. Receive this towel as a sign that you also must serve, for the one who would be first must be the servant of all.' Alternatively, the college representative may present a different gift as a symbol of ministry.

The congregation then says

**The Lord bless you and keep you.
The Lord make his face to shine upon you
and be gracious to you.
The Lord lift up the light of his countenance upon you
and give you peace. Amen.**

ADDITIONAL MATERIAL

CONFESSING FAITH AND PROMISING FAITHFULNESS: ORDINATION VOWS

The presiding minister addresses the ordinand

My *brother/sister*, do you believe in one God,
Father, Son and Holy Spirit,
and do you confess Jesus Christ
as your Saviour and Lord?

**I do.
This is the God in whom I trust.**

The call of Jesus Christ to all who follow him
is to go and make disciples of all nations,
baptizing them in the name
of the Father, the Son and the Holy Spirit.
Will you proclaim the good news of Jesus Christ
through your words and deeds
and seek the coming kingdom of God?

I will, for Jesus Christ has called me.

Jesus said to Peter 'feed my sheep'.
Will you serve and lead the people of God
through pastoral care, gentle nurture and faithful teaching?
Will you set before them the whole counsel of God,
serving after the pattern of Jesus himself,
the good shepherd, whose people they are?

Abiding in the love of God, I will.

Paul, the apostle, writes,
'set the believers an example in speech and conduct,
in love, in faith, in purity.'
Will you endeavour to lead a godly life,
setting an example to all people,
especially the flock of Christ committed to your charge,
and will you be diligent in prayer,
in reading the Scriptures
and in all studies that will deepen your faith and ministry?

With the Lord's help, I will.

Paul, the apostle, writes
that we are to 'make every effort
to maintain the unity of the Spirit in the bond of peace.'
Will you exercise your ministry
in all humility and patience,
serving the people of God and not lording it over them;
welcoming the stranger and building up the body of Christ
until we all 'come to the unity of the faith
and of the knowledge of the Son of God, to maturity,
measured by nothing less than the full stature of Christ?'

In the power of the Holy Spirit, I will.

Jesus challenged his disciples to leave self behind,
take up a cross and follow him.
Will you follow Christ wherever he leads you,
remaining faithful to your Lord
until he comes or calls you to your heavenly rest?

With the Lord's help, I will.

May the God of grace
keep you steadfast
in the vows you have made,
living and serving
in the power of the Holy Spirit
as a faithful disciple of Jesus Christ.

ORDINATION PRAYERS

Loving God,
who sent your Son into the world
to be the Servant of all
and the Saviour of the world,
fill your servant *A* with your Holy Spirit
as we ordain *him/her* in your name
to share in the ministry of Christ.

Fill *him/her* with all grace and truth
that *he/she* might lead your people in their mission
to proclaim the gospel of Jesus Christ
and to care with the compassion of Christ.
Send upon *him/her* the Spirit of wisdom
to lead your people into all truth,
in accordance with the scriptures,
and to maintain the truths of the faith
against error and falsehood.

As a faithful pastor to the flock of Christ,
give *him/her* patience with the weak
and love for all
as *he/she* cares for those committed to *his/her* charge.
Enable *him/her* to bring healing to the broken,
strength to the weary and hope to the despairing.
May *he/she* lead your people faithfully in worship and prayer,
baptizing disciples and sharing bread and wine,
always setting forth the word of life before your people.

Defend *him/her* from all evil,
keeping *him/her* faithful in times of trial,
abounding in hope and filled with mercy.
Send your Holy Spirit upon *A*,
that *he/she* may empowered for ministry
and filled with your love,
though Jesus Christ our Lord. **Amen.**

Or

Loving God, in the name of Jesus Christ
we now set apart your servant *A*
for the work of ministry
as a *pastor/evangelist/youth specialist.*

Send your Spirit, we pray,
that *she/he* may be empowered for service
and formed in the likeness of Jesus.
Guide and direct *her/him*
as *she/he* seeks to lead and serve your people.
Give *her/him* the gift of wisdom
for teaching the mind of Christ,
and guide *her/his* steps
that others might be led in the way of Christ.
Grant *A* an abiding sense of your presence
and fill *her/him* with the love of Christ
that *she/he* may be his true disciple.

Those sharing in the laying on of hands or others in the congregation may add brief extempore prayers, asking for God's blessing upon the ordinand and her or his ministry.

INDUCTING INTO MINISTRY

The act of induction of a minister to the pastoral leadership of a congregation, or other forms of ministry, marks a new beginning for the church and is an opportunity for both minister and church to renew their commitment to God and God's mission in the world.

The person leading the service is often the moderator of the church, appointed to serve during its period of pastoral vacancy, and a regional minister normally presides in the act of induction, though this may be led by someone else who represents the wider Church. The act of induction should include the following elements

1   *Welcome and Introduction* – stating the purpose of the event
2   *Telling the Story* – an account of the church's call of this minister
3   *Confessing Faith and Promising Faithfulness* – including the induction vows by the minister
4   *Confessing Faith and Promising Faithfulness* – including the induction vows by the church
5   *Induction Prayer, usually with the laying on of hands*
6   *Declaration of induction and Blessing*
7   *Greetings*

When an induction follows the ordination of the minister in the same service, care should be taken to avoid repetition, such as the confession of faith. Additional material for such an act of induction is offered below.

Two full acts of induction for a pastor within the local church are included below, together with the additional material mentioned above and resources appropriate for other spheres of ministry, ordered according to the relevant numbered sections.

INDUCTING A MINISTER

1 WELCOME AND INTRODUCTION

After opening worship, the presiding minister greets the congregation and introduces the service

You, the members of … Baptist Church
have called *AB* to be your pastor,
and believing this call to be of God,
he/she has accepted,
and comes now to be inducted into this office.
At this significant time
in the life of both church and minister
I invite you all to renew your commitment
to Christ and this Church,
as together you share in God's mission
of saving love to the world.

First we shall hear how God has led
both church and minister
to issue and accept this call.

2 TELLING THE STORY

The church secretary, or other representative of the local church, describes how the church came to call this person to be its minister.

The minister elect gives an account of the call to this particular ministry.

3 CONFESSING FAITH AND PROMISING FAITHFULNESS: THE MINISTER

The presiding minister questions the minister elect

All Christians are called to be disciples of Jesus Christ
and to follow in his way.
A, as a Christian minister,
you are first a disciple of Christ,
and so I ask you to affirm afresh
your faith and trust in God,
a faith which you have already confessed in baptism.
Do you believe in one God,
Father, Son and Holy Spirit,
and do you confess Jesus Christ
as your Saviour and Lord?

I do.

A, you have been called to be the pastor
of this church and congregation.
Do you accept the charge from Christ
to care for his people with all diligence and compassion?
Will you care for the weak,
bring Christ's healing to the brokenhearted,
lift up the downcast,
and pray regularly for those committed to your care?

I will, God's Spirit empowering me.

Will you 'equip the saints for the work of ministry,
for building up the body of Christ'?
Will you lead and enable God's people
in their mission to the world,
seeking God's kingdom,
proclaiming the gospel in word and deed
and seeking to make Christ known in every way?

I will, the risen Christ inspiring me.

Will you 'make every effort to maintain the unity of the Spirit
in the bond of peace'?
By your example,
will you lead this church
in all godly living and devotion to Christ
through prayer and the reading of scripture?
Will you be faithful in the leading of worship,
in presiding at the table of the Lord
and in preaching the word of God?

**In the name of God who is
the Father of all,
the living Word
and the Spirit of unity, I will.**

Optional question for minister's partner

You have heard the promises made by *A* today.
Will you join in that commitment to Christ and his people,
promising to support ~~and~~ encourage ~~him/her in his/her ministry~~ *and work with him in his ministry*
~~in~~ *among* this church and community?
I will.

4 CONFESSING FAITH AND PROMISING FAITHFULNESS: THE CHURCH

The presiding minister addresses those who will share in leadership with the minister, such as elders, deacons or other ministerial staff

Do you believe you have been called by God
to work together humbly and willingly
in serving this church and community?

We do.

Do you promise to honour and respect one another,
'doing nothing from vain conceit,
but in humility regarding others as better than yourselves,'
and do you promise to work with the members of this church
in its calling to seek the kingdom of God?

We will.

I invite the members of this church to stand.

My sisters and brothers,
a new chapter in the life of this church is opened today.
I invite you now to renew your commitment
to Christ and this church,
to affirm again the vows of your baptism.
Do you believe in one God,
Father, Son and Holy Spirit,
and do you confess Jesus Christ
as your Saviour and Lord?

We do.

Do you accept and welcome *A*
as your *minister/pastor*,
and do you promise to honour and support *him/her*
with your love and prayers,
working together with *him/her* in your shared calling
to witness to Christ in this place?

We do.

Paul, the apostle, says 'You were bought with a price.'
Will you serve Jesus Christ as Lord,
bearing witness to him
and daily taking up your cross to follow him?

We will.

Would the whole congregation please stand.

As representatives of the wider church and community,
will you offer your support at this new beginning
in the life of church and minister,
and will you join in praying for them all?

We will.

5 INDUCTION PRAYER

*The congregation remains standing and prayer is offered, either extempore by those who now
gather round the minister to lay hands on him/her, or, using the following*

Merciful God,
whose steadfast love is renewed every morning,
we give you thanks for this day of new beginnings
in the life of this minister (and *his/her* family),
and for this new chapter in the story of this church.
You have led pastor and people together,
guiding them by your Spirit,
and we ask that your guiding and strengthening hand
will remain upon them
as together they enter this covenant partnership with you,
for the sake of the gospel.

For *A,* we pray that you will renew within *him/her*
the gifts and graces of your Holy Spirit,
that *he/she* may lead a life worthy of the calling of Christ.
So fill *him/her* with your Spirit
that *he/she* may lead those committed to *his/her* charge
in proclaiming the gospel of Christ
and together with all your people
serve Christ and his world
in all compassion and faithfulness.

Fill *him/her* with wisdom,
understanding and strength
and keep from *him/her* all evil,
error, arrogance and self-seeking,
that *he/she* may 'set the believers an example
in conduct, speech, love,
faith and purity.'

And for your church here,
we pray that the mutual love and trust expressed today
might grow through all the chances and changes of this life.
Help all who gather here in the name of Christ
to maintain the unity of the Spirit in the bond of peace,
that together they might become for all to see,
'a letter of Christ written with the Spirit of the living God.'
Prosper all that is the work of your Spirit,
that the members of this church may be blessed
and given to your world in costly service and fruitful ministry,
to your praise and glory.
This we ask in the name
of the ascended and interceding Christ. **Amen.**

6 DECLARATION AND BLESSING

The presiding minister then says

AB, in the name of our Lord Jesus Christ,
in the name of the Baptist Union of Great Britain
and on behalf of this church,
I declare you inducted to the pastorate of this church and congregation.
As you lead the people of God and care for them,
as you serve and pray for this community,
may the Lord richly bless and sustain you.

Either the presiding minister or the whole congregation says

**The Lord bless you and keep you.
The Lord make his face to shine upon you
and be gracious to you.
The Lord lift up the light of his countenance upon you
and give you peace. Amen.**

7 GREETINGS

*The church secretary and others may now welcome the minister and his/her family, or this may
be reserved for a less formal occasion following the service. The service continues.*

A COVENANT PATTERN OF INDUCTION

At the heart of this induction service is an act of covenant between the church and the new minister. This replaces the traditional question and answer format and has the church and minister speaking directly to each other and to God as they affirm their faith and make a commitment to each other. It incorporates a statement of purpose based on the 'Five Core Values for a Gospel People'.

1 GREETING AND INTRODUCTION

After opening worship, the presiding minister greets the congregation and introduces the service

We have gathered
to induct a new minister, *AB*,
to work with the community of Christ here
at ... Church.

We come to affirm our belief
that as this church and minister
have explored the possibilities of life together here in ...,
they have been brought to this mutual commitment
through the movement and calling of God's Spirit.

Today we have come to witness the covenant
which this church and this minister are making with each other
to walk together as people of Christ.

So let us hear from the church and from *A*
as they share with us something of this story.

2 TELLING THE STORY

This might take the form of a scripted conversation between church and minister or else a simple statement by a representative

3 & 4 CONFESSING FAITH AND PROMISING FAITHFULNESS: THE COVENANT OF CHURCH AND MINISTER

The new minister invites the local church congregation to stand. They speak alternately, the congregation using the words in bold type

Today we stand with each other,

recognizing the Christ in our midst,

affirming our faith in the God who loves us
with a love that transforms us,

and who calls us to work for a transformed world.

Today we stand with each other,

recognizing the Christ in each other,

affirming the calling of the Spirit

who has brought us together this day.

Today I bring myself and the gifts I have,
and I covenant to serve and encourage
this church and community:
to respect and care for you,
to journey with you,
to take responsibility among you,
to seek God with you,
to listen to God in you,
and to work with you to be Christ in this world.

Today we bring ourselves and the gifts we have,
and we covenant to serve and encourage
this church and community:
to respect and care for each other,
to take responsibility for the people we are
and the people we hope to be in Christ,
and to encourage you as our minister
as we make this journey together.

What kind of people does Christ call us to be?

We are called to be a prophetic people,
working for justice, resisting violence
and challenging the abuse of power.

We are called to be an inclusive people,
pulling down the walls of prejudice
and welcoming the stranger.

We are called to be a sacrificial people,
risking uncertainty, becoming vulnerabe,
and reflecting the generosity of God.

We are called to be a missionary people,
demonstrating in word and action
the redeeming love of God in the world.

We are called to be a worshipping people,
seeking and celebrating the God who journeys with us,
and open to the Spirit in the whole of life.

God of life,
you call us and envision us,
we give ourselves today
to each other and to you,
trusting that as you call us
so you covenant
to share this journey with us,
to nurture and sustain our life together
and to guide our paths. **Amen.**

RECOGNITION

The presiding minister invites all to stand

As friends and representatives of the wider church and community,
we have heard this church and minister
affirm their faith and make a covenant
with each other and with God.

If you will recognize
and support this new relationship,
then say with me

Today we stand with you,
recognizing the commitment you have made,
offering our encouragement
for the challenges that lie ahead of you,
and sharing in your hope for a new day.

5 INDUCTION PRAYER FOR THE CHURCH AND MINISTER

*In the spirit of the covenant that has just been made between church and minister, these prayers
are not only for the minister, but for the minister and the church together. Any symbolic
gesture, such as the laying on of hands, if this is agreed by all parties, may be received by both
the minister and the representative(s) of the church.*

6 DECLARATION AND BLESSING

In the name of Jesus Christ
and his church here at …,
and in the name of the Baptist Union of Great Britain,
I now declare that *AB* has been inducted
to the pastorate of this church and congregation,
to work with them, and they with *her/him*,
in the ministry to which Christ has called them all.
As a token of this, I now offer a hand of fellowship.

*The hand of fellowship may be offered to both minister and representative(s) of the
local church.*

*The presiding minister invites the visiting members of the congregation, as representatives of
the wider church, to bless the new minister and congregation*

The covenant God
bind you in grace and love,
the faithful God
keep you faithful through all things
and the God of hope and peace
sustain you in the way of Jesus,
this day and every day. Amen

The service continues.

7 GREETINGS

INDUCTING DURING AN ORDINATION SERVICE

Where induction takes place in the same service as ordination, the repetition of statements and vows should be avoided. Here is material suitable for such an occasion.

1 WELCOME AND INTRODUCTION

The following words may be inserted after the second paragraph of the Introduction and Welcome *in the ordination service on page 121.*

You, the members of ... Baptist Church
have called *A* to be your pastor here,
and believing this call to be of God,
he/she has accepted,
and comes to be inducted to this office.

2 TELLING THE STORY

Earlier in the service, before the ordination vows, the ordinand and the secretary or representative of the calling church will have given accounts of the call to ministry and the call to serve in this particular local church.

3 CONFESSING FAITH AND PROMISING FAITHFULNESS: THE MINISTER

The regional minister addresses the newly ordained minister

A, as you serve within this church community,
will you commit yourself
to both giving to its members
and to receiving from them as members of the Body of Christ?
Will you lead and serve this fellowship
in your calling as a pastor,
seeking the kingdom of God
and always following our Lord Jesus Christ
who is the head of the Church?

**As a disciple of Jesus Christ,
and in the power of the Spirit,
I will.**

(Optional question for minister's spouse)

C, you have heard the commitment that *A* has made to this church.
Do you promise to encourage and support *him/her*
as *he/she* seeks to exercise *his/her* ministry
in this church and community?

As a disciple of Jesus Christ,
and in the power of the Spirit,
I will.

4 CONFESSING FAITH AND PROMISING FAITHFULNESS: THE CHURCH

The regional minister invites the deacons and/or elders of the church to stand and asks them

Do you believe in your hearts
that you have been truly called by God
to work with this minister
and with this church and congregation?

We do.

Do you welcome and accept *A* as your pastor,
and do you promise to honour and support *her/him*
with your love and prayers,
working together with *her/him* in your shared calling
to witness to Christ in this place?

As disciples of Jesus Christ,
and in the power of the Spirit,
we will.

The regional minister invites all the members of the calling church to stand

My sisters and brothers,
as members of this church,
I invite you now to renew your commitment
to Christ and his church,
and to affirm again the vows of your baptism.
Do you believe in one God,
Father, Son and Holy Spirit,
and do you confess Jesus Christ
as your Saviour and Lord?

We do.

Believing that you are called by God to work with this minister,
do you now acknowledge and receive *AB* as your minister?

Gladly, we do.

Will you honour and support *her/him,*
praying and working together in the unity of the Spirit
as the people of God?

As disciples of Jesus Christ,
and in the power of the Spirit,
we will.

The regional minister then invites the visiting members of the congregation to stand and, as
representatives of the wider church, asks them

As friends of this church
and as representatives of the wider Church of Jesus Christ,
do you support this new beginning in the life of ... Baptist Church
and *A* as its minister?

We do.

Will you all offer your love, prayer and encouragement
to this fellowship in the days ahead?

As disciples of Jesus Christ,
and in the power of the Spirit,
we will.

The service continues with the induction prayer.

INDUCTING A YOUTH SPECIALIST

1 INTRODUCTION

After opening worship, the presiding minister greets the congregation and introduces the service

God gives a variety of ministries to the Church.
Today we give thanks for the gifts
which God is giving to this local church
through the ministry of *AB* as a youth specialist.
We thank God for *his/her* gifts and training
and today set *him/her* apart for work with young people
in this congregation and beyond it.
Here we celebrate the whole people of God, young and old,
especially thanking God for the presence of young people,
for their contribution to this fellowship
and for their own journeys of faith.
We shall together make promises
and together pray for *A* and for one another.

2 TELLING THE STORY

A statement explaining the invitation of the local church will be given by the church secretary or other representative.

A statement by the youth specialist of how they have discerned the guidance of God leading them towards this particular ministry will be given.

3 CONFESSING FAITH AND PROMISING FAITHFULNESS: YOUTH SPECIALIST

The presiding minister invites the youth specialist to respond to the following questions

A, we have heard how you have been called by God
to serve as *youth pastor/youth worker* here at ... Baptist Church.
Now you should reaffirm your faith in God.

Do you believe in one God, Father, Son and Holy Spirit,
and do you confess Jesus Christ as your Saviour and Lord?

I do.

Will you carry out the ministry to which you have been called
with enthusiasm and dedication,
introducing young people to Jesus Christ
and discipling them,
working within the church and in the community?

Relying on God's help, I will.

Will you work in partnership
with the other minister(s) of this church
with the deacons, youth team and members of the fellowship?
Will you encourage and enable them
to carry out Christ's mission in the local community and the world?

I will, with God's help and guidance.

Will you be faithful in prayer,
in reading the scriptures
and in study,
that your faith may be deepened
and that you may live out the truth of the gospel?

Relying on God's help, I will.

The presiding minister invites the other minister(s) and deacons and/or elders to stand and asks them

Will you accept *A* to lead and serve alongside you
in *his/her* calling as a youth specialist in this church,
honouring and supporting *his/her* work?

Gladly, we will.

4 CONFESSING FAITH AND PROMISING FAITHFULNESS: THE CHURCH

The presiding minister invites the church members to stand and asks them

Brothers and sisters in Christ,
will you acknowledge and receive *A*
as your *youth pastor/youth worker*?
Will you pray for *him/her*,
encourage and support *him/her* in the days ahead?

We will.

The presiding minister invites the young people and then the whole congregation to stand, and asks them

Will you encourage and support *A*
in *his/her* ministry amongst you,
and will you play your part alongside him
in forwarding the work of the kingdom of God?

Gladly, we will.

Those laying hands on the new youth pastor/youth worker may now be invited to gather around him/her and may offer prayer after the induction prayer.

5 INDUCTION PRAYER

Loving God,
we thank you for the guidance of your Holy Spirit
which has brought church and youth pastor together today.
Bless them in their life together
as followers of Jesus Christ.
We pray that their partnership in the gospel
may bring blessing to many young people
and praise to your name.

For *A,* we pray that you will keep *her/him* faithful to *her/his* calling,
in good times and bad.
Equip *him/her* with all the wisdom
and spiritual gifts that are needed.
Grant *him/her* patience, joy, self-control
and all the harvest of the Spirit
that *he/she* might become more like Jesus Christ.
Give *him/her* courage in proclaiming the good news of Jesus
and in demonstrating the values of the Kingdom.

To you be glory,
in the church and in Christ Jesus,
from generation to generation for evermore. **Amen.**

6 DECLARATION AND BLESSING

In the name of our Lord Jesus Christ,
and on behalf ... Baptist Church
and the wider Christian community,
I declare you to be inducted
as *youth pastor/youth worker* of ... Baptist Church.

May the Lord bless you and guard you,
fill you and enfold you,
guide you and sustain you
now and always. **Amen.**

Prayers may be offered for the youth specialist, church and local community as the service continues.

7 GREETINGS

COMMISSIONING FOR WIDER MINISTRY

Baptist ministers are often called to service beyond the local church, serving in chaplaincies, associations and colleges, as well as national denominational bodies and other Christian organizations. There follows sample material which may be adapted for a variety of purposes and included in order to modify appropriately the induction patterns already given above. The section numbers and titles of the induction pattern are included in order to guide their use.

COMMISSIONING FOR SECTOR MINISTRY

Increasingly, Baptists are ministering in various 'sectors' beyond the local church. Industrial, commercial and retail workplaces, further and higher education, prisons, the armed forces and health care: all these provide settings within which people are commissioned to minister and most are ecumenical in nature.

Arrangements for recognition of such ministries are many and varied, reflecting the diversity of contexts, and the variety of forms of ministry, as well as the Baptist people undertaking them – be they ordained and accredited Baptist Union ministers, or Baptist church members. With such diversity, the language in a service of commissioning needs to be chosen with some care so that all the parties involved may be respected and enabled to participate.

Reflection continues among Baptists about how the ministry of those in sectors beyond a local congregation is to be understood and, consequently, what kind of liturgical action might best inaugurate the ministry and express its meaning. The notion of *commissioning* is one which has wide ecumenical acceptance and considerable Baptist support. Implied in this word, is a theology of mission in which sector ministers share in the mission of God in the world. This is a ministry into which they are sent by the people of God, as representatives of the gospel of Jesus Christ, a representation which in turn implies a continuing relationship with the Church as a gospel community.

INDUCTING A CHAPLAIN
INTO A CHAPLAINCY TEAM

A Baptist regional minister, or other minister appointed for the task by the association, should preside over this part of what will usually be an ecumenical service.

3 CONFESSING FAITH AND PROMISING FAITHFULNESS: THE CHAPLAIN

All Christians
are called to be disciples of Jesus Christ
and to follow in his way.
AB, you are first a disciple of Christ,
and so I ask you to affirm afresh
your faith and trust in God,
a faith which you have already confessed in baptism.

Do you believe in one God,
Father, Son and Holy Spirit,
and do you confess Jesus Christ
as your Saviour and Lord?

**As a disciple of Jesus Christ,
this is the God in whom I trust.**

A, you are about to take up a work of ministry
within this ecumenical team,
which offers Christian ministry to *[name of institution]*.

Will you fulfil your calling
as a minister of the gospel of Jesus Christ
in the company of these colleagues,
and serving the people of this
[college/university/hospital/city centre etc.]
with love and in obedience
to the pattern of Christ?

I will, the risen Christ inspiring me.

A, will you seek the Kingdom of God in this place,
promoting values of justice, peace and the integrity of creation,
looking out for signs of God's Spirit at work amongst its people,
and offering your friendship and care to any who seek it?

I will, God's Spirit empowering me.

A, will you maintain the integrity of your own faith,
while recognizing the freedom of others to practise theirs,
being ready always to explain the hope that is in you?

I will, God's word sustaining me.

A, will you pray for the good of this
[college/university/hospital/city centre etc.] and its people,
witnessing together with all who witness to Christ here,
to what is good, just and true in God's sight?

**In the name of God
who is Father of all,
the living Word
and the Spirit of unity, I will.**

4 CONFESSING FAITH AND PROMISING FAITHFULNESS: THE CHAPLAINCY

The presiding minister then addresses the members of the chaplaincy team

My Christian brothers and sisters,
I commend A to you as
*an accredited minister of the Baptist Union
[or: a member in good standing of … Baptist Church].*
Will you, together with *her/him,*
maintain the spirit of unity in the bond of peace
through the work of this chaplaincy,
and seek ways to embody that unity
in your common life and work?

**Gladly, we will,
the Lord being our helper.**

The presiding minister then addresses a representative of the institution

CD, as a representative of … *[name of institution]*
we offer you the ministry of A
on behalf of Baptists locally *[and/or nationally],*
asking that you will extend to *her/him*
the freedom to practice that ministry
within this place.
Will you join with us
in affirming A in this role?

Gladly, I will.

6 DECLARATION AND BLESSING

On behalf of … Baptist Association
and as a representative of the Baptist Union of Great Britain,
I affirm you in your new ministry,
charging you to maintain your covenant relationship with us,
and offering you our pastoral care and oversight.

As an association we recognize your ministry
and will support you in prayer,
seeking, with you,
the furtherance of God's kingdom in this place.

The everlasting God shield you,
east and west and wherever you go,
and the blessing of God be upon us,

the blessing of the God of life.

The blessing of Christ be upon us,

the blessing of the Christ of love.

The blessing of the Spirit be upon us,

the blessing of the Spirit of grace.

**The blessing of the Trinity be upon us
Now and for ever more. Amen.**

ADDITIONAL MATERIAL FOR SECTOR MINISTRY

When a minister leaves the pastoral charge of a local congregation to undertake a sector ministry, it may be appropriate to include an act of 'sending' within her or his concluding service. Here is a prayer which may be used on such an occasion.

Loving God, you have called us
to ministry and mission in church and world.
Now, as *A* begins a new ministry
beyond the walls of the church
in which *she/he* has previously served,
we ask you to fill *her/him* afresh
with your Spirit who broods over creation,
bringing life out of death
and fruitfulness out of everyday things.

As Christ ministered to those around him,
however close or far away they were to your Kingdom,
so help *A* to minister according to Christ's greater pattern.

Give *her/him* courage where difficulties must be faced.
Encourage *her/him*
where results are not easily seen.
Lead *her/him*
through the cost, pain, and privilege of this ministry,
and always hold before *her/him*
the vision of your kingdom that cannot be shaken,
where there is wholeness, healing, and new creation.

We pray for all those who serve here,
that they also may know
your challenging, guiding, enlivening Spirit,
and we pray for all who work here,
that through your Spirit's work
they may see the vision of your kingdom
and come to know the peace and love of Christ,
in whose name we pray. **Amen.**

INDUCTING A REGIONAL MINISTER

The presiding minister should be a representative of the wider church, such as the general secretary of the Baptist Union, or someone recognized within the association as having a wider ministry.

1 INTRODUCTION

After opening worship, the presiding minister greets the congregation and introduces the purpose of the gathering.

You, the members of … Association,
have called *AB* to be one of your regional ministers,
and, believing this call to be of God,
he/she has accepted, and comes now to be inducted into this office.
This is a special day in the life of this association
and I invite you all to renew your commitment
to Christ and his church,
and to a sharing in God's mission of saving love to his world.

3 CONFESSING FAITH AND PROMISING FAITHFULNESS

After inviting the new regional minister to confess anew their faith in God, the presiding minister calls on the new minister to respond to the following questions

A, you have been called to the office of regional minister
and *team leader/mission enabler/charged with responsibility for pastoral care*
for this association, its churches and ministers.
Do you accept the charge from Christ
to care for his people with all faithfulness and compassion,
watching over the life of the churches with all humility?
Will you care for the weak,
bring Christ's healing to the brokenhearted,
lift up the downcast,
and pray regularly for those committed to your care?

**As a disciple of Jesus Christ, I will,
God's grace enabling me.**

Will you share in leading and equipping God's people
for mission to the world,
proclaiming the gospel in word and deed
and seeking to make Christ known in every way?

I will, the risen Christ inspiring me.

Will you 'make every effort
to maintain the unity of the Spirit in the bond of peace',
and by your example serve this association
in holy living and devotion to Christ?
Will you be faithful in prayer
and the reading of God's word,
in the leading of worship,
and the preaching of the word?

I will, God's Spirit empowering me.

You are called to share in building up the common life
of the Baptist Union of Great Britain,
its fellowship and its mission.
Will you commit yourself to serving God
through this national community of his people?
Will you be diligent in its service,
faithful in your support and encouragement
of colleagues and partners in the gospel
and will you support and pray for the whole union
of churches, associations and colleges?

**In the name of God who is Christ,
the head of the Church, I will.**

You are called to share with brothers and sisters
from other Christian traditions
in the oversight of the whole church of Jesus Christ;
to share with them in mission
and to care for the communities
within the *county/counties* of your association.
Will you work and pray for the unity of the church
and its mission to God's world?

**Through the grace of God
who is the Spirit of unity, I will.**

The presiding minister then invites the other members(s) of the association team to stand and asks them and the new regional minister to respond to the following questions

Do you believe you have been called by God
to work together humbly and willingly in serving this association?

We do.

Do you promise to honour and respect one another,
'in humility regarding others as better than yourselves,'
and do you promise to work
with the members of this association and its councils
in its calling to serve the churches and their mission?

As disciples of Jesus Christ,
and in the power of the Spirit,
we will.

Optional question for the regional minister's partner

You have heard the promises made by *A* today.
Will you join in that commitment to Christ and his people,
promising to support and encourage *him/her*
in *his/her* ministry in this association and its churches?

As a disciple of Jesus Christ,
and in the power of the Spirit,
I will.

4 CONFESSING FAITH AND PROMISING FAITHFULNESS

The presiding minister then invites the members of the churches of the association to stand,
and says

My brothers and sisters,
today God offers this association a new beginning.
I invite you to renew your commitment to Christ and his church,
asking you to affirm afresh your baptismal vows.
Do you believe in one God,
Father, Son and Holy Spirit,
and do you confess Jesus Christ as your Saviour and Lord?

We do. This is the God in whom we trust.

Do you accept and welcome *AB*
as one of your regional ministers with responsibility for
leading the team/enabling mission/pastoral care,
and do you promise to honour and support *him/her*
with your love and prayers,
working together with *him/her*
in your calling to serve Christ in this region?

Gladly, we do.

The presiding minister then invites the ecumenical representatives to stand, and asks them

Will you welcome and accept *A* to work with you
in the varied tasks of oversight and leadership
in the church of Jesus Christ?
Will you work and pray together
for the coming kingdom of God,
the unity of the church
and its mission to God's world?

**Through the grace of God
who is the Spirit of unity, we will.**

The presiding minister invites the whole congregation to stand and asks

As representatives of the wider church and community,
will you offer your support in this new beginning
for this association and new regional minister,
and will you join in praying for them?

Gladly, we will.

*The congregation remains standing and prayer is offered, by the presiding minister and by some
of those who gather round the regional minister to lay hands on him/her. Prayer should include
thanksgiving for God's guidance and grace, an invocation of the Spirit on the new regional
minister, the team and the churches and a dedication to future service and faithfulness.*

6 DECLARATION

The presiding minister then addresses the new regional minister

AB, in the name of our Lord Jesus Christ,
and on behalf of the Baptist Union of Great Britain
and this association,
I declare you inducted to the office of regional minister
within the ... Association.

INDUCTING A COLLEGE TUTOR OR PRINCIPAL

Baptist colleges have both a regional and a national role within the union of Baptist churches and the presiding minister may be a regional minister, a representative of the Baptist Union, an officer of the college or, in the case of a tutor, the college principal.

3 CONFESSING FAITH AND PROMISING FAITHFULNESS: THE TUTOR OR PRINCIPAL

My *sister/brother*,
do you believe in one God,
Father, Son and Holy Spirit,
and will you confess again Jesus Christ
as your Saviour and Lord?

**This is the God in whom I trust
and Jesus Christ is my Savour and Lord.**

Do you believe that God has called you
to serve God and the Church of Jesus Christ
as *principal/a tutor* in this college?

**As a disciple of Jesus Christ, I do.
I believe that God has called me
to share in the preparing of people for Christian ministry,
for the strengthening of those in ministry,
the building up of the Church of Christ
and the service of the kingdom of God.**

Will you faithfully care for those in your charge?
Will you teach the full counsels of God,
continually sharing the love of Christ
and encouraging dependence on the Holy Spirit?

**I will, the Lord being my helper.
I will give of my best and ask the same of others,
for the sake of the kingdom.
I will preach the gospel of Christ,
invite disciples to follow him more closely
and encourage all who are called to minister
to consecrate themselves and their gifts to God,
for the sake of the Church, the body of Christ.**

Will you always seek to live a godly life,
fulfilling your high calling in Jesus Christ,
with wisdom, diligence and love?
Will you faithfully study the scriptures
and the witness of God's Church in every time and place,
listening for the voice of Christ among his people and in the world?

In the name of God who is
the Father of all,
the Living Word
and the Spirit of life,
I will.

4 CONFESSING FAITH AND PROMISING FAITHFULNESS: THE COLLEGE COMMUNITY

The congregation stands

As members and friends of the college community,
and as representatives of the churches of Christ,
do you acknowledge *A* as *principal/a tutor* of this College,
and do you offer your prayers and support to *her/him*
in this ministry amongst us?

Gladly, we do.

The other members of the college team join their new colleague and are asked

Those of you who are tutors and staff of this college,
do you acknowledge one another as brothers and sisters in Christ,
called to share in the ministry of the college amongst the churches?

**We do. We are disciples of Jesus Christ
and, by his grace, we will follow him together.**

Will you support and encourage one another
in all that you are called to do for the glory of God?
Will you display the love of Christ
in your relationships one with another,
that others might see in your teamwork
a sign of the kingdom of God
and an expression of the Body of Christ?

**As disciples of Jesus Christ,
and in the power of the Spirit,
we will.**

There follows the induction prayer with the laying on of hands, in which representatives of the college community, local churches and the wider church may share.

In the name of our Lord Jesus Christ
and on behalf of this college and the churches it serves,
I declare *AB* inducted as *principal /a tutor* of ... College.
As a token of this, I now give the hand of fellowship.

Prayers for the life and work of the college may now be offered as worship continues.

FORMING MINISTERS

Increasingly, the majority of those preparing for ordained ministry within the Baptist Union of Great Britain are doing so on congregation-based courses. Although under supervision, they carry all the responsibilities of local ministry, their ordination and accreditation as Baptist ministers will not normally take place until the completion of their college course. While they are not ordained, they need to be inducted or commissioned with prayer and the laying on of hands and welcomed into a covenant relationship with the congregation they will serve and with whom they will learn.

The pattern which follows is also suitable for a person beginning a period of formation for locally recognized ministry through pastoral care of a local congregation.

The presiding minister may be a regional minister, a representative of the college, a local minister, or a church member invited for that purpose by the church meeting. The act of commissioning and welcome should include the following elements

1 *Welcome and Introduction* – stating the purpose of the event
2 *Telling the Story* – including testimony by the student concerning his or her call to ministry and commendations by the student's home church and someone involved in their training, either in person or by letter read aloud
3 *Confessing Faith and Promising Faithfulness: the minister in training*
4 *Confessing Faith and Promising Faithfulness: the church*
5 *Induction Prayer with the laying on of hands*
6 *Declaration of induction and Blessing*
7 *Greetings*

INDUCTING A MINISTER IN TRAINING

1 WELCOME AND INTRODUCTION

After opening worship the leader greets the congregation and introduces the act of welcome and commissioning.

Today we welcome *AB*
into the life and ministry of this church
at the beginning of *her/his* formation for pastoral ministry.
It is right that both church and pastor
should make promises to each other,
as the sign of covenant relationship between us,
a covenant which we pray will bear fruit
in effective ministry and growth in grace.

2 TELLING THE STORY

The minister in training may be invited to give an account of God's call to ministry and a testimony of the personal journey thus far.

A commendation may be given, in person or through the reading of a letter, from the student's home church and from the college.

3 CONFESSING FAITH AND PROMISING FAITHFULNESS

The minister in training is invited to stand and respond to these questions

A, do you believe in one God,
Father, Son and Holy Spirit?
And do you confess Jesus Christ
as your Saviour and Lord?

**This is the God I trust
and Jesus is my Saviour and Lord.**

Do you believe that God has called you,
through his church,
to this time of preparation
here in this congregation
and to a life of ministry in the wider Church?

**As a disciple of Jesus Christ,
I believe that God has called me here.**

A, you have responded to God's call
to Christian ministry
and set out now to prepare for it here.
Do you promise
to live a life worthy of your calling,
offering your gifts
of body, mind, and spirit to the service of Christ
through the life of this church and its community?

I do, the Lord being my helper.

A, will you be open to change
and obedient to what you learn
from congregation and college?
Will you seek to form relationships of care and respect
with the people you meet here,
and pray with them and for them
for the sake of Christ's purposes in all our lives?

I will, God's Spirit empowering me.

A, in the ministry of preaching and teaching
and pastoral care in this place,
do you promise to apply
what you have learned and will learn
about God's word and God's world.

I will, the risen Christ inspiring me.

An optional question may be addressed to the spouse of the minister in training.

C, will you support *A* in this ministry
and play your own part in the fellowship of this church,
so that we may, together,
discover further signs of God's love amongst us?

As a disciple of Jesus Christ,
and with the help of God's Spirit,
I will.

4 CONFESSING FAITH AND PROMISING FAITHFULNESS: THE CHURCH

The congregation is invited to stand

Brothers and sisters, do you believe in one God,
Father, Son and Holy Spirit?
And do you confess Jesus Christ
as your Saviour and Lord?

**This is the God we trust
and Jesus is our Saviour and Lord.**

Will you, the members of this church and congregation,
give to *A* your love and support,
allowing *her /him* the space to learn and grow,
and encouraging *her/him [together with C]*,
as *she/he* continues to respond
to God's call to Christian ministry?

Gladly, we will.

A question is then asked of church and student together

Will you all, from this day forward,
covenant together to further the work of Christ's kingdom
in the ministry and mission of this church,
though the developing ministry of *A*
and the shared ministry of *us/you* all?

**This is the ministry of Jesus Christ
in which we are glad to share.
Thanks be to God.**

5 INDUCTION PRAYER

Prayer is offered, extempore or as follows

God of grace,
you have brought together
this church and this minister in training.
We pray that you will give to *A*
a fresh outpouring of your Holy Spirit
for the work that *she/he* now begins,
and to ... Baptist Church a new awareness
of the presence of Christ for what lies ahead.

In Christ's name, and trusting in your guidance,
we commission *A* as a minister in training in this church.

Grant to its members a shared ministry
of encouragement and care,
and to *A* the humility and confidence
of a true disciple of Jesus Christ.
Keep us true to our promises
and open to your Holy Spirit,
that Jesus Christ may be exalted
and your kingdom proclaimed,
through Jesus Christ our Lord. **Amen.**

6 DECLARATION AND BLESSING

A, I declare you to be minister in training
in this church and congregation.

The Lord bless you and keep you:

**The blessing of the Father who made us,
the blessing of the Son who saves us,
the blessing of the Holy Spirit who gives us life
be with you and all of us
as we look for your coming kingdom. Amen**

7 GREETINGS

Greetings may be offered either now or at the close of the service.

COMMISSIONING FOR LOCALLY RECOGNIZED MINISTRY

In some associations, there are churches which receive pastoral leadership from people who have been called by God to that role within a particular local church, but who may not exercise that ministry more widely and are recognized by the local Baptist association rather than accredited by the Baptist Union for national ministry. If their names are to be included in a national register of locally recognized ministers, they will also have engaged in a programme of theological education and ministerial formation approved by the Baptist Union of Great Britain. Baptists differ as to the theological distinction between this local ministry of pastor and the wider role of an accredited minister. However, because those exercising this ministry are called by God through the local church meeting, exercise a ministry of pastoral care, spiritual leadership (including presiding at the Lord's Table) and preaching, a service of ordination is appropriate.

It is likely that a service of ordination to locally recognized ministry will take place in the church to which the person has been called. However, circumstances may vary. The ordinand may already be exercising ministry in that church or may be about to begin ministry there. Decisions will need to be taken as to whether or not the service is to include an act of induction. The pattern below does include an act of induction which will need to be omitted when not appropriate. However, even when an act of induction is not appropriate, some form of affirmation and commitment by the congregation might be considered desirable at this new beginning in the life and ministry of the one already serving there. Induction material may therefore be amended for use in such circumstances.

The commendations early in the service will also vary according to particular circumstances, though what follows will include a commendation from the association, incorporating reference to gifting, character and call. This commendation should also refer to what training has taken place, or the training to which the person is committing himself or herself. There should also be a commendation from the church of which the person is currently a member, whether that is the receiving church or another.

The person presiding will normally be a regional minister and the following elements should be included

- *Introduction* – including a statement on the meaning of local ordination
- *Telling the Story* – an opportunity for testimony by the ordinand concerning his or her call to this ministry and commendations by the association and the church of which the ordinand is currently a member.
- *Confessing Faith and Promising Faithfulness: the Ordination Vows.*
- *Presentation of the ordination Bible* by the receiving church.
- *Confessing Faith and Promising Faithfulness: the induction promises* of the church.
- *Ordination and Induction Prayer with the laying on of hands.*
- *Declaration of ordination, of induction (where appropriate) and Blessing.*

ORDAINING AND INDUCTING
A LOCALLY RECOGNIZED MINISTER

Where the person to be ordained is already the pastoral leader of the local church, the induction elements of the following pattern may be omitted.

After opening worship, the presiding minister greets the congregation and introduces the act of ordination and induction

Sisters and brothers,
we have come together in the name of Jesus Christ,
the head of the Church,
to set apart and to ordain for local ministry
our *sister/brother AB.*
We believe that God has called *A* to stand before us,
to serve as a pastor to this people,
a witness in this community
and a teacher of the good news of Jesus Christ
in this church and within this association.
We pray that *she/he* may *continue to be/be* a channel of God's grace
to the Church and to the world.

Here we welcome and receive *A* as a gift from God,
enabling *her/him* to fulfil that calling among us.
Here we call for God's gracious Holy Spirit
to anoint and empower *A* for service,
praying that *she/he* may continue to be formed
in the likeness of Jesus Christ.

All God's people are called to ministry.
All who are baptized into Jesus Christ
and have received the Holy Spirit
are called to serve our Lord Jesus Christ,
and one another,
in the fellowship of the Church.
God gives gifts to all, so that, like a body,
all may share in the purposes of Christ for the world
which God has made
and for which Jesus Christ has died.

Yet within this fellowship of service,
some are called by Christ to particular forms of ministry.
All are called to be disciples.
All are called to be servants of God in Christ Jesus
through the power of the Holy Spirit.
Yet God calls some to servant leadership in the Church
and these are to be honoured among us.

For this reason,
none may take this office upon themselves.
Only God can call to ministry,
so today we acknowledge
our dependence upon God
and seek to do his will.
We have sought God's guidance
and prayerfully tested the calling of *A*
within the local church and the association.
Today we gather as the Church of God
to ordain *A* for pastoral ministry
and to seek God's blessing.

TELLING THE STORY

In ordination we recognize and receive this call of God,
so we invite *A* to declare *her/his* confidence
that *she/he* is called by God to this local ministry of pastor.

The one to be ordained testifies to the call of God upon his or her life.

Every call must be tested,
and then, under God,
the gifts must be developed
and the person formed for ministry.
Let us hear from those who have shared
in this process of discernment.

A statement may be given by the church of which the ordinand is currently a member. If the ordinand is already ministering in the receiving church, then the statement may be made on behalf of that fellowship.

A statement should be made by a representative of the association with special reference to the association's recognition of the person's gifting, character and call. Reference should also be made to past and future training and formation.

If the person has not yet ministered in the receiving church and an act of induction is to take place in this service, then a statement should be made by the local church which has called the ordinand for ministry.

Believing this ministry to be the will of God,
we now invite *A* to declare *her/his* faith in God
and *her/his* commitment to the way of life of a Christian minister
as we set *her/him* aside for the work of local ministry
with prayer and the laying on of hands.

CONFESSING FAITH AND PROMISING FAITHFULNESS: THE ORDINATION VOWS

Christian ministry is a sharing in the ministry of Jesus Christ,
through the power of the Holy Spirit
and in response to the call of God.
A, you are already a disciple of Jesus Christ,
do you now acknowledge this further call on your life?
Do you willingly and joyfully submit yourself to God
as his servant and as a minister in his Church?

**I believe that God has called me
to follow and to serve.**

Do you believe in one God,
Father, Son and Holy Spirit,
and do you confess Jesus Christ
as your Saviour and Lord?

**This is the God in whom I believe
and in whom I place my trust.**

Do you believe that you are called by God to local ministry
as a pastor in this church and association?

I believe that God has called me here.

Do you accept the scriptures
as revealing the salvation of God in Jesus Christ
and will you open yourself to the ministry of the Holy Spirit
who will lead us into all truth?

**I will be faithful
in reading the word of God
and preaching the word of life.
I will seek to be open
to God's leading and direction
for this congregation, for the local community
and for my own walk of faith.**

Will you share with God's people here
the breadth and length and height and depth of the love of Christ,
that together you may become ministers of reconciliation
and servants of God's grace to the world?

**As a disciple of Jesus Christ
and with the help of God's Spirit, I will.**

If the ordinand is already ministering in the receiving church, an act of induction may well not be appropriate. In these circumstances the service should move to the presentation of the ordination Bible.

CONFESSING FAITH AND PROMISING FAITHFULNESS: THE CHURCH

The presiding minister invites the members of the receiving church to stand.

Sisters and brothers,
it was by the calling of God that you came to faith,
and it is by the calling of God
that you are members of this church and congregation.

Will you therefore confess your faith in God,
revealed in Jesus Christ by the Holy Spirit
and your trust in that same God as your Saviour and Lord?

**This is the God in whom we believe
and in whom we place our trust.**

Do you acknowledge and receive *AB* as your pastor?

Gladly, we do.

Will you pray for *her/him* as *she/he* prays for you?
Will you work with *her/him*
to know, to do and to bear the mind of Christ?
Will you follow with *her/him* in the way Christ leads?

Through the grace of God, we will.

The presiding minister invites the whole congregation to stand.

You have heard from *A* and this church
of their calling to ministry together.
You have heard the promises they have made
to live Christ's life together.

Do you, as representatives of the wider church,
acknowledge this calling
and will you support them in their promises?

**We have heard and we are witnesses.
We will pray and we will care.**

Together you are disciples of Jesus Christ.
Today you have covenanted
to care for one another
and to serve God
through the gifts he has lavished on you
and the Spirit he has poured out upon you.

ORDINATION PRAYER WITH THE LAYING ON OF HANDS

Following the practice of the early Church,
we formally set *A* apart with the laying on of hands.
In this act of ordination,
both the local fellowship and the wider Church will share,
for we are ordaining *A* to Christian ministry
in the wider fellowship of our association.

*The ordinand kneels or stands and representatives of those who are sharing in the service,
ministerial and lay, gather around and lay hands on her/him. The presiding minister then prays
extempore, or as follows*

Loving God, in the name of Jesus Christ
we now set apart your servant *A*
for ministry in the church of Jesus Christ
and as a pastor in this church and within this association.

Send your Spirit, we pray,
that *she/he* may be empowered for service
and formed in the likeness of Jesus.
Guide and direct *her/him*
as *she/he* seeks to lead and serve your people here.
Give *her/him* the gift of wisdom
for teaching the mind of Christ,
and guide *her/his* steps
that others might be led in the way of Christ.

Grant *A* an abiding sense of your presence
and fill *her/him* with the love of Christ
that *she/he* may be his true disciple.
This we pray in the name of Jesus Christ,
the head of the Church and Saviour of all. **Amen.**

If the prayer is extempore, it should contain

- *an invocation of the Spirit of God*
- *a setting aside for the work of ministry*
- *prayer for God's blessing and an enduing with wisdom, discernment, and spiritual power.*

Further prayers may be offered by those sharing in the laying on of hands, and by others.

DECLARATION AND BLESSING

In the name of God
the Father, the Son and the Holy Spirit,
we declare you, *AB*, to be ordained
to ministry in the church of Jesus Christ
and we commission you to serve in this association.
May the Lord richly bless and sustain you
as you lead the people of God and care for them
and as you serve and pray for this local community,

If an act of induction has not taken place, then the presiding minister and others should give the hand of fellowship to the new minister.

If the induction vows have been made in this service then the presiding minister should also say

I offer you a hand of fellowship
and declare you inducted
to the pastorate of this church and congregation,
to work with the members
in the ministry to which Christ has called you all.

PRESENTATION OF THE ORDINATION BIBLE

If an act of induction has not taken place, a representative of the church in which the ordinand is already serving, may present the gift of a Bible with the words

A, we are grateful to God
for your ministry amongst us.
A, we entrust this Bible to you
as a symbol of your commission
and of your responsibility as a minister of the gospel.

If induction promises have just been made, a representative of the receiving church may present a gift of a Bible to the ordinand with the words

A, we entrust this Bible to you
as a symbol of your commission
and of your responsibility as a minister of the gospel

Other symbols of ministry may also be presented with appropriate words.

The congregation may then say

**The Lord bless you and keep you.
The Lord make his face to shine upon you
and be gracious to you.
The Lord lift up the light of his countenance upon you
and give you peace. Amen.**

The congregation may greet the new pastor in an appropriate way and the service continues.

COMMISSIONING FOR MINISTRY OVERSEAS

A valedictory or commissioning service is usually held before a new missionary goes abroad for the first time. This is an opportunity to express the call of God to the new missionary (or missionaries) and for those present to surround them with love and prayer.

When a missionary couple has children whose lives will be greatly affected by this new step, it is important that each of the family is named and feels that they too will be supported by prayer. While the form of words here is in the singular, it should be adapted if there is more than one missionary or if there is a couple where both will be serving.

The presiding leader should be a person who has had pastoral oversight of the missionary, preferably within the context of the local church.

A representative of the mission organization with which they will serve should normally be invited to share in the service

- Introduction to the work to which the missionary is called.
- Testimony to his or her call by the new missionary.
- Questions enabling an affirmation of faith, a commitment to the work and a commendation by the mission agency or receiving body.
- Prayer with the laying on of hands.
- Prayers for the missionary and the family, whether accompanying the missionary or remaining behind.

Suitable scripture readings: Joshua 1.1–9; Isaiah 6.1–8; 42.1–8; 49.1–7; 60.1–7; 61.1–4; Jeremiah 1.1–10; Matthew 9.35–10.16; 28.18–20; Luke 10.1–12; John 20.19–23; Acts 1.1–11; 13.1–5; 16.6–10; Romans 10.1–17; 2 Corinthians 5.11–21.

COMMISSIONING A MISSIONARY

After opening worship, the leader greets and congregation and introduces the act of commissioning

We gather today to give thanks to God
that he has chosen and set apart *AB*
to work in partnership with this church in ...
We gather in order to surround *him/her*
with our love and prayers
as *he/she* prepares to leave the familiar
and take this step of faith and obedience.

A representative of the mission organization or, if possible, of the church or receiving body to which the missionary is going, should outline what this new work will entail. This may be done by words alone or by the use of visual or other resources.

The missionary testifies to the way in which he or she came to hear the call of God.

QUESTIONS AND PROMISES

Do you believe in one God,
Father, Son and Holy Spirit,
and do you confess Jesus Christ as your Saviour and Lord?

**This is the God in whom I trust,
for I am a disciple of Jesus Christ.**

Do you believe
that Jesus Christ calls you and all people everywhere
with the words 'Follow me',
and do you believe that at this time
he calls you to work with ... in ...?

**I do. I am a disciple of Jesus Christ
and I will follow where he leads.**

Jesus told his followers,
'Go and make disciples of all the nations.'
In your ministry,
will you seek to ensure that the gospel of Jesus Christ
is proclaimed and demonstrated
in such a way that many may hear and understand the good news?

**I am a disciple of Jesus Christ
and I will seek to make disciples.**

You have heard God's call.
Will you continue to listen to him speaking to you
through people of a different language and culture?

I am a disciple of Jesus Christ,
and I will listen for his voice.

You have opened yourself to God.
Do you believe that he has prepared you to go to …
to work in partnership with others?
Do you go willingly to give and to receive,
to teach and to be taught?

I do. I am a disciple of Jesus Christ
and I rejoice that I am called to follow in company with others.

A, you have committed yourself to share Christ with others.
Do you now recommit your life to him?
Do you promise to be faithful in prayer,
in reading the scriptures,
and in seeking the mind of Christ
through reflection and fellowship,
that all you do may be firmly rooted
in the love and knowledge of our Lord Jesus Christ?

I do. I am a disciple of Jesus Christ
and I gladly and wholeheartedly embrace his call
to follow in love and faithfulness.

The leader then addresses a representative of the receiving or sending body. If a person is not available, part of a letter may be read.

E, as the representative of … present here today,
Do you believe that this offer of service
is within the will of God
and do you believe that *she/he* is ready for this step of faith?

We do.

The leader invites the congregation to stand.

We have gathered
because we believe that God has called *A* to work in …
We have come as a sign of fellowship
and to surround *A* and the family of *A* *[and partner]*
with our prayers.
Do you now commit yourselves to be faithful in prayer,
continuing to pray for *A* and the whole family
and to support them in practical ways?

We do.
This is our calling in Christ.

You send *A* to … in love
and this departure makes possible
a deepening of fellowship
with sisters and brothers in Christ in that place.
Are you willing to learn from, and be enriched by, this fellowship?

We are, for we are one in Christ Jesus
and he is Lord of all.

PRAYER WITH THE LAYING ON OF HANDS

Prayers are offered for the missionary or missionary family, for their extended family and close
friends, for the work to which they go, their future colleagues and the church in that place.
These prayers may be extempore or as follows, may be led by different people, and may be
accompanied with the laying on of hands.

Gracious God,
your love sustains us through all things
and, confident of this,
we pray for *A* and *C* *[name all directly affected]*.

In all the things that *she/he* finds hard about this new work,
we pray that *she/he they* may know your faithful love
and empowering presence.
Defend *her/him* from all evil,
keep *her/him* faithful in times of trial,
abounding in hope and filled with mercy,
a disciple of Jesus Christ
and an ambassador of the gospel.

Send your Holy Spirit to empower and equip *A* for service,
to transform *her/him* into the likeness of Jesus
and to be ever his true disciple.
This we ask in the name of our Lord Jesus Christ,
the head of the church and Lord of all. **Amen.**

PRAYERS

Lord of all the world,

Bless your children we, pray.

We pray for the family and friends of *A*.
As they face the pain of separation,
we pray that they may know your peace
which passes all understanding.
Lord of all the world,

Bless your children, we pray.

Gracious God,
we thank you for the church in ...
As *A* arrives and begins to share in the work,
we pray that trust and understanding may grow quickly,
and that the love of Christ might shine
through all that is said and done.
Lord of all the world,

Bless your children, we pray.

Missionary God,
you send your Son before you send us.
Help us never to close our ears to your call.
Remove our fear and self-absorption,
that we may listen for your invitation to new challenges;
and when we hear,
help us to say 'Yes'.
Lord of all the world,

Bless your children, we pray.

The service continues and at the close the leader may say

A, go in peace.
Love and serve the Lord,
rejoicing in the power of the Holy Spirit.

In the name of Christ. Amen.

The Grace is said together.

LIVING AND CARING

ENTERING AND CELEBRATING CHRISTIAN MARRIAGE

PASTORAL AND LEGAL NOTES

Planning a wedding service with an engaged couple can be an important part of the pastoral care offered in preparation for marriage, and there is considerable freedom of choice to exercise and enjoy. However, there are a number of legal requirements that a wedding service in a nonconformist church must fulfil.

The following legal notes apply to England and Wales at the time of publication in 2005. The law may change (more than once) soon afterwards and those responsible for marriage services need to be clear as to the legal requirements in force at the time of the service.

In other parts of the world, legal arrangements will differ and it is most important that those conducting wedding services should be aware of, and comply with, the requirements of the law currently in force in the place where the marriage service is to be conducted.

LEGAL NOTES

1   The church must be registered for marriages (though this requirement may change).

2   The legal preliminaries before marriage should have been completed and applicable document(s) produced. Details of registration and the necessary documents(s) are not given here as they belong to the responsibility of the Authorized Person or Registrar (and may in the future be subject to change).

3   The marriage service itself must be held between 0800 and 1800.

4   A marriage ceremony is a public event. The doors must not be so closed as to prevent people from entering.

5   An Authorized Person or Registrar must be present to witness and register the marriage.

6   There must be present at least two people who are able to act as witnesses, apart from the couple, Authorized Person, the Registrar or the person conducting the service.

7   During some part of the ceremony, the couple must each make a declaration of no impediment as follows

Either

In response to the question
Are you *AB* free lawfully to marry *CD*?

Replying
I am

Or

**I do solemnly declare that I know not
of any lawful impediment why I *AB*
may not be joined in matrimony to *CD*.**

Or

**I declare that I know of no reason why I *AB*
may not be joined in marriage to *CD*.**

8   Various forms of the vows are possible, and there is no reason why a couple should not compose their own, providing of course that they contain the legal form of words required below and do not contradict the Christian understanding of marriage embodied in the services in this book. The couple's vows must include the following words

Either

**I call upon these persons here present
to witness that I, *AB*,
do take thee, *CD*,
to be my lawful wedded wife/husband.**

Or

**I, AB, take you, *CD*
to be my wedded wife/husband.**

In these legal forms of words, the names used should be the full names, including surnames, which the parties use and by which they are generally known. If these names are different from the names given on the certificate(s) (or schedule), this difference must be cleared by the Authorized Person or Registrar prior to the marriage taking place.

If the law in England and Wales changes in order to allow denominational variation, those conducting marriage services 'according to the rites and ceremonies of the Baptists' should still comply with these legal notes or else with replacement guidelines issued by the ministry department of the Baptist Union of Great Britain.

9   There are special provisions to enable marriages to take place in the homes of those who are housebound, for marriages for those who are detained, and how deaf and dumb persons are to make their declarations and vows. For these matters the advice of the Authorized Person or Registrar should be sought.

PASTORAL NOTES

There are various customs attached to the wedding service which need not be followed and may well be questioned in the light of contemporary views of marriage. For example, the custom of the bride arriving after the bridegroom may be varied by both the man and woman entering the church at the beginning of the service and entering together, or by walking down either side to meet at the front. The custom of the bride being given away by her father may be omitted, repeated for the groom, or extended by including other members of the couple's families and the whole congregation. Alternatives are offered in the following material.

As an alternative to repeating the words after the minister, the couple may wish to read them from previously prepared cards.

Since marriages are very different in character, depending on the age and circumstances of the man and woman, it is important that, before use, the following material is carefully examined for any inappropriateness to the wedding taking place.

The following section offers two basic patterns for the marriage service. In the first, the ceremony is integrated into an act of worship, with the introduction and declarations being followed by the ministry of the Word and then the marriage vows and prayers. In the second, traditional pattern, the marriage ceremony takes place early in the service and is followed by the opportunity to reflect and pray on what has taken place. Words may be taken from either pattern, or from the additional material offered later, provided the legal requirements outlined above are observed.

In addition, a pattern is offered for the blessing of a civil ceremony and a pattern for an act of thanksgiving. Both provide opportunity for the reaffirmation of marriage vows.

SCRIPTURE READINGS

Genesis 1.26—31a; 2.4b—8, 18—24; Psalms 8; 33.2—9; 67; 95; 100; 103.1—5, 15—18; 117; 121; 128, 136.1—9, 26; 144.8—10, 15, 17—18; 145; 148; 150; Proverbs 3.3—6; Song of Songs 2.8—10, 14, 16; 8.6—7; Isaiah 54.5—8; Jeremiah 31.31—34; Matthew 5.13—16; 7.21, 24—27; 19.3—6; 22.35—40; Mark 10.6—9; John 2.1—11; 15.1—17; Romans 12.1—2, 9—13; 1 Corinthians 13; Ephesians 3.14—21; Philippians 1.9—11; Colossians 3.12—17; 1 Peter 3.1—12; 1 John 3.18—24; 4.7—12; Revelation 19.1, 5—9a.

FIRST PATTERN FOR CHRISTIAN MARRIAGE

WELCOME

Having met the bride and bridal party at the door, the minister goes to the front of the church and extends a welcome, such as

On behalf of ... *[name of church]*,
I welcome you all to this service
to celebrate the Christian marriage
of *A* and *C*.

Would you please stand for the entry of the bride.

Alternatively, the bride may enter during the singing of the first hymn.

OPENING WORSHIP

The service may begin with a call to worship, hymns, songs and prayers of praise, confession, thanksgiving and trust. The minister may then state the meaning of Christian marriage and lead the couple in their initial declarations.

PRELIMINARIES

STATEMENT OF PURPOSE

Either

Unless the Lord builds the house,
its builders labour in vain.

Psalm 127.1

We are gathered as a congregation
of God's people,
to witness the joining together
of *A* and *C* in marriage.

Marriage reveals the loving nature
and wise purpose of God.
Man and woman were created
in the image of God,
so that the love and community of God's own nature
may be reflected in the human family.

Christian marriage is an image
of the union of Christ and his Church.

Through his cross,
our broken relationships
with God and with one another
are forgiven and healed,
and we are reconciled.

Our Lord Jesus Christ
was himself a guest
at a wedding in Cana of Galilee.
Through his Spirit he is with us now,
to enrich our love
and to give us his joy and peace.

Or

We gather in the presence of God
to give thanks for the gift of marriage,
to witness the joining together of *A* and *C*,
to surround them with our prayers,
and to ask God's blessing upon them,
so that they may be strengthened to their life together
and nurtured in their love for God.

God created us male and female,
and gives us marriage
so that husband and wife may help and comfort each other,
living faithfully together in need and in plenty,
in sorrow and in joy,
in sickness and in health,
throughout all their days.

God gives us marriage
for the full expression of the love between a man and a woman.
In marriage a woman and a man belong to each other,
and with affection and tenderness
freely give themselves to each other.

God gives us marriage
for the well-being of human society,
for the ordering of family life,
and for the birth and nurture of children.

God gives us marriage as a holy mystery
in which a man and a woman are joined together
and become one,
just as Christ is one with the church.

In marriage,
husband and wife are called to a new way of life,
created, ordered, and blessed by God.
This way of life must not be entered into carelessly,
or from selfish motives,
but responsibly, and prayerfully.

We rejoice that marriage is given by God,
blessed by our Lord Jesus Christ,
and sustained by the Holy Spirit.
Therefore, let marriage be held in honour by all.

LEGAL DECLARATIONS

Either

The minister turns to the couple and says

If either of you knows of any reason
why you may not lawfully marry,
you should say so now.

The groom either reads or repeats after the minister

**I declare that I know of no legal reason
why I, AB,
may not be joined in marriage
to CD.**

Similarly, the bride repeats or says

**I declare that I know of no legal reason
why I, CD,
may not be joined in marriage
to AB.**

Or

The minister says to the congregation

A and C are now to make the declarations which the law requires.

The minister says to the man

Are you, AB, free lawfully to marry CD?

I am.

Are you, *CD*, free lawfully to marry, *AB*?

I am.

STATEMENT OF INTENT

The minister says to the man

A, are you willing to give yourself in marriage to *C*?

I am.

Will you love her and comfort her,
honour and keep her,
in sickness and in health,
and be faithful to her
as long as you both live?

With God's help, I will.

The minister says to the woman

C, are you willing to give yourself in marriage to *A*?

I am.

Will you love him and comfort him,
honour and keep him,
in sickness and in health,
and be faithful to him
as long as you both live?

With God's help, I will.

Or

A and *B*, have you come here
to give yourselves
to each other in marriage?

We have.

THE MINISTRY OF THE WORD

Suggested scripture readings may be found in the introduction on page 187.

A sermon may be preached and a hymn, or worship songs, sung.

MARRIAGE CEREMONY

AFFIRMATIONS OF THE FAMILIES

The minister addresses the families of the bride and groom

Either
Do you, the families *[and friends]* of A and C,
give your blessing to them,
and do you promise, in good times and bad,
to do everything in your power
to support them in their marriage?

**We give our blessing
and promise our support.**

Or
Do you, the families *[and friends]* of A and C,
give your love and blessing to this new family?
If you do, then please stand.

The members of the families stand.

Affirmations of the Congregation

The minister addresses the whole congregation

Either
Will all of you witnessing these vows
do everything in your power
to support A and C in their marriage?

We will.

Or
Will all of you in this congregation,
by God's grace,
do everything in your power
to uphold and care for these two in their life together.
As a sign that you will, please stand.

The congregation stands.

PRAYER

A prayer asking for God's help and blessing may now be offered, extempore or as follows

Gracious God,
we give you thanks and praise
for all your gifts of goodness and grace.
We praise you for your gift of love,
blessing our lives
and enfolding us all our days.

We praise you for your guidance
in the lives of *A* and *C*,
for the joy they find in each other,
and for the love and trust they bring
to the happiness of this day.

And since we know that without you
nothing is strong, nothing is holy,
we pray that, as they make their vows,
you will sustain and surround them.

May your Spirit of love
sanctify their joy and enrich their love.
Guide them by your grace
and keep them in your love,
through Jesus Christ our Lord. **Amen.**

MARRIAGE VOWS

The minister invites the couple to face each other and to join hands. The man and the woman are each in turn invited to make their vows

Either

The groom says, either reading or repeating after the minister

Before God
and in the presence of this congregation,
I give myself to you as your husband.
I, *AB*, take you, *CD* to be my wedded wife.
I promise you my love,
my loyalty, and my trust
for as long as we both shall live.

Similarly, the bride says

Before God
and in the presence of this congregation,
I give myself to you as your wife.
I, *CD*, take you, *AB* to be my wedded husband.
I promise you my love,
my loyalty, and my trust
for as long as we both shall live.

Or

Before God,
and in the presence of this congregation,
I, *AB*, take you, *CD*, to be my wedded wife.
I give myself to you as your husband,
for better, for worse,
for richer, for poorer,
in sickness and in health,
to love and to cherish, until we are parted by death,
and to this end
I give you my word.

The bride says

Before God,
and in the presence of this congregation,
I, *CD*, take you, *AB*, to be my wedded husband.
I give myself to you as your wife
for better, for worse,
for richer, for poorer,
in sickness and in health,
to love and to cherish, until we are parted by death,
and to this end
I give you my word.

GIVING OF RINGS

The minister invites the rings (or ring) to be placed on an open book or cushion, and says

As a token of the covenant into which you have entered,
these rings *[this ring]* are *[is]* given and received.

Taking the rings, the minister says

Either

God of steadfast love,
by your blessing
may these rings *[this ring]*
be to *A* and *C*
symbols *[a symbol]* of the vow they have made this day
and of the covenant into which they have entered.
By your grace,
help them to be faithful to each other
in unbroken love,
through Jesus Christ our Lord. Amen.

The groom and the bride may each place a ring on the other's finger, and say in turn

I give you this ring as a sign of our marriage.
With my body I honour you,
all that I am I give to you,
and all that I have I share with you
within the love of God,
Father, Son and Holy Spirit.

Or

Each may say in turn

I give you this ring
in God's name,
as a sign and seal of our marriage.
May God's love encircle us,
together or apart.
May this ring
be a sign to all
that I pledge you
my life-long love and loyalty.

DECLARATION OF MARRIAGE

Before God
and in the presence of this congregation,
A and *C* have made their solemn vows to each other.
They have joined hands
and given and received rings *[a ring]*,
binding themselves in the covenant of marriage.
I therefore pronounce them husband and wife,
in the name of God,
Father, Son and Holy Spirit.

MARRIAGE BLESSING

Either

Blessed be God the Father
who gives joy to the bridegroom and bride.
Blessed be the Lord Jesus Christ,
who brings new life to the world.
Blessed be the Holy Spirit of God,
who brings us together in love.
Blessed be the Father, Son and Holy Spirit,
one God to be praised for ever. **Amen.**

Or

Blessed be the God of bride and groom
who pours out love on man and woman.
Blessed be the God of wedding feast
who turns water into wine.
Blessed be the God of love and loyalty
who makes from two
one new creation.

The minister then addresses the couple

The Lord bless you and keep you,
the Lord make his face to shine upon you and be gracious to you:
the Lord lift up the light of his countenance upon you,
and give you his peace. Amen.

PRAYERS

Prayers may be offered for the couple, extempore or as follows

God of grace and source of all love,
we pray for *A* and *C*
that they may live together in love and faithfulness.
to the end of their lives.

Lord of life,
hear us in your love.

Enrich their friendship,
that each may be for the other
a companion in joy
and a comforter in sorrow.

Lord of life,
hear us in your love.

Help *A* and *C* to be patient, gentle and forgiving,
that their marriage may reflect
Christ's love for all people.

Lord of life,
hear us in your love.

Enable them to make their home
a place of welcome and friendship,
that their life together
may be a source of strength to others.

Lord of life,
hear us in your love.

Other intercessions may be included, concluding with

By your grace,
enable us,
who have witnessed these vows today,
to be signs of your love in the world,
through Jesus Christ our Lord. **Amen.**

Or

Gracious God,
for the promise,
for the hope,
and for the love of this day,
we praise you.

Bless your children now
with the gift of your Holy Spirit,
that they may build a life of joy and fulfilment
on the foundations of commitment and love.

By your grace,
sustain them through the love and support
which surround them now.
Fill them with your love,
that they may remain open-hearted,
courageous and strong.
Give them understanding and a generosity of spirit,
patience and delight with each other,
forbearance and friendship.

Grant that they may go forward from this day
delighting in their love,
abounding in forgiveness and hope.

May others see in them
a symbol of your love
from which nothing can separate us
and which nothing can overcome.

Be with them now
and remain with them for ever. **Amen.**

The Lord's Prayer may be said here.

SIGNING OF THE REGISTER

The wedding party and witnesses leave for the vestry so that the register may be signed. Music may be played until their return.

CLOSING WORSHIP AND BLESSING

A closing hymn, or worship songs, may be sung, followed by the words of dismissal and blessing, such as

Either

As God's own,
clothe yourselves with compassion,
kindness and patience.
Bear with one another
and forgive one another
as the Lord has forgiven you,
and crown all these things with love,
which binds everything together in perfect harmony.

see Colossians 3.12–14

Or

Go in peace to love and serve the Lord.

And either

The grace of Christ attend you,
the love of God surround you,
the Holy Spirit keep you,
that you may live in faith,
abound in hope,
and grow in love,
now and always. **Amen.**

Or

The blessing of God,
creator, redeemer and sustainer
be with you
now and always. **Amen.**

SECOND PATTERN FOR CHRISTIAN MARRIAGE

WELCOME

Having met the bride and bridal party at the door, the minister goes to the front of the church and extends a welcome, such as

On behalf of … [name of church],
I welcome you all to this service
to celebrate the Christian marriage
of A and C.

Would you please stand for the entry of the bride.

Alternatively, the bride may enter during the singing of the first hymn.

CALL TO WORSHIP

HYMN

PRAYER

A prayer of approach should be offered, such as

God of love, we praise you.
You made the world in love,
giving us freedom;
in Christ you lived by love,
accepting all its hurt and sharing all its healing;
by your Spirit you are present in love,
everywhere and always, here and now.
As we respond to your great love,
accept the worship and commitment we all bring,
and bless the commitment of A and C.
Let the love of Christ be present in everything done and begun today;
through Jesus Christ our Lord. **Amen.**

Or general prayers of praise and confession may be offered, after which the couple and attendants should remain standing.

STATEMENT OF PURPOSE

Either

We have come together in the presence of God,
to witness the marriage of *A* and *C*,
to ask God's blessing on them,
and to share in their joy.

God has made us in his own image,
male and female,
and marriage is his gift,
a holy mystery
in which man and woman become one flesh,
united in love,
and called to be faithful to each other throughout their lives.

Marriage is founded in God's loving nature,
and in his covenant of love with us in Christ.
Husband and wife,
in giving themselves to each other in love,
reflect the love of Christ for his Church.

Marriage is given
so that husband and wife may comfort and help each other,
living faithfully together in need and in plenty,
in sorrow and in joy.
It is given that with delight and tenderness
they may know each other in love,
and through the joy of their bodily union,
may strengthen the union of their hearts and lives.
It is given so that the stability it imparts to their relationship
may be a source of strength to others
[and the foundation of a secure family life
for any children they may have.]

In marriage husband and wife belong to one another,
and they begin a new life in the community.
It is a way of life that all should honour;
it must not be undertaken carelessly, lightly or selfishly,
but reverently, responsibly and after serious thought.
This is the way of life,
created and hallowed by God,
that *A* and *C* are now about to enter.
Therefore anyone who can show any reason
why they may not lawfully be married
should say so now.

Or

We are here to witness the marriage of *A* and *C*.

The Bible says that God has made us in his image,
male and female.
We are separate and different
yet able, in love, to meet, know, and delight in one another.
In Christian marriage two people
trusting in this mystery of love
commit themselves to live faithfully together for life,
in plenty or need, joy or sorrow.

For this purpose *A* and *C* are here today.
It is our privilege not only to witness this,
but to celebrate it with them,
and to acknowledge their marriage ourselves.
In marriage wife and husband belong to one another
and begin a new life together in the community.
We shall offer them our support.
All this we do before God the source of life and love.
All who trust their lives to one another
are relying on the power of love and the faithfulness of God,
so we shall ask God to send his blessing on *A* and *C*
that their new life together may be filled with joy,
may bring them ever closer to one another,
and may make them ever more open to God
whose love gives meaning to theirs.

This is the way of life, which *A* and *C* are now about to begin.
Anyone who can show any reason
why they may not lawfully be married
should say so now.

LEGAL DECLARATIONS

Either

The minister turns to the couple and says

If either of you knows
of any reason why you may not lawfully marry,
you should say so now.

The minister then invites the man to say after him/her or the man says

**I do solemnly declare
that I know not
of any lawful impediment
why I, AB,
may not be joined in matrimony
to CD.**

Similarly, the woman repeats or says

**I do solemnly declare
that I know not
of any lawful impediment
why I, CD,
may not be joined in matrimony
to AB.**

Or

The minister says to the congregation

A and *C* are now to make the declarations which the law requires.

The minister then says to the man

Are you, *AB*, free lawfully to marry *CD*?

I am.

The minister says to the woman

Are you, *CD*, free lawfully to marry, *AB*?

I am.

DECLARATION OF INTENT

With rephrasing, this question could be asked to both together.

A, will you take C as your wife in Christian marriage?
Will you love her,
comfort her,
honour, and keep her,
in sickness and in health,
and be faithful to her as long as you both live?

I will.

C, will you take A as your husband in Christian marriage?
Will you love him,
comfort him,
honour, and keep him,
in sickness and in health,
and be faithful to him as long as you both live?

I will

PRESENTATION FOR MARRIAGE

Either

Here the minister may ask

Who presents this woman to be married to this man?

The relative or friend presenting the woman may say

I do.

The minister may then ask

Who presents this man to be married to this woman?

The relative or friend presenting the man may say

I do.

Or

Inviting first the families (or parents), and then the congregation to stand, the minister may then ask

Will you, the families and friends of *A* and *C*,
do all in your power
to support and encourage them in their marriage?

The congregation replies

With God's help, we will.

PRAYER

Prayers for the couple may be offered, such as

Either

Father, hear our prayers for *A* and *C*
who, with faith in you and in each other,
pledge their love today.
May they be as aware of your presence as they are of ours,
and confident that you are able to help them
fulfil their promises in their life together;
through Jesus Christ our Lord.

Or

Living God,
you have commanded us to love each other.
We thank you now for the love
which grows between a man and a woman,
which has brought these two together here
to declare themselves one before you and their families and friends.
As they make their promises to each other,
may they do so humbly and penitently
[and in the confidence that you will forgive all their failures of the past].
May they begin their life together
with your own love in heart and mind,
and may we all continue, all our lives,
to walk with you and glorify your name;
through Jesus Christ our Lord.

All sit. The minister invites the couple to turn and face one another, join their hands, and make the following promises.

The man repeats after the minister, or says

I, *AB*, do take thee, *CD*,
to be my wedded wife,
to have and to hold,
from this day forward,
for better for worse,
for richer for poorer,
in sickness and in health,
to love and to cherish,
until we are parted by death,
and this is my solemn vow.

Similarly the woman repeats or says

I, *CD*, do take thee, *AB*,
to be my wedded husband,
to have and to hold,
from this day forward,
for better for worse,
for richer for poorer,
in sickness and in health,
to love and to cherish,
until we are parted by death,
and this is my solemn vow.

THE GIVING OF THE RING(S)

The following form of words may be used at the exchange of rings

Either

I give you this ring as a sign of our marriage.
With my body I honour you,
all that I am I give to you,
and all that I have I share with you
within the love of God,
Father, Son, and Holy Spirit.

Or

**I give you this ring in God's name,
as a symbol of all that we shall share.**

If there is only one ring, the woman may respond,

**I receive this ring in God's name
as a symbol of all that we shall share.**

DECLARATION OF MARRIAGE

A and *C* have declared
in the presence of God and this congregation
that they will live together in Christian marriage,
they have made their promises to each other,
and symbolized their marriage by joining hands,
and by exchanging rings (giving and receiving a ring).
I therefore pronounce them husband and wife
in the name of the Father, the Son, and the Holy Spirit.
Those whom God has joined together,
let no one separate.

A hymn or worship song may be sung.

*A scripture reading should be read and a sermon may be preached. Suitable Scripture readings
may be found on page 187.*

PRAYER AND BLESSING

A prayer (for which the couple may wish to kneel) may be offered, extempore or as follows

Eternal God, Creator and Father of us all,
we praise you for creating humanity male and female,
so that each may find fulfilment in the other.

We praise you for the ways in which love comes into our lives,
and for all the joys that can come to men and women through marriage.

Today, we thank you for *A* and *C*,
for your gift to them of life,
and for bringing them together in marriage.

We thank you for the love and care of their parents,
which has guided them to maturity
and prepared them for each other.
We thank you for their commitment to one another

and to a life planted in love and built on love.
With them we pray for their parents,
that at this moment of parting
they may find new happiness as they share their children's joy.

Help *A* and *C* to keep the promises they have made,
to be loyal and faithful to each other,
and to support one another throughout their life together;
may they bear each other's burdens and share each other's joys.

Help them to be honest and patient with each other,
to be loving and wise parents (of any children they may have),
and to make their home a place of welcome and peace.
In their future together,
may they enjoy each other's lives
and grow through each other's love;
through Jesus Christ our Lord.

The blessing may be said by the minister or the whole congregation and may be accompanied
by the laying on of hands.

A and *C*, the Lord bless you and keep you;
the Lord make his face to shine upon you
and be gracious to you;
the Lord lift up the light of his countenance upon you
and give you peace.   *Numbers 6.24–26*

A hymn or worship song may be sung.

BENEDICTION

Go in peace and in the joy of the Lord.

And the blessing of almighty God,
Father, Son and Holy Spirit,
be with you all. **Amen.**

SIGNING OF THE REGISTER

The minister, the couple, the best man and bridesmaids, the couple's parents and any others
required to act as witnesses, now leave the church in order to sign the registers, or sign them in
the church.

At this point it is traditional for an organ voluntary to be played, or a solo to be sung.
Alternatively, the congregation could be led in prayer and praise.

When the signing is completed, the couple lead the congregation from the church.

BLESSING A CIVIL MARRIAGE

This pattern must not be used for the solemnization of a marriage. It is for use when a couple, already married in law seek God's blessing for their continuing marriage. It may take place in a special act of worship or comprise part of Sunday worship.

After opening worship, the minister reads scripture sentence, such as

Jesus said,
'This is my commandment:
love one another, as I have loved you.'   *John 15.12*

Unless the Lord builds the house,
those who build it labour in vain.   *Psalm 12.1*

God is love;
and those who abide in love abide in God,
and God abides in them.   *1 John 4.16b*

STATEMENT OF PURPOSE

We rejoice in the marriage
of *A* and *C*
will ask God to bless it.

A and *C* have been married
according to the law of the land.
They have pledged their love and loyalty
to each other.
Now, in faith, they come before God
and this congregation
to acknowledge their covenant of marriage.

In Christian marriage,
a man and a woman
bind themselves to each other in love,
and become one,
even as Christ is one with the Church.
They are committed to love each other
as Christ loved the Church
and gave himself for it.

A and *C*,
you have already entered this way of life
which God has created
and, in Christ, blessed.
Today we pray that the Holy Spirit

will guide and strengthen you
that you may fulfil God's purposes
for the rest of your lives.

DECLARATION OF INTENT

The minister says to the couple

You have heard how God has given and blessed
the covenant of marriage.
Now in the presence of God and this congregation,
do you wish to affirm the vows
of Christian marriage?

The couple respond together

We do.

PRAYER

Living God,
we thank you for all the ways
by which your love reaches us:
through family and relations
whose care and trust have helped us;
through friends and companions
whose patience and concern
have brought us strength and hope.

We thank you for the love *A* and *C.*
Fill their hearts with the presence of Christ
as they recommit themselves to each other.
We pray that the new joy he brings
will make their lives new,
through Jesus Christ our Lord. **Amen.**

AFFIRMATION OF THE CONGREGATION

The minister addresses the congregation

Will all of you witnessing these vows
do everything in your power
to uphold *A* and *C* in their marriage?

We will.

REAFFIRMATION OF MARRIAGE VOWS

Either

The man says

C, you are my wife.
Before God and these witnesses,
I promise to love you,
and to be faithful to you,
as long as we both shall live.

The woman says

A, you are my husband.
Before God and these witnesses,
I promise to love you,
and to be faithful to you,
as long as we both shall live.

Or

The man says

C, you are my wife.
Before God,
and in the presence of this congregation,
I give myself to you as your husband,
for better, for worse,
for richer, for poorer,
in sickness and in health,
to love and to cherish,
until we are parted by death,
and to this end
I give you my word.

The woman says

A, you are my husband.
Before God,
and in the presence of this congregation,
I give myself to you as your wife.
for better, for worse,
for richer, for poorer,
in sickness and in health,
to love and to cherish, until we are parted by death,
I give you my word.
and to this end
I give you my word.

PRAYER

> God of love and grace,
> *these rings are symbols*
> of the love, trust and commitment
> between *A* and *C.*
> Bless them in their life together
> and help them to keep the promises
> they have made,
> through Jesus Christ our Lord. **Amen.**

MARRIAGE BLESSING

> Blessed be God the Father
> who gives joy to the bridegroom and bride.
> Blessed be the Lord Jesus Christ,
> who brings new life to the world.
> Blessed be the Holy Spirit of God,
> who brings us together in love.
> Blessed be the Father, Son and Holy Spirit,
> one God to be praised for ever. **Amen.**

> The Lord bless you
> and guard you;
> the Lord make his face shine upon you
> and be gracious to you;
> the Lord look kindly on you
> and give you peace. **Amen.**

DECLARATION

> *A* and *C* are husband and wife.
> They have now pledged
> their love and loyalty for one another
> before God and this congregation.

> Those who God has joined together,
> no one must separate.

Worship may continue with a reading from scripture, sermon, prayers for the couple and concluding praise.

THANKSGIVING FOR MARRIAGE
WITH THE RENEWAL OF MARRIAGE VOWS

This pattern may be used at an anniversary; or after a time of separation; or when a couple has experienced difficulty in their marriage; or when several couples request, or are invited to make, a public reaffirmation of marriage.

It may be used at home or in public worship, whether at a special act of worship or as part of a Sunday service.

The pattern is prepared for use with one couple only and the text will need to be varied if more than one couple use it on the same occasion.

The minister may give a suitable introduction by explaining the circumstances that lead to the occasion.

OPENING WORSHIP

A call to worship may be followed by the singing of a hymn or worship songs and the offering of prayer.

SCRIPTURE SENTENCES

God created humankind in his own image;
male and female he created them;
and God blessed them.

from Genesis 1.27f.

God is love;
and those who abide in love abide in God,
and God abides in them.

1 John 4.16b

Unless the Lord builds the house,
those who build it labour in vain.

Psalm 127.1

STATEMENT OF PURPOSE

Marriage is a way of life founded in God.

It is his gift to us,
to help man and woman find
companionship, help and comfort.
It is also a means of grace
in which husband and wife,
living faithfully together,

may find the fulfilment of human love
in tenderness and respect.
In Christian marriage,
God makes his servants one.
Their life together is a witness to his love
in this troubled world,
a love by which unity overcomes division,
forgiveness heals injury,
and joy triumphs over sorrow.

By marriage God enriches society
and strengthens the sanctity of family life.
A and *C* are here today
to celebrate their marriage
(on its . . . th anniversary)
and to reaffirm their commitment
to this way of life
which God has provided and Christ has blessed.
We rejoice with them,
and support them with our prayers

PRAYER

Prayer is offered, extempore or as follows

Living God,
we thank you for all the ways
by which your love reaches us:
through family and relations
whose care and trust have helped us;
through friends and companions
whose patience and concern
have brought us strength and hope.

We thank you for the love *A* and *C*.
Fill their hearts with the presence of Christ
as they recommit themselves to each other.
We pray that the new joy he brings
will make their lives new,
through Jesus Christ our Lord. **Amen.**

RENEWAL OF VOWS WITH THANKSGIVING

This section is for use when the dominant note is thanksgiving.

The husband and wife face each other and join hands.

The husband says

I, *AB*,
in the presence of God,
renew my commitment
to you, *CD*,
as your husband.
I give thanks
that you have shared my life.
All that I am
and all that I have
I continue to share with you.
Whatever the future holds,
I will love you
 and stand by you,
as long as we both shall live.

The wife says

I, *CD*,
in the presence of God,
renew my commitment
to you, *AB*,
as your wife.
I give thanks that you have shared my life.
All that I am
and all that I have
I continue to share with you.
Whatever the future holds,
I will love you
and stand by you,
as long as we both shall live.

RENEWAL OF VOWS FOR RECOMMITMENT

This section is for use when the dominant note is recommitment.

The husband and wife face each other and join hands.

The husband says

I, **AB**,
in the presence of God,
renew my commitment
to you, **CD**,
as your husband.
I give thanks
that you have shared my life.
All that I am
I give to you,
and all that I have
I share with you.
Whatever the future holds,
I will love you
and stand by you,
as long as we both shall live.

The wife says

I, **CD**,
in the presence of God,
renew my commitment
to you, **AB**,
as your wife.
I give thanks that you have shared my life.
All that I am
I give to you,
and all that I have
I share with you.
Whatever the future holds,
I will love you
and stand by you,
as long as we both shall live.

Whichever form of renewal has been used, the service then continues

AFFIRMATION BY THE PEOPLE

The minister says

Will you,
the family and friends of *A* and *C*,
who have gathered here today,
continue to uphold them in their marriage?
If you will promise this, then please stand.

The congregation stands.

PRAYERS

Prayers may be offered by the minister or others, extempore or as follows

Generous God,
your Son has shown us how to love
and invites us to love one another
as he loves us.

We pray for *A* and *C*,
with their shared memories of the past;
of joy and laughter,
sadness and disappointment,
forgiving and being forgiven.
By your Spirit,
help them to put their trust in you
to guide and guard them in the future.

Loving God,
we thank you that in our earthly life
you may speak to us of eternal life.
Help us to
know you more clearly,
love you more dearly
and follow you more nearly,
day by day;
through Jesus Christ our Lord. **Amen.**

The Lord's Prayer may be said together.

BLESSING

The couple may kneel while the minister blesses them

The riches of God's grace be upon you,
that you may continue in faith and love
and receive the blessing of eternal life.

The Lord bless you
and guard you;
the Lord make his face shine upon you
and be gracious to you;
the Lord look kindly on you
and give you peace. **Amen.**

*The service continues, or reaches its conclusion with closing worship. If there is continuing
worship, then the couple may return to their places in the congregation.*

ADDITIONAL MATERIAL

OPENING PRAYER

Faithful God,
with eager anticipation we gather for this wedding celebration.
We pray that you will bless *A* and *C*,
the families who have nurtured and guided them
and all who have come here today to show love and support.
Thank you for drawing *A* and *C* together
in love, friendship and commitment.
You are the giver of life
 and your love transforms all we do and are.
Take all we bring and do today,
in worship and in celebration,
and bless us with your grace,
through Jesus Christ our Lord. **Amen.**

DECLARATION OF NO IMPEDIMENT

The traditional form may still be used thus

The minister turns to the couple and says

If either of you knows of any reason
why you may not lawfully marry,
you should say so now.

The minister invites the man to say after him/her or the man says

**I do solemnly declare
that I know not
of any lawful impediment
why I, *AB*,
may not be joined in matrimony
to *CD*.**

Similarly, the woman repeats or says

**I do solemnly declare
that I know not
of any lawful impediment
why I, *CD*,
may not be joined in matrimony
to *AB*.**

WORDS TO THE CONGREGATION BEFORE THE VOWS ARE EXCHANGED

On this life-changing day of outward glory,
of wedding finery and bouquets,
of fine music and inspiring words,
let us remember the true meaning of Christian marriage,
which begins with this step of faith and trust,
and leads into the faithful, loving, caring commitment
of partnership for life.
For those who have eyes to see,
Christian marriage may reflect the faithful love of God
in a human relationship.

Some of us were too nervous on our own wedding day
to take in the full meaning of the solemn vows,
so in coming as guests to this wedding
we may reflect on their deep significance.
All of you who are married couples here,
listen intently to the promises,
and renew them in your own hearts and lives.

MARRIAGE VOWS: THE PROMISE OF LOVE

These words are to be said by groom and bride in turn to each other.

I call upon God to be my witness
and on those gathered here
to hear my promise.
I, *AB*,
take you, *CD*,
to be my wedded *wife/husband*.

I promise you love and loyalty
in dark times as well as light,
in ill-health as well as strength and vigour,
in hard times and in good.

I promise to stay with you
through thick and thin,
good and bad,
sorrow and joy,
tears and laughter.
I promise to love you
and to be faithful to you
now and for ever.
I do not promise in my strength alone:
I promise in the name of God,
Father, Son and Holy Spirit.

PRAYERS

Prayers for the bride and groom

Loving God,
on this day of celebration we come to you
in trembling and in trust.
Thank you for the delights of loving,
for *A* and *C* and their desire to work for each other's happiness,
seeking each other's fulfillment
and committing themselves to all that is good and life-giving.
Thank you for the excitement and comfort of home-making,
love-sharing and mutual trust.

We pray that the solemn vows of Christian marriage
may reveal to *A* and *C*
more of your covenant with us:
to honour and keep us for better for worse,
for richer for poorer,
in sickness and in health,
cherishing us faithfully throughout time and eternity,
so that even death cannot separate us from your love.
We ask these prayers in the name of our Lord, Jesus Christ. **Amen.**

Or

Creator God,
who formed us out of stardust,
and breathed life into our bodies,
as *A* and *C* entrust their lives to one another,
we see their everyday existence
shot through with threads of gold.

By your grace,
weave the fine, glistening strands
of confident hope, trusting love and sparkling dreams
into a strong and shining ribbon of lifelong love –
where shade and light,
dark and bright,
day and night
are encompassed by your love
and transformed by your gospel,
through Jesus Christ our Lord. **Amen.**

God of fresh beginnings,
we thank you for offering *A* and *C* this new opportunity
to commit themselves in a loving and creative partnership.
We pray that any mistakes in the past
may lead them to insight, wisdom and compassion.

Loving God,
who understands us better than we understand ourselves,
you know us through and through
and love us completely.
We entrust to you our past hurts
and ask for your healing;
we come in trembling trust,
with tender hopes,
and ask for your help.

Show *A* and *C* that
your mercy stretches to the heavens,
your grace reaches to the depths of the sea
and your love enfolds them,
though Jesus Christ our Lord. **Amen.**

Where there are children involved

God, father and mother of us all,
we pray for the children, … and …
which this new family bond has forged.
Help them to know that they belong,
that are loved and treasured by you,
and by those who care for them.
We ask these prayers in the name of Jesus,
who was once a child. **Amen.**

Prayer following the reading of the marriage at Cana

Lord Jesus,
the true and fruitful vine,
you brought joy to a wedding at Cana in Galilee,
transforming water into the finest wine.
Take the cup of our human existence,
and fill it with life in all its fullness —
rich, sparkling and heady, like wine,
brimming with love.
Inspire *A* and *C*
to yearn for the best —
your abundant life at the heart of their marriage. **Amen.**

Prayer following the reading of 1 Corinthians 13

God of grace,
giver of faith, hope and love,
we pray for *A* and *C,*
that their love for one another
may be patient, kind, and caring,
faithful and overflowing with hope.
Show them how to bear all things,
believe all things,
hope all things,
endure all things,
by the power of your love,
which never ends;
through Jesus Christ our Lord. **Amen.**

Alternative Prayer and Blessing

Lord God, Heavenly Father,
in your great love you created us male and female
and made the union of husband and wife
an image of the covenant
between you and your people.

Send your Holy Spirit
to pour out your blessing on *A* and *C*
who have this day
given themselves to each other in marriage.

Bless them in their work and in their companionship;
in their sleeping and in their waking;
in their joys and in their sorrows;
in their life and in their death.

Let their love for each other
be a seal upon their hearts,
a mantle about their shoulders,
and a crown upon their heads.

Bless them so that all may see,
in their lives together in the community of your people,
a vision of your Kingdom on earth.

And finally, in the fullness of time,
welcome them into the glory of your presence;
through your Son Jesus Christ. **Amen.**

A responsive blessing

May God, the Father, give you his joy.
Amen.

May the Son of God guide and help you in good times and bad.
Amen.

May the Holy Spirit always fill your hearts with his love.
Amen.

May almighty God bless you,
the Father, the Son, and the Holy Spirit.
Amen.

REAFFIRMATION OF MARRIAGE VOWS

Couples who wish to reaffirm their marriage vows, for whatever reason, may wish to use the vows printed in one of the patterns above.

Alternatively, or in addition, they may wish to use a form of words such as

Husband

C, I will love you in good times and bad.
I will love you when it is easy and when it is not.
I will love you when love brings us close,
and when love pushes us apart.
I will love you when my love is obvious
and when it is hidden by my faults.
Please go on trusting me.

Wife

A, I will go on trusting you and loving you
in good times and bad.
I will love you when it is easy and when it is not.
I will love you when love brings us close,
and when love pushes us apart.
I will love you when my love is obvious
and when it is hidden by my faults.
Please go on trusting me.

Husband

I will.
Rich or poor, well or ill, strong or weak:
I will, till death parts us.
It is God's purpose.
I give my word.

Wife

I will.
 Rich or poor, well or ill, strong or weak:
I will, till death parts us.
It is God's purpose.
I give my word.

In an act of reaffirmation, the question of intent might be modified by substituting the words

A, do you acknowledge C
to be your *wife/husband* in Christian marriage?
Do you promise to go on loving her ... *[etc]*.

I do.

If the legal forms of words is to be used it can be adapted similarly

**I call upon these persons here present
to witness that I, AB,
have taken you, CD,
to be wedded husband/wife...**

CONFRONTING DEATH
CELEBRATING RESURRECTION

Christian funeral services are distinctive: beyond the solemn farewell that any person's death evokes, they enable us to relate human death and bereavement to God.

In the funeral service we begin with the one who has died. We confront death itself, and we rejoice in the resurrection promised and known in Christ. In our pastoral care (of which the funeral service is a part) we confront the reality of death with the hope of the resurrection. For the deceased, death is the gateway to judgement and to life. For the bereaved, the journey through grief will not lead back to 'normal', to a past that cannot be recaptured. In our funeral services we point to a new experience of God beyond death. For the deceased there is the hope of deliverance and of glory; for the bereaved there is opportunity for the past to be remembered with forgiveness and for the future to be embraced with freedom.

To accomplish all this (and more) we need to remember that it is the task of the funeral to map the journey that lies ahead, not to travel it in its entirety. A funeral at a church or chapel may include all the elements suggested here. If we remember that the dead from whom we part were made in the image of God, and that the death of Jesus touches their death, we will be strengthened in our ministry. 'Truly, I tell you, just as you did it to one of the least of these my brothers (my sisters), you did it to me.'

Two basic funeral patterns are offered here, plus additional material for particular situations. In the first pattern, the public service of worship leads to the act of committal (burial or cremation). This may be followed at a later date with a memorial service or other form of thanksgiving. In the second pattern, the service begins with the act of committal, (usually at the chapel in the crematorium/cemetery) and may, but need not, involve only the immediate family and a few close friends. After the committal the mourners may move on to the local church for a public service of thanksgiving.

Both patterns, in different ways, hold pastoral opportunities for those mourning: the reality of death is confronted, thanksgiving is expressed for the life of the person who is remembered and the hope of life eternal within the gospel story is affirmed and celebrated. Careful reflection and sensitive guidance will help plan a pattern of remembrance and hope which best meet the needs of the family and expresses the promises of God.

Suggested readings for use within the funeral service:
Psalms 8; 16; 23; 27; 30; 42.1–8; 43.3–5; 46; 90; 103; 116; 118.14–21, 28–29; 121; 130; 138; 139.1–14, 17–18, 23; John 5.19–25; 6.35–40; 11.17–27; Romans 8.18, 28, 35, 37–39; 1 Corinthians 15.1–4, 20–26, 35–38, 42–44, 50, 53–58; 2 Corinthians 4.7–18; 4.16–5.18; Philippians 3.10–21; 1 Thessalonians 4.13–18; 1 Peter 1.3–9; Revelation 7.9–17.

FIRST FUNERAL PATTERN
FOR A SERVICE FOLLOWED BY
AN ACT OF COMMITTAL

The service may begin in church and then be completed at the cemetery, or it may all take place at the cemetery or crematorium chapel.

SCRIPTURE SENTENCES

The minister may lead the coffin into the church or chapel. During the procession, or on arrival at the front, one or more of the following sentences may be read

Praised be the God and Father
of our Lord Jesus Christ!
In his great mercy by the resurrection
of Jesus Christ from the dead,
he gave us new birth into a living hope.   *1 Peter 1.3 REB*

Things beyond our seeing,
things beyond our hearing,
things beyond our imagining,
have all been prepared by God
for those who love him.   *1 Corinthians 2.9 REB*

In the tender compassion of our God
the dawn from heaven will break upon us,
to shine on those who live in darkness,
under the shadow of death,
and to guide our feet into the way of peace.   *Luke 1.78f. REB*

Or

John 11.25f.; Romans 8.38f.; I Thessalonians 4. 14,17b—18; 1 Timothy 6.7; Job 1.21b; Lamentations 3.22f.; Matthew 5.4; John 3.16

INTRODUCTION

We meet in the presence of God,
who holds the keys of life and death.
We meet to remember the life of *N*, who has died,
to give thanks,
to forgive,
and to look forward.

We meet to commit *N* and ourselves to God
whose son, Jesus, has passed through death before us.
Hear now words of faith and hope.

Or

We are here now to honour *N* who has died.
We are here because in one way or another, this death affects us all.
We are here to listen again
to some of the great words of the Christian faith.
To consider, to remember,
and in quiet gratitude,
to give thanks for his/her and our own continuing lives.
We are here to renew our trust in God
who has said: I will not fail you or desert you.

A hymn may be sung

OPENING PRAYER

One or more of these prayers may be used

Eternal God,
maker of all that is,
we come before you in our need.
On this day of parting
do not abandon *N* whom we love
do not desert us in our grief.
Give us courage and strength for today
and hope and peace for tomorrow.
This we ask through Jesus Christ our Lord. **Amen.**

Or

God, your love is stronger than death.
By you we are all being brought to life.
Help us as we hear the promises of your word
to believe them and to receive the comfort they offer.
You are the giver of hope:
fill us with joy and peace in believing
that our fears may be dispelled,
our loneliness eased,
and our hope reawakened;
through Jesus Christ our Lord. **Amen.**

Words of confession and forgiveness may be offered here

Loving God,
in our pain,
we remember with sorrow
how we have failed one another
and grieved your heart.
In your kindness,
forgive our past sins,
set us free from guilt,
and make us strong to live our lives in love;
through Jesus Christ your Son our Saviour.

God of grace and power
send your Holy Spirit among us,
that we may hear your promises
and know them to be true,
and so receive the comfort and peace they bring;
through Jesus Christ our Lord. **Amen.**

Or

If only, Lord God,
if only we had taken time,
if only we had said more,
if only we had said less.
We confess to you our regrets,
we acknowledge what is past.
In this moment give us grace to receive
and to offer forgiveness;
through Jesus Christ our Lord. **Amen.**

When a tribute is to be offered, it may be given here. The proclamation of the Christian hope then takes its rightful place at the heart of the service in the reading of scripture and a sermon.

Suggested passages for Scripture readings are listed above.

A sermon follows.

PRAYERS

At this point, prayers should be offered to include: thanksgiving for victory over death, remembrance of the departed, and prayers for those who mourn. Two options for covering these three themes is offered below: a LITANY and concluding prayer covering these three themes or, alternatively, three distinct prayers. A combination of either of these options or extempore prayer is also possible.

LITANY

Let us pray to the Lord our God,
making known our heart's desire for *N*.

God of our journey,
you have called us to follow in the way of Christ,
even to death.
By the victory of the cross
lead *N* through death to resurrection
where Christ has gone before.

Lord, in your mercy,
Hear our prayer.

Righteous God,
you call us to judgement –
the living and the dead,
to the place where right and truth prevail.
Examine us with love,
and show *N* your mercy,
for without it none of us may stand.

Lord, in your mercy,
Hear our prayer.

Saving God,
you have promised your salvation
to all who trust in you.
Bring *N* with all your saints
to your eternal presence.

Lord, in your mercy,
Hear our prayer.

Ever-living God,
you have promised new life
to all who are found in Christ.
Clothe *N* with the life of Christ,
whom not even death could hold.

Lord, in your mercy,
Hear our prayer.

Eternal God
all our days depend on you,
for you are the giver of all good gifts.
Grant to us with *N*
the life of your eternal joy and peace.

Lord, in your mercy,
Hear our prayer.

CONCLUDING PRAYER

The following may be said after the litany

Eternal God,
we pray for ourselves as we pray for *N*.
We stand where earth and heaven meet,
where life is brought to death,
and death is made the gate to glory.
Deliver us from fear and doubt,
from despair and unbelief,
and bring us to the light of your presence.
Grant us that peace which the world cannot give,
so that we with *N* may trust in you
and find our life in you.
We make our prayer through Jesus Christ,
our Saviour in life and death,
who lives and reigns with you
in the unity of the Holy Spirit,
God for ever and ever. **Amen.**

A PRAYER TRILOGY

Prayer of thanksgiving for victory over death

Living God, we praise you for Jesus Christ
who, for the joy that was in the future
went into the darkness of death
so that we might continue to hope and rise above despair.
Thank you for his death
which has opened up the future for us.
Thank you for his living among us now as risen Lord
leading us through death to undying life.
Keep convincing us that his resurrection
means life for us,
and that neither death nor life,
nor anything in all creation,
can deprive us of the future you are making for us.

Prayer of remembrance and thanksgiving for the deceased

Eternal God,
source of all life
and inspiration for living,
you are
too mysterious to understand,
too awesome to behold.
Further from us
you could not be,
yet nearer to us
than we are to ourselves.

Thank you
for dwelling in us
and being present for us
in each other
and in the life of *N* who has died

Thank you
for all the achievements in *N*'s life
for the love given by *her/him*
and the love received among family and friends.
Thank you
that where frustration and disappointment
diminished their joy in life
that time is now past.

Help us through their death
to grasp more firmly the hope
that life is longer than our years,
and the love you have shown to us in Christ
is stronger than death.
Through Jesus Christ our Lord. **Amen.**

Prayer for those who mourn

To your loving care, O God,
we commend those who mourn,
especially … and all the family.
Sustain them in the days to come
with treasured memories of the past
and radiant hopes for the future.
And bring us all at the last to fullness of life
with your saints in the Kingdom of heaven;
through Jesus Christ our Lord. **Amen.**

Or

Almighty God,
deal graciously we pray with those who mourn,
that casting all their care on you,
they may know the consolation of your love;
through Jesus Christ our Lord. **Amen.**

THE LORD'S PRAYER

Our Father in heaven,	Our Father,
hallowed be your name,	who art in heaven,
your kingdom come,	hallowed be thy name.
your will be done,	Thy kingdom come,
on earth as in heaven.	thy will be done
Give us today	on earth as it is in heaven.
our daily bread.	Give us this day
Forgive us our sins	our daily bread
as we forgive those	and forgive us our trespasses,
who sin against us.	as we forgive those
Save us from the time of trial	who trespass against us.
and deliver us from evil.	Lead us not into temptation,
For the kingdom, the power,	but deliver us from evil.
and the glory are yours	For thine is the kingdom,
now and forever. Amen.	the power and the glory,
	for ever and ever. Amen.

PRAYER OF FAREWELL

Eternal God,
go before us to lead our ways from death to life,
go with us to keep us in the paths of peace.
Gather us with *N* into the company
of those who praise you for ever;
through Jesus Christ our Lord,
who lives and reigns with you
in the unity of the Holy Spirit,
now and for ever. **Amen.**

Or

Gracious God,
by your power you gave us life,
and in your love you are giving us new life
in Jesus Christ.
We entrust *N* to your safe keeping,
in the faith of Jesus Christ your Son our Lord,
who died and rose again to save us,
and to bring us all
to a joyful resurrection
and the glory of your eternal kingdom. **Amen.**

Rest eternal, grant *N*, O Lord,
and let light perpetual shine upon *her/him*.

*If the committal is to take place elsewhere, this part of the service may end with a scripture
sentence, an ascription of glory, and a blessing.*

FINAL SCRIPTURE

We may be certain of this: neither death, nor life, no angel, no ruler,
nothing that exists, nothing still to come, not any power, or height or
depth, nor anything created, can ever separate us from the love of God
which we have seen in Christ Jesus our Lord.   *Romans 8.38–39*

ASCRIPTION OF GLORY

Now to the One who can keep you from falling,
and set you in the presence of his glory,
jubilant and above reproach,
to the only God and Saviour,
be glory and majesty, power and authority,
through Jesus Christ our Lord. **Amen.**

A blessing may be said.

THE COMMITTAL

If the committal is conducted in a different place to the first part of this service it may be helpful to start with scripture sentences, and an opening prayer. At a burial, the mourners are invited to gather round the grave. At a crematorium, the congregation may be invited to stand and curtains may be drawn or left open as desired.

SCRIPTURE SENTENCES

We exult in the hope of the divine glory
which is to be ours.
Such hope is no fantasy:
through the Holy Spirit,
God's love has flooded our hearts.   *Romans 5.2, 5 REB*

We brought nothing into this world
and we can take nothing out.   *1 Timothy 6.7 REB*

As in Adam all die,
so in Christ all will be brought to life.   *1 Corinthians 15.22 REB*

Do not be afraid,
I am the first and the last, says the Lord,
and I am the Living One;
I was dead and now I am alive for evermore.   *Revelation 1.8, 17f. REB*

There is nothing in death or life,
in the world as it is, or the world as it shall be,
nothing in all creation that can separate us
from the love of God in Christ Jesus our Lord.   *Romans 8.38f. REB*

THE WORD OF RESURRECTION

Lord, you renew the face of the earth;
gather to yourself *N* whom we have loved,
and grant to *her/him* those things
which eye has not seen, nor ear heard,
nor the human heart imagined.

The following prayers may be used in addition as desired and as appropriate

At a graveside

From the dust you made us, O God,
to the dust we return.
Here is your *daughter/son N.*
Awaken *her/him* from the sleep of death,
and feed *her/him* at the table of eternal life.

Love is stronger than death,
hope is stronger than despair:
So we entrust *N*, to you, our God;
set *her/him* as a seal upon your heart
and bring *her/him* to life eternal.

CONCLUDING PRAYERS

One or more prayers may be said, such as

Eternal God,
in Jesus Christ
you have given to us a sure faith and a true hope.
Help us to live
as those who believe and trust
in the communion of saints,
the forgiveness of sins,
and the resurrection to life eternal.
Strengthen this faith and hope in us
all the days of our life;
then bring us at our last awakening
to the house and gate of heaven,
to enter into that gate
and to dwell in that house,
where we shall be one with you
and with all your saints for ever;
through Jesus Christ or Lord. **Amen.**

Or

Jesus said,
'Peace I leave with you;
my peace I give to you.'
Loving God, we long for peace:
peace to leave *N* with you,
peace to strengthen us for today and tomorrow,
peace with ourselves, with each other and with you.
Grant us that peace which the world cannot give:
through Jesus Christ, your Son. **Amen.**

SECOND FUNERAL PATTERN
FOR A SERVICE OF COMMITTAL
FOLLOWED BY A SERVICE OF THANKSGIVING

This pattern begins with a service of committal followed by a thanksgiving service. The committal will usually be an intimate service for the family and close friends and may, for practical reasons, take place in a crematorium or cemetery chapel. The thanksgiving service will normally take place in a church building and will reflect the pattern of worship familiar to the local congregation.

SERVICE WITH COMMITTAL

The committal should provide an opportunity for 'letting go' of the person who has died and also be an occasion for ministering to the needs of those left behind. If it precedes the thanksgiving service, it may include prayers asking for strength to help the mourners through the difficulties of the more public event.

WELCOME

We have come here to say farewell to N,
to thank God for *his/her* life
and to commit *her/him* and ourselves
into God's loving care.

Listen now to the promises of Scripture:
draw strength and comfort from them,
that you might face this hour
trusting in the love and faithfulness of God.

SENTENCES

The steadfast love of the Lord never ceases, his compassion never fails;
every morning they are renewed.

Lamentations 3.22f.

Blessed are those who mourn for they will be comforted.

Matthew 5.4

'As a mother comforts her child so I will comfort you,' says the Lord.

Isaiah 66.13

Praise be to the God and Father of our Lord Jesus Christ who in his mercy gave us new birth into a living hope through the resurrection of Jesus Christ from the dead! The inheritance to which we are born is one that nothing can destroy or spoil or wither.

1 Peter 1.3f. NEB

I am convinced that there is nothing in death or life, in the realms of spirits or superhuman powers, in the world as it is or the world as it shall be, in the forces of the universe, in heights or depths – nothing in all creation that can separate us from the love of God in Christ Jesus our Lord.

Romans 8.38f. REB

OPENING PRAYER

Prayers expressing trust and asking for strength and assurance may be offered extempore or as follows

Heavenly Father,
in your Son Jesus Christ
you have given us true faith
and a sure hope.
Strengthen this faith and hope within us
that we may live believing in the
communion of saints,
the forgiveness of sins
and the resurrection to eternal life
through Jesus Christ our Lord. **Amen.**

Or

Eternal God,
the Lord of life,
the conqueror of death,
our help in every time of trouble,
comfort us who mourn.
Give us grace, in the presence of death,
to worship you;
and enable us to put our whole trust
in your goodness and mercy.
Through Jesus Christ our Lord. **Amen.**

Or

Loving God,
we come to you in our need.
You have given us birth
and now we face the mystery of death.
Help us to find you in the whole of life,
its beginning and its ending.
Help us to discover you
in our pain as well as our joy,
and in our doubts as well as our believing,
that we might find
comfort in your word
and light for our darkness.
In the name of Jesus. **Amen.**

A hymn may now be sung, or a psalm read together.

When a tribute is to be offered, it may be given here. This may particularly be the case if there is no service of thanksgiving following. The proclamation of the Christian hope then takes its place at the heart of the service in the reading of scripture and a sermon.

Scripture passages and a brief address follow.

PRAYERS

Extempore or otherwise, prayers should now express thanks for all that God has done in Christ, and for the life of the deceased, and should seek the comfort of God for those who are bereaved.

THANKSGIVING FOR VICTORY IN CHRIST

Eternal God,
you are the Creator, the Giver of Life.
In Jesus Christ,
you have given us a new life which nothing can destroy.
In the resurrection of Jesus
you have shown us that the grave is not the end,
for your love holds us through all things.
We thank and praise you for this hope,
not based on vain and wishful thinking,
but on the message of Easter
and on the life-giving power of your Spirit at work in your people
through Jesus Christ,
the life and hope of the world. **Amen.**

REMEMBRANCE AND THANKSGIVING

Loving God,
we thank you for the gift of life.
Today we thank you for the life of *N*
and all that *she/he* was.
We thank you for the memories of *N*
which we can keep,
as a source of comfort and continuing thankfulness.
We thank you for those aspects
of *his/her* life which meant so much to us;
for ...

By your grace,
help us this day to commit *N* into your hands
and as we do, grant us your peace,
in the name of Jesus Christ our Saviour. **Amen.**

The Lord's Prayer may now be said, after which the minister invites the congregation to stand.

THE ACT OF COMMITTAL

O Death, where is your victory? O Death, where is your sting? Thanks be to
God! He gives us victory through our Lord Jesus Christ.

1 Corinthians 15.55, 57 REB

Our Lord Jesus Christ said,
'I am the resurrection and the life.
Whoever has faith in me shall live,
even though he dies;
and no one who lives and has faith in me
shall ever die.

John 11.25f GNB

Words of committal such as

Now that the earthly life of *N* has come to an end,
we commit *his/her* body to be *cremated/buried*,
confident of the resurrection to eternal life;
through our Lord Jesus Christ.

Or

Nothing can separate us from God's love,
so we commend *N* into God's hands.
We commit the body of our *sister/brother* to be *cremated/buried*,
trusting in God's mercy and compassion.

God will wipe every tear from their eyes. There shall be an end to death,
and to mourning and crying and pain, for the old order has passed away.

Revelation 21.4 REB

A brief silence may be followed by suitable prayers.

REFLECTIONS AND PRAYERS

At the grave

We have entrusted our *sister/brother*, *N*
into the hands of God.
We therefore commit *her/his* body to the ground,
earth to earth, ashes to ashes, dust to dust,
in the sure and certain hope
of the resurrection to eternal life,
through our Lord Jesus Christ,
who died, was buried,
and rose again for us,
and is alive and reigns for evermore.

At the crematorium

We have entrusted our *sister/brother*, *N*
into the hands of God.
We therefore commit *her/his* body to be cremated,
ashes to ashes, dust to dust,
in the sure and certain hope
of the resurrection to eternal life,
through our Lord Jesus Christ,
who died, and rose again for us,
and is alive and reigns for evermore.

O Lord,
support us all the days
of this troubling life,
until the shadows lengthen
the evening comes,
the busy world is hushed,
the fever of life is over

and our work done.
Then, Lord, in your mercy
grant us safe lodging,
a holy rest,
and peace at the last
through Jesus Christ our Lord. **Amen.**

Or

Eternal God,
in Jesus Christ
you have given to us a true faith and a sure hope.
Help us to live
as those who believe and trust in
the communion of saints,
the forgiveness of sins,
and the resurrection to eternal life.
Strengthen this faith and hope in us
all the days of our life;
then bring us at our last awakening
to the house and gate of heaven,
to enter into that gate
and to dwell in that house,
where we shall be one with you
and with all your saints for ever;
through Jesus Christ our Lord.

THE BLESSING

God of peace, you brought back from the dead our Lord Jesus,
the great shepherd of the sheep, by the blood of the eternal covenant.
Show us the peace we should seek;
show us the peace we should try to give;
show us the peace we may keep;
show us the peace you have given;
and make us what you want us to be;
through Jesus Christ, to whom be glory for ever.

Or

Deep peace of the running wave to you,
deep peace of the flowing air to you,
deep peace of the quiet earth to you,
deep peace of the shining stars to you,
deep peace of the Son of peace to you.

SERVICE OF THANKSGIVING

As this will take place either later in the same day as the committal or at a later date, the mourn-
ers will take their places in church in the same way as other members of the congregation. This is
a more public event than the committal and, although there will be prayers for the bereaved, the
emphasis of the service will be: thanksgiving for what God has done in Christ; for the life of the
deceased; and prayers for those things which the deceased believed to be important. In the case of
the death of a church member, it may well be helpful for the prayers or other parts of the service
to be led by various members of the fellowship. Materials from the other patterns in the funeral
section may be used here, as may material from the general or Easter sections.

A call to worship may be given and a hymn of praise sung.

PRAYERS OF PRAISE AND CONFESSION

Extempore or as follows

Loving God,
you have made the world in which we live
and you have given us life.

Eternal Word,
we praise and adore you.

Generous God,
you have shown us in your Son the wonder and the cost of love
through his life and through his death upon the cross.

Risen Lord,
we praise and adore you.

Creator God,
through your life-giving Spirit, you renew and empower us
to live as the children of God.

Spirit of love, hope, joy and peace,
we praise and adore you. Amen.

Servant God,
forgive us
our squandering of life and its possibilities.

We have missed opportunities
for service and witness;
we have misused and neglected gifts
which you have entrusted to us.

Our love of you has been half-hearted
and our love of others pitiful.

Let the glory of loving service shown to us in Christ
shine through our lives
restoring us
and renewing us
to your ways.

Grant us the confidence we lack
in your life-giving Spirit,
to do a new thing amongst us and within us.

ASSURANCE OF FORGIVENESS

Here is a saying you must trust, one that merits full acceptance: 'Christ
Jesus came into the world to save sinners.' Thanks be to God!

*Scripture may be read and a sermon given. The emphasis will be on thanksgiving for the
person's life and on a triumphant proclamation of the resurrection hope.*

A hymn or songs of faith may be sung

PRAYERS

*Thanksgiving may be offered here for new life in Christ, for the life of the deceased, and for
our own continuing lives.*

Loving God,
you have given us life
with all its possibilities for growth
and all its opportunities for service.
You have made us
in your own image
as men and women
responsible and creative,
open to great visions,
and capable of great imagination.
In Jesus Christ you have shown us,
what we might be.
When you raised him to life
you showed us that death is not the end
for those who put their trust in you.
Thank you for this new life in Christ
and for the hope of its future fullness.

This day
we thank you especially for the life of *N*.
We thank you for all that *she/he* meant to us.
We especially remember with gratitude ...
We thank you for *her/his* faith in you
and all that we saw of you through *her/him*.

As we remember,
help us to commit ourselves anew to your service,
so that our thanksgiving for *N*
might show itself
in a readiness to be faithful to your will.
This we pray
in the name of Jesus Christ our Lord. **Amen.**

A hymn of commitment may be sung.

DISMISSAL AND BLESSING

May the love of the Lord Jesus draw us to himself;
may the power of the Lord Jesus strengthen us in his service;
may the joy of the Lord Jesus fill our souls.

May the blessing of God Almighty,
the Father, the Son, and the Holy Spirit,
be among you and remain with you always.

PATTERN FOR
THE BURIAL OR SCATTERING OF ASHES

This brief service, usually in the open air, has no fixed pattern. It may include a reading of scripture, words of committal or commendation and a prayer.

PREPARATION

The minister greets the people in these or other suitable words

Either

This is a time to remember with affection and gratitude the one who has died, to hold in prayer those who are left behind, and to recall the mystery of faith which connects the mortality of life as we know it, with the miracle of life as we shall know it.

Or

Though we are dust and ashes,
God has prepared for those who love him
a heavenly dwelling place.
We have already commended *N* into the hands of Almighty God.
Here we prepare to commit *N* to the earth;
dust to dust and ashes to ashes,
we entrust ourselves and all who love God to his loving care,
we open ourselves to the mystery of creation, its frailness and its glory
and we name the miracle of life eternal, as both a future reality
and a present tense experience.

SCRIPTURE SENTENCES

We brought nothing into this world,
and we can take nothing out.
The Lord gives and the Lord takes away;
blessed be the name of the Lord.

1 Timothy 6.7; Job 1.21 REB

The Lord is faithful to all his promises
and loving towards all he has made.
The Lord upholds all those who fall
and lifts up all who are bowed down.

Psalm 145.13f. NIV

All you have made will praise you, O Lord;
your saints will extol you.
They will tell of the glory of your kingdom
and speak of your might,
so that all may know of your mighty acts
and the glorious splendour of your kingdom.
The Lord is near to all who call on him,
to all who call on him in truth.
My mouth will speak in praise of the Lord.
Let every creature praise his holy name
for ever and ever.

Psalm 145.10–12, 18, 21 NIV

SCRIPTURE READING

This or another reading may be used

The Lord is full of compassion and mercy,
slow to anger and of great goodness.
For he knows of what we are made:
he remembers that we are but dust.
Our days are like grass;
we flourish like a flower of the field;
when the wind goes over it, it is gone
and its place will know it no more.
But the merciful goodness of the Lord endures
for ever and ever toward those who fear him
and his righteousness
upon their children's children.

PRAYER

God our maker,
in your loving care
your hand has created us,
and as the potter fashions the clay
you have formed us in your image.
Through the Holy Spirit
you have breathed into us the gift of life.
In the sharing of love you have enriched our knowledge
of you and of one another.
We claim your love today,
as we return these ashes to the ground
in sure and certain hope of the resurrection to eternal life. **Amen.**

The Lord's Prayer may be said.

INTERMENT OR SCATTERING OF ASHES

We have entrusted our *sister/brother N*
to God's merciful care.
We now commit *his/her* ashes to the earth,
trusting in God
whose Spirit is at work
fashioning a new creation.

PRAYER

O God,
we remember *N* with gratitude and affection,
and give thanks for *her/him*.
We say again that this is not the end,
for our God is the God who raised Jesus from the dead
and will bring us all to life.

Lord, we remember your love
toward us and all people,
especially your love for *N*.
We give you thanks
that your love never comes to an end,
that whether we live or die
we belong to you.
We give you thanks for all that *N* still means to us,
and we pray for ourselves,
that we may continue to grow in love
until we reach the full stature of Christ,
in whom all things are one;
we ask it in his name. **Amen.**

Heavenly Father
we thank you for all those whom we love but see no longer.
As we remember *N* in this place,
hold before us our beginning and our ending,
the dust from which we come
and the death to which we move,
with a firm hope in your eternal love and purposes for us,
in Jesus Christ our Lord. **Amen.**

THE DISMISSAL

May God the mysterious Trinity
direct our lives
and, after our journey through this world,
grant us eternal rest with all the saints. **Amen.**

ADDITIONAL MATERIAL

FOR THE FUNERAL FOR
A STILL-BORN OR NEWLY-BORN CHILD

In the funeral for a baby it is important to recognize and express the belief that the baby was a person. Even if he or she never lived outside the womb, he or she was a loved child who has died. The use of the child's name will therefore be important when a name has been given. The care and love given to the child should be affirmed, especially if there are lingering feelings of guilt on the part of the parents about the quality of care they gave.

SCRIPTURE SENTENCES

The Lord's true love is surely not spent, nor has his compassion failed; they are new every morning, so great is his constancy. *Lamentations 3.22f. NEB*

Cast your burden on the Lord, and he will sustain you. *Psalm 55.22*

God has said, 'I will never leave you: I will never abandon you.'
Hebrews 13.5 GNB

The Lamb at the centre of the throne will be their shepherd,
and he will guide them to springs of the water of life,
and God will wipe away every tear from their eyes. *Revelation 7.17*

Scripture readings might include part of Psalm 139; Mark 10.13–16; John 1.1–5; Ephesians 3.14–19.

PRAYERS

One or more of the following prayers may be used

Living God,
loving Father,
be with us,
and give us this day
the courage and hope
of your promises.
You have invited us
to unload our burdens on to you
because you will support us:
we call on your promise now.
Be present with us
as we offer these last words
of love and farewell.
Assure us again
that you are our home,

and that underneath us
are the everlasting arms.
Help us to leave the one we love in your keeping,
believing that you are bringing *her/him* and us
to undying life
with Jesus Christ our Lord. **Amen.**

Or

Father in heaven,
healer of broken hearts,
we ask you to look with pity and compassion
upon your servants
whose joy has been turned into mourning.
Comfort them
and grant that they may be drawn closer together
by their common sorrow.
Dwell with them and be their refuge
until the day breaks
and the shadows flee away;
through Jesus Christ our Lord. **Amen.**

Or

Heavenly Father,
you have given us life
and in Jesus
you promise us new life
which nothing can destroy.

We entrust *N*
into your loving care.
Greet *her/him* with your love
and surround *her/him* with your healing power,
that *she/he* may live in your presence
as a whole child of God,
for your glory and delight;
through Jesus Christ our Lord. **Amen.**

Or

Almighty God,
you make nothing in vain,
and love all that you have made.
Comfort these parents in their sorrow,
and console them by the knowledge of your unfailing love;
through Jesus Christ our Lord. **Amen.**

ON THE DEATH OF A CHILD

If other children are present at this service, their grief should be recognized and the language used should enable them to share as much as possible. The following prayers try to take account of this pastoral need.

SCRIPTURE SENTENCES

The Sovereign Lord is coming to rule with power.
He will take care of his flock like a shepherd;
he will gather the lambs together and carry them in his arms.

Isaiah 40.10f. GNB

Jesus said, 'Never despise one of these little ones.
It is not your heavenly Father's will
that one of these little ones should be lost.'   *Matthew 18.10, 14 NEB*

Scripture readings might include Matthew 18.1–5; 18.10–14; Mark 10.13–16; 2 Corinthians 1.1–3.

PRAYERS

Father God,
we are glad
that *N* no longer has to know pain or fear,
but we are sad for ourselves
that *she/he* is no longer with us
to share things together
and to have fun with us.
Father God,
we are sad
for we cannot understand
what has happened to *N*.
Please help us to know
that however hard it is for us,
she/he is being looked after by you
and that you love *her/him* still more
than we do.

Even as you look after *her/him*;
please look after us as well;
through Jesus Christ our Lord. **Amen.**

Father God,
we thank you for *N*.
We thank you for all the enjoyment
she/he found in ...
[Here favourite activities or games may be mentioned.]

Thank you for all the pleasure and love
N brought to us
and the way in which caring for *her/him*
helped us to grow.

We thank you
for the things *she/he* taught us
and the things which *she/he* said and did
that will stay with us for ever.
Thank you for giving N to us.
Help us to learn to live without *her/him*,
whilst still remembering *her/him*
with love and gratitude;
through Jesus Christ our Lord.

In the awfulness of life cut short,
let us turn to God,
the Father of our Lord Jesus Christ
and our Father.

We try so hard to be strong before others,
but, in the presence of God
who understands all things,
let us admit our weakness
and our need of help.

Silence

Gracious God,
we pray for ourselves
and especially for those
who suffer most at N's death.

Even if we can grasp
nothing else at this time,
help us to know that you are near
and that you will lead us onward
through Jesus Christ our Lord. **Amen.**

AFTER SUICIDE

In these circumstances it is pastorally dangerous to ask too many questions in the service or seem to be making judgements about what led to the ending of the person's life or its consequences.

Mourners may be carrying a heavy burden of guilt and opportunity for confession may be important with a stress on God's forgiveness.

It is important that the manner of a person's death should not overshadow all that has been good in their life. Their qualities and gifts deserve as much affirmation as those of any other person.

SENTENCES

A voice cries out:
'In the wilderness prepare the way of the Lord;
the uneven ground shall become level,
and the rough places a plain.'

Isaiah 40.3, 4

Lord, you have examined me
and you know me.
You know me at rest
and in action;
you discern my thoughts from afar.
You trace my journeying and my resting-places,
and are familiar with all the paths I take.

Examine me, O God,
and know my thoughts;
test me and understand my misgivings.

Psalm 139.1–3, 23 NEB

I will not leave you bereft.
I am coming back to you.
Peace is my parting gift to you,
my own peace,
such as the world cannot give.

Set your troubled hearts at rest,
and banish your fears.

John 14.18, 27 REB

Scripture readings may include Psalms 22.1–4; 23.1–4; Wisdom 3.1–3

PRAYERS

Lord, we do not understand
what has happened.
There seems to be
no sense in the ending of this life
so we are puzzled
and distressed.

In the crucifixion of Jesus,
you have shown us
that your love is alongside us
even when we feel abandoned.

As we remember *N*
and think of the despair
which engulfed *her/his* end,
help us to realize
that in you
light outshines darkness.
Nothing, not even death,
is more powerful
than your love.

We thank you
for the good things in *N*'s life
and ask forgiveness
for those times when we let *her/him* down.
Forgive us our sins
and heal our guilt,
we pray.

Redeemer God,
take what has happened
and weave it into your loving purpose,
so that *N*
may not have lived or died in vain.
This we ask
in the name of Jesus our Saviour. **Amen.**

Or

Lord Jesus Christ,
you spoke of your Father's love for all people;
help us to know that your love
will never be withdrawn from *N* or from us.

Lord Jesus Christ,
you wrestled with questions of life and death
in Gethsemane;
help us to know that you understand
and are present where there is anguish of mind.

Lord Jesus Christ,
you gave hope beyond death
to a dying man on a cross;
help us to know that you did not withdraw hope from *N*.

Lord Jesus Christ,
we pray for ourselves
and for all who are bereft at this time,
knowing that you have experienced
all the depths of life and believing
that you still call us to experience its everlasting heights. **Amen.**

AFTER SUDDEN OR VIOLENT DEATH

Where death is very sudden, the prevailing emotion of the mourners may well be one of shock and disbelief. The funeral may be an important opportunity for friends and family to be set free from that initial disbelief and to begin to grieve.

If a person is the victim of a criminal act or of carelessness on the part of others, the feelings of the family towards those who may be responsible should be dealt with sensitively. Care must be taken with the manner in which the Christian call to forgive is expressed.

SENTENCES

God is our refuge and strength,
a very present help in trouble.
Therefore we will not fear, though the earth should change,
though the mountains shake in the heart of the sea;
though its waters roar and foam,
and though the mountains tremble.

Psalm 46.1–3

Christ died for us while we were yet sinners,
and that is God's proof of his love towards us.

Romans 5.8 REB

Scripture readings may include Psalm 22.19–27 or Romans 8.18, 28, 35, 37–39.

PRAYERS

Our Father,
we believe your promises of victory,
but we did not want to hear them for *N* just yet.
So much remains unsaid and unfinished.

It is hard to accept
that it will not now be completed
as we would have wished.

Help us in this act of worship
to allow you
to come near to us
in the aching void of loss,
through Jesus Christ our Lord. **Amen.**

Or

Lord, we thank you for *N.*
Thank you for *her/him* as a person;
for all *his/her* qualities
and for all *she/he* meant to us.

We entrust *her/him* into your hands,
knowing that you alone
are the one to satisfy the longings of *his/her* heart.

Lord, you are the one who brings good out of evil,
so now we pray that you will bring something good
out of *N's* tragic death.

We pray for all those
touched by *N's* life and death.
Help us to hear what you are saying to us
through this tragedy.
Turn us away from all that we know to be wrong.
Help us to show love and understanding
to those around us.

Forgive us
for any ways in which we may have hurt *N.*
Help us to know
that you are always ready to forgive us
and offer us a new beginning when we turn to you.
Keep us in your grace,
guide and protect us,
until with *N* and with all your children
we find ourselves truly at home in your great love;
through Jesus Christ our Lord. **Amen.**

Or

Compassionate God,
you know us better than we know ourselves.
You understand what we are feeling
and are with us in our grief.
Bind the wounds of our sorrow
and surround us with your love;
through Jesus Christ our Lord. **Amen.**

FOR THE VICTIM OF VIOLENCE

Eternal God,
the savagery that has taken *N*
has wounded us as well.
We are reeling under the blow,
unable to think clearly
and aware of the cruel ways life can end.
In all the anger and
perplexity of this time,
help us to cling to you
as the calm at the centre of the storm
through Jesus Christ our Lord. **Amen.**

Or

Almighty God,
we know that we should forgive
those who violate the sanctity of human life,
but the pain and the anger are too great.

For now, and maybe for always,
we ask you to do for us
what we cannot do for ourselves:
forgive where regret is real
and heal those whose flaws
have led to this crime.

We also pray for ourselves,
that we may be set free from bitterness
to know your peace
and to live your forgiveness
through Jesus Christ our Lord. **Amen.**

GATHERING AND PRAYING FOR HEALING

Healing was central to the ministry of Jesus. It was a sign of God's kingdom in which broken lives received healing and transforming. Jesus shared this ministry with his disciples, sending them out 'to proclaim the kingdom of God and to heal' (Luke 9.2).

The ministry of healing can, and will, take place in various settings outside worship, but when the community gathers for worship it affirms who God is and how generous and comprehensive is the grace of God. In every act of worship, the Christian community celebrates the grace of God who desires wholeness of body, mind and spirit for all people, as well as the healing of communities and relationships. In a service of healing, we focus on this aspect of God's character. We bring our own frailty and brokenness – felt not just in physical illness, but in guilt, anxiety, and all the burdens which weigh us down. We also bring our concerns for others and for the world. Above all, we come to God who knows our needs before we ask, and whose love revealed in Jesus Christ is stronger than suffering and death.

So worship is the natural place to come and seek God's healing in our lives and in our communities. Such ministry is not restricted to people with particular gifts of healing. Indeed, all healing is the work of the Holy Spirit and whether we come as a leader or minister to speak and act on behalf of God, as a community of intercessors beseeching God on behalf of others, or as a wounded and hurting child of God in search of God's healing for ourselves, we are demonstrating our dependence on divine grace.

Within worship, the ministry of healing may take place in various ways. A whole service may be designated as 'A Healing Service', a general service may contain prayers for healing or a service may close with an invitation for individuals to receive the ministry of prayer. Many will want this ministry of healing to take place within the setting of a communion service.

Normally, there will be an opportunity for individual members of the congregation to be prayed for individually, though the way in which this happens may vary. So individuals may be invited to come forward and, in full view and hearing of the congregation, they may be named and prayed for, with the laying on of hands or anointing. Alternatively, people may come forward and be prayed for quietly, outside the hearing of the congregation or, indeed, taken aside in order to ease the access to prayer of those who are fearful.

Seeking and celebrating the healing of God in worship, enables us to see clearly how much we are in need of God's help. Leaders come with empty hands and those seeking healing come powerless in search of the gracious God who is sovereign over all and powerful to save.

A service for healing may include the following elements
- Scripture words concerning God's grace and the ministry of healing.
- Prayers which praise God and seek God's forgiveness.
- A scripture reading and meditation.
- Prayers of dependence asking for the Spirit's help in our very praying for healing.
- Intercessions for a broken and hurting world.
- Prayers of commitment and submission.
- The laying on of hands.
- Anointing.
- Blessing.

As with other acts of worship, prayer may take place with the laying on of hands. Here the action is a sign of acceptance and solidarity, as Jesus reached out to those who were often rejected or ignored. But here also is a sign of our faith, for our prayers are focused on this person, at this time, with this need. Our faith is shown in our readiness to be specific in our praying, open to the possibility of what God can do but also ready for what he will, or will not, do. For such faith and such pray we need the Spirit's help and our need leads us to a depth of encounter with grace which is beyond our explaining.

Some may wish to precede or follow a prayer for healing with the anointing of a person's forehead with oil. This biblical symbol expresses, as a sign of consecration, that we place ourselves in God's hands and, as a symbol of the Spirit, reminds us who is the one who heals. It can also remind us of Jesus the Christ, the anointed one, in whose name we pray, and to apply the oil in the shape of a cross may also be a helpful sign.

The following section includes a pattern for a healing service, a pattern of prayer which is concerned with the healing of communities, and additional material. which can, as well as additional material. All this material may, of course, be incorporated into various services or situations, or adapted and used in pastoral situations outside worship.

A PATTERN FOR A HEALING SERVICE

This pattern may be adapted according to the worship practices of the local congregation. The main sections are listed below so as to ease local use and the incorporation of other material.

PREPARATION

Scripture verses may be read which focus the worship on God and our faith in him, such as

Be still before the Lord, and wait patiently for him.

Psalm 37.7

Great is the Lord, and greatly to be praised;
his greatness is unsearchable.

Psalm 145.3

But this I call to mind,
and therefore I have hope:

The steadfast love of the Lord never ceases,
his mercies never come to an end;
they are new every morning;
great is your faithfulness.

'The Lord is my portion,' says my soul,
'therefore I will hope in him.'

The Lord is good to those who wait for him,
to the soul that seeks him.

Lamentations 3.21–25

That evening they brought to him many who were possessed with demons; and he cast out the spirits with a word, and cured all who were sick. This was to fulfil what had been spoken through the prophet Isaiah, 'He took our infirmities and bore our diseases.'

Matthew 8.16f.

Then Jesus went about all the cities and villages, teaching in their synagogues, and proclaiming the good news of the kingdom, and curing every disease and every sickness. When he saw the crowds, he had compassion for them, because they were harassed and helpless, like sheep without a shepherd.

Matthew 9.35f.

'Come to me, all you that are weary and are carrying heavy burdens, and I will give you rest. Take my yoke upon you, and learn from me; for I am gentle and humble in heart, and you will find rest for your souls. For my yoke is easy, and my burden is light.'

Matthew 11.28f.

'For where two or three are gathered in my name, I am there among them.'

Matthew 18.20

When the crowds found out about it, they followed him; and he welcomed them, and spoke to them about the kingdom of God, and healed those who needed to be cured.

Luke 9.11

The Lord is near. Do not worry about anything, but in everything by prayer and supplication with thanksgiving let your requests be made known to God. And the peace of God, which surpasses all understanding, will guard your hearts and your minds in Christ Jesus.

Philippians 4.5b—7

Time might be offered for brief reflection on these or other verses.

PRAISE

A hymn of praise may be sung, or a series of songs interspersed with prayer.

INVOCATION

Prayer may be offered asking for God's help.

Loving and gracious God,
we come in our need
to knock on heaven's door
and to ask for you help.
We are weak and you are strong,
we are empty and your grace overflows,
we are fearful and you are faithful.

Come to us now,
that our prayers might take wing
and be the flight of your Spirit;
that our faith might be strengthened
and our trust in you made firm;
that our hope in your kingdom
be reawakened;
for you are our saviour
and we pray in the name of Jesus. **Amen.**

Lord Jesus Christ,
God's anointed proclaimer of the kingdom,
you brought good news to the poor
and proclaimed release to those in prison
and recovery of sight to the blind.
Demonstrate your kingdom here
in healing and renewal
that we might sing again of the Lord's favour
and share the story of your love
with all who need your grace. **Amen.**

CONFESSION

A prayer of confession may be offered, extempore or as follows

Our Lord Jesus Christ said:
'Anyone who comes to me I will never turn away.'
In the presence of God, let us confess our sins:

Lord Jesus,
you came to reconcile us to God and to one another.
Lord, have mercy.
Lord, have mercy.

Lord Jesus,
you heal the wounds of sin and division.
Christ, have mercy.
Christ, have mercy.

Lord Jesus,
you offer us a new beginning.
Lord, have mercy.
Lord, have mercy.

Or

Father eternal, giver of light and grace,
we have sinned against you and against our neighbour,
in what we have thought,
in what we have said or done,
through ignorance, through weakness,
through our own deliberate fault.
We have wounded your love,
and marred your image in us.

We are sorry and ashamed,
and repent of all our sins.
For the sake of your Son Jesus Christ,
who died for us,
for give us all that is past;
and lead us out from darkness
to walk as children of light. **Amen.**

An assurance of forgiveness may be announced

God is love.
Through Jesus our sins are forgiven.
Let us live in the power of the Spirit. **Amen.**

Or

Almighty God,
who forgives all who truly repent,
have mercy upon you,
pardon and deliver you from all your sins,
confirm and strengthen you in all goodness,
and keep you in life eternal;
through Jesus Christ our Lord. **Amen.**

THE SHARING OF PEACE

God's desire for our wholeness includes our relationship with him and our relationship with others. The wholeness of the community may be both expressed and sought in worship with a sharing of the peace. The leader may invite the congregation to greet one another with a word and sign of peace. This may be introduced with a scripture sentence such as

Greet one another with a kiss of love. Peace to all of you who are in Christ.

1 Peter 5.14

Live in harmony with one another; do not be haughty, but associate with the lowly; do not claim to be wiser than you are. Do not repay anyone evil for evil, but take thought for what is noble in the sight of all. If it is possible, so far as it depends on you, live peaceably with all.

Romans 12.16—18

'Salt is good; but if salt has lost its saltiness, how can you season it? Have salt in yourselves, and be at peace with one another.'

Mark 9.50

Christ is our peace.
He has reconciled us to God in one body by the cross.

from Ephesians 2.13—16

SCRIPTURE READING

A testimony of God's goodness in someone's life may be shared.

MEDITATION ON THE READING

A reflection which focuses on the grace of God may be given.

PRAYERS FOR HEALING

Intercessions may happen here or after the laying on of hands.

Those who are seeking prayer for themselves, or on behalf of another, may be invited to come forward, or to another specified place, during the singing of hymn or song of faith.

Pray may be offered asking for God's help in our praying and trusting, extempore or as follows

God of grace,
in your love and compassion
strengthen our faith
and enliven our hope.

God of grace,
by your Spirit's breath
help us to pray
and to trust you
now and every day,
through Jesus Christ our Lord. **Amen.**

LAYING ON OF HANDS

As each person is prayed for, with the laying on of hands, these words may be said as an accompaniment to prayer for that person's need.

Lord, you can do all things.
Send your Spirit of life and health
on you servant, *A*,
in the name of Christ. **Amen.**

Or

A, the grace of Christ bring you wholeness
and give you peace. **Amen.**

Or

May the Spirit of the living God
present with you now,
heal you of all that harms you,
in body, mind and spirit;
in the name of Jesus Christ. **Amen.**

ANOINTING

If prayer is accompanied with the anointing with oil, these words may be said

A, know God's healing and God's blessing.
In the grace of God there is hope,
in the cross of Christ there is peace
and in the Spirit of God there is life. **Amen.**

PRAYERS FOR OTHERS

*Names of others may be shared and prayer offered. General intercession may take place in
open or extempore prayer, or as follows*

Christ our Saviour, born for us,
bring healing and peace to all people.

Lord, have mercy.
Christ, have mercy.

Christ our Saviour, baptized in the Jordan,
give hope to all who come to you.

Lord, have mercy.
Christ, have mercy.

Christ tested in the desert,
give courage to those who are tempted.

Lord, have mercy.
Christ, have mercy.

Christ, who comforted and healed,
bring wholeness to all who are broken.

Lord, have mercy.
Christ, have mercy.

Christ, who hung in agony on the cross,
bring strength to those who suffer.

Lord, have mercy.
Christ, have mercy.

Christ, who died to save us,
give peace to all who face death.

Lord, have mercy.
Christ, have mercy.

Christ, raised from the tomb,
bring light and life to all the world.

Lord, have mercy.
Christ, have mercy.

Christ, present among your disciples,
unite all your people in love.

Lord, have mercy.
Christ, have mercy.

Silence

The grace of Christ attend us,
the love of God surround us,
and the Holy Spirit keep us,
this day and for ever. **Amen.**

The service may continue with the Lord's Supper or closing worship.

A PATTERN OF PRAYER
FOR HEALING IN PEOPLE AND PLACES,
IN CHURCH AND WORLD

The leader greets the congregation and informally introduces what is to follow. This introduction may conclude with the following explanation or an appropriate summary

Our prayer is for the healing
of people, communities, nations
and our planet.

The healer is God by the Holy Spirit.
We are sharing in what God is already seeking to do.
Our prayers and our lives are part of his response
to the needs of our world.

Anyone can receive prayer
with the laying-on of hands
for themselves, another or for a current crisis or need.

We mention people and situations by name
only because all that they are is known by God.
They are not a problem for us to explore or solve
but a focus for God's compassion and reconciliation.

PRAYER

God of our hidden depths,
we come before you as people of our time and place.
We confess our faults and recognize our weaknesses.
We are complex creatures;
deep within us are patterns, experiences,
conflicts we do not understand
and we do not always know
what to do with them.

We are silent before you and pray:
understand us, unburden us.
We are silent before you and pray:
help us to understand and unburden each other.
We are silent before you and pray:
help us not to fear what is deep within us
that is hurting and hurtful, that breaks and is broken.

Spirit of God's deep peace,
show us that we are forgiven so that we may forgive;
touch our wounds with your healing
so that we may be people who heal;
and help us to be at peace with ourselves
so that we may become makers of your peace for others,
though Jesus Christ our saviour. **Amen.**

READING AND REFLECTION

A passage of scripture reading may be read, followed either by a reflection on the nature of God the healer, or a healing story of Jesus.

CONFESSION

A prayer asking for God's forgiveness may be offered, or the following

Let us be with God in a spirit of repentance
and make our confession.

Father you have been there, listening deeply,
both when we think of you and when we do not;
you know well what we fear and question,
what we long for and from whom we turn away...

It is just like us to ...*
Or
Together with many others we ...*
Or
In common with the whole world we ...*

> *   *The leader may make suggestions arising from local or contemporary events or from suggestions previously made by the congregation.*

In silence,
in honest regret,
in trust,
we admit our mistakes and recognise our frailty.

Lord of truth and forgiveness,
by your gentle spirit
move us from guilt to grace,
and from darkness to light,
that our lives may proclaim
the transformation of the peace of Christ. **Amen.**

Or

Almighty God, maker of all,
have mercy on us.

Jesus Christ, Son of God,
have mercy on us.

Holy Spirit, breath of life,
have mercy on us.

Let us in silence remember our own faults and failings.

Silence, after which the leader makes confession, saying

I confess to Almighty God,
and in the presence of all God's people,
that I have sinned
in thought, word and deed,
and I pray, Almighty God,
that you will have mercy on me.

May Almighty God have mercy on you,
pardon and deliver you from all your sins,
and give you time to amend your life. Amen,

The congregation makes confession, saying

We confess to Almighty God,
and in the presence of all God's people,
that we have sinned
in thought, word and deed,
and we pray, Almighty God,
that you will have mercy on us.

May Almighty God have mercy on you,
pardon and deliver you from all your sins,
and give you time to amend your life. **Amen.**

AFFIRMATION OF THE FAITHFULNESS OF GOD

Hymns or songs may be sung, testimonies shared, and scripture verses read, such as

Blessed are those who trust in the Lord,
whose trust is the Lord.

Heal me, O Lord, and I shall be healed;
save me, and I shall be saved;
for you are my praise.   *Jeremiah 17.7, 14*

Blessed are the poor in spirit,
for theirs is the kingdom of heaven.
Blessed are those who mourn,
for they will be comforted.
Blessed are the meek,
for they will inherit the earth.
Blessed are those who hunger and thirst for righteousness,
for they will be filled.
Blessed are the merciful,
for they will receive mercy.
Blessed are the pure in heart,
for they will see God.
Blessed are the peacemakers,
for they will be called children of God.
Blessed are those who are persecuted for righteousness' sake,
for theirs is the kingdom of heaven.
                                                          Matthew 5.3—10

Come to me, all you that are weary
and are carrying heavy burdens,
and I will give you rest.
Take my yoke upon you, and learn from me;
for I am gentle and humble in heart,
and you will find rest for your souls.
For my yoke is easy, and my burden is light.
                                                          Matthew 11.28—30

For to this you have been called,
because Christ also suffered for you,
leaving you an example,
so that you should follow in his steps.
He himself bore our sins in his body on the cross,
so that, free from sins,
we might live for righteousness;
by his wounds you have been healed.
                                                          1 Peter 2.32, 24

PRAYERS

Intercessions may be made for the world, and prayers asking for God's help for those gathered, extempore, open, or as follows

God our Father, as disciples of Jesus
we join him in his ministry of healing.
He is the saviour of the world;
and nothing in our world
is beyond the touch of your love and grace.
We seek now to make here a healing space.
We come with the fragility of faith
and the burden of our sinfulness.
We know our capacity to hurt and damage.
Yet in this healing space
there is no greater power than your compassion and mercy.
Nothing in our past or present
is greater than gift of your presence with us now.

May this healing space be a place of your blessing.

With us come
　　people haunted by their past,
　　people obsessed by the present,
　　people dreading the future.

They are poor in spirit:
with them may we see your kingdom among us.

With us come
　　people crushed by war and terror,
　　people bruised by oppression and persecution,
　　people wounded by bigotry and ignorance.

They mourn:
with them may we receive comfort.

With us come
　　people weary of their pain ,
　　people burdened by their fear,
　　people worn-down by distress.

They are meek:
with them may we receive the gifts of your goodness.

With us come
>   people frustrated by complacency,
>   people ground down by manipulation,
>   people hemmed in by despair.

They hunger and thirst for righteousness and so do we:
may we be filled.

With us come
>   people caring for the wounded,
>   people holding the hand of the dying,
>   people weeping with the grief-stricken.

They are the merciful and so are we:
may we receive mercy.

With us come
>   people struggling with doubts,
>   people confused by questions,
>   people diminished by the certainty of others.

They are the pure in heart and so are we:
may we see God.

With us come
>   people who have turned the other cheek,
>   people who have stood in the way of hatred,
>   people who absorbed another's violence.

They are the peacemakers and so are we:
may we be called the children of God.

With us come
>   people who are excluded because they are different,
>   people who speak the truth when others do not,
>   people who peace through justice.

They are persecuted for righteousness sake and so are we:
may we receive your Kingdom among us.

THE LAYING ON OF HANDS

The words which accompany the laying on of hands may be said by the leader or by all

A, the grace of Christ bring you wholeness
and give you peace. **Amen.**

Or

Spirit of the living God,
present with us now,
enter you, body, mind and spirit,
and heal you of all that harms you.
in Jesus' name. **Amen.**

The service may continue, or close with further prayer and songs, after which all say

**The grace of our Lord Jesus Christ,
the love of God
and the fellowship of the Holy Spirit
be with us all, evermore. Amen.**

ADDITIONAL MATERIAL

INVITATION

The LORD is the everlasting God,
the Creator of the ends of the earth.
He does not faint or grow weary;
his understanding is unsearchable.

He gives power to the faint,
and strengthens the powerless.

Even youths will faint and be weary,
and the young will fall exhausted;

but those who wait for the LORD shall renew their strength,
they shall mount up with wings like eagles,
they shall run and not be weary,
they shall walk and not faint.

Isaiah 40.28–31

CONFESSION

Lord Jesus,
you came to reconcile us to God
and to one another.

Lord, have mercy.
Lord, have mercy.

Lord Jesus,
you heal the wounds of sin and division.

Christ, have mercy.
Christ, have mercy.

Lord Jesus,
you offer us a new beginning.

Lord, have mercy.
Christ, have mercy.

Silence

God is love;
and through Jesus our sins are forgiven.
Let us, then, live in the power of the Spirit. **Amen.**

BLESSING

I bless you, precious one,
in the name of the Sacred Three,
the Father, the Son, and the Holy Spirit.
May you drink deeply from God's cup of joy.
May the night bring you quiet,
and when you come to the Father's palace,
may his door be open and the welcome warm.
In the name of Christ. **Amen.**

Or

May the Father of life pour out his grace upon you;
may you feel his hand in everything you do,
and be strengthened by the things he brings you through:
this is my prayer for you.

May the Son of God be Lord in all your ways;
may he shepherd you the length of all your days,
and in your heart may he receive praise:
this is my prayer for you.

May his Spirit comfort you and make you strong,
may he discipline you gently when you're wrong,
And in your heart may he give you a song:
this is my prayer for you.

May Jesus be Lord in all your ways;
may he shepherd you the length of all your days,
and in your heart may he receive the praise:
this is my prayer for you, my prayer for you. **Amen.**

INTERCESSION

Holy God,
we pray for all those
whose minds are broken
through trauma or mental illness.

We remember those who are bewildered and disorientated,
whose minds are shattered and confused.
We ask that they might find reflected in their carers
the love that draws the broken pieces together
and cherishes each tiny part of the whole.

Lord, in your mercy,
Hear our prayer.

We lift to you those
who because of guilt, anxiety or failure
feel they can't live with themselves.
Enable them to find the forgiveness that brings peace
and the hope that's founded on your eternal love.

Lord, in your mercy,
Hear our prayer.

We hold to you those
whose minds are tortured
by memories of violence, hatred or death.
We pray that finding the suffering Christ
in the depth of their despair,
they might also in that same place
hear the words of the risen Christ:
'Peace be with you.'

Lord, in your mercy,
Hear our prayer.

We lift to you those
who seek to harm themselves or others
wad all who are drawn into cycles of abuse.
We pray that rediscovering their own precious value
they might recognise also the value of others.

Lord in your mercy,
Hear our prayer.

We remember those
whose pain is so deep
that they cannot speak of it or share it with another.
We pray that in the silence of your surrounding love
they might know the touch that holds and heals.

Lord in your mercy,
Hear our prayer.

And for ourselves,
that we might know your healing
in body, soul and mind,

**Lord in your mercy,
hear our prayer. Amen.**

VISITING THE SICK
AND PRAYING WITH THOSE NEAR DEATH

PRAYERS AT HOME OR IN HOSPITAL

In ministering to those who are sick it is important

- to give comfort and to lift the spirit
- to give a sense of the surrounding love and prayers of the church
- to give the assurance of God's presence and his grace which is sufficient for all our needs.

It is helpful to concentrate on positives rather than negatives, on spiritual resources and God's gift of wholeness rather than on symptoms. Let the main focus be on God's promises, power, faithfulness, understanding, nearness and peace.

Frequent use of 'we', 'us' and 'our' will help to create a feeling of being together, sharing prayer in a loving Christian family, not 'praying over' someone. It is also reassuring when prayer if offered, to remember members of the family, as well as doctors, nurses, and all involved in the caring and healing ministry.

1   Living God,
    when we feel sad and helpless,
    assure us that you are our light and salvation,
    and therefore we need not be afraid.
    Grant us, we pray, a firm faith in the apostle's message:
    we do not live to ourselves alone
    and we do not die to ourselves alone.
    If we live, we live to the Lord;
    and if we die, we die to the Lord.
    May we know in our hearts,
    that whether we live or die, we belong to you,
    because the risen Jesus is Lord of the dead and of the living.
    Grant this assurance to … *[name of sick person]*
    whom we specially pray for now,
    and to us all, as we commit *her/him* into your gracious care.
    In Jesus' name. **Amen.**

2   Eternal God, our Father,
    we thank you that from our earliest days,
    your love has surrounded us and blessed us,
    beyond what we deserved.
    We thank you for the energy and excitements of youth,
    for the gifts and opportunities of our middle years,
    and for the way you have provided, guided and protected us
    as the years have passed.
    Now in these closing days,
    we pray especially for … *[name of sick person]*,
    may *she/he* know that your promise of eternal life stands firm.
    In the hour of death hold *her/him*
    and all *she/he* loves, safely in your hands,
    now and for ever. **Amen.**

3   *A prayer for someone suffering long illness or disability, and feeling cut off and isolated from*
     the church family and work, with which she/he was once fully involved. This can be preceded
     by a brief sharing of church news and issues for which to give thanks, and people and events
     needing our prayer.

Lord Jesus Christ,
head of the church and Lord of all,
we thank you for all the blessings we have received
through being in the family of the church.
In times of illness and infirmity
it is easy to feel cut off and useless.
Teach us that we need not feel like that,
for we can pray for one another,
we can remember those who are busy as we used to be,
encourage them and prosper their efforts.
In our frustration and disappointment
may we know through our prayers,
and our times of trouble
that we still can be of useful service.
Even as others pray for us,
may we pray for them,
so that together we bear one another's burdens
and so fulfil the law of Christ,
in whose name we pray. **Amen.**

4   Living Lord Jesus,
the same yesterday, today, and for ever,
we recall the stories of your earthly ministry
to people in all sorts of sickness and sorrow.
We thank you for the confidence
that in your resurrection power
you still minister to us today.
Therefore we ask you to lay your hands of compassion
and healing on ... *[name of sick person]*
May the Holy Spirit give *her/him* faith
that by your power at work within us
you are able to do far beyond all that we can ask or think.
We lift *her/him* up to you,
praying that you will work out your perfect will.
Free *her/him* from doubt and fear,
and give *her/him* grace to leave with you
all pain, weakness or despair,
and receive the blessing which only you can give.
We ask this for your name's sake. **Amen.**

5   Our Father of mercy
and God of all comfort,
we pray for … *[name of sick person]* in this time of sickness.
Enfold and keep *her/him* in your unfailing love,
so that *she/he* may be strengthened in weakness and be full of hope.
Help *her/him* to know your nearness in any long and sleepless night.
Give wisdom and skill to those who care for *her/him*.
Support the family and friends if they feel the strain and grow tired.
And may we all put ourselves and one another in your loving care,
knowing deep within that that is the best place for us to be.
May the peace of God, which is beyond our understanding,
keep us all safe in Jesus Christ our Lord. **Amen.**

6   Gracious God,
we praise you for your love which never lets us go.
We thank you that you love each of us
as if there were only one of us to love.
Let us be awake to your presence by day and by night,
even if we feel helpless and alone.
May we experience what our Saviour promised:
'I will be with you always.'
May that give … *[name of sick person]* a trust which nothing can shake,
a peace which can weather every storm,
and your grace which can enter the depth of *his/her* being,
bringing wholeness of body, mind and spirit.
We pray in the name of Jesus
who is able now and for ever
to save those who come to God through him. **Amen.**

PART TWO

PRAYERS IN
THE COMMUNITY OF DISCIPLES

COMMUNITY IN PRAYER

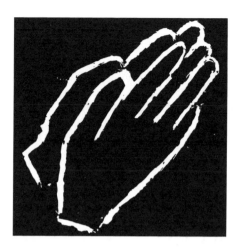

COMMUNITY IN PRAYER

Here are prayers which you may find helpful in the leading of worship. This section includes prayers for various points in the journey through a service, as the community of disciples gathers before God and is sent out into God's world. These prayers may be spoken by one voice, by several, or responsively between leader and congregation or between sections of the congregation: the division into stanzas and the selective use of bold type are intended as guides to help in such local use.

OPENINGS: DECLARATIONS AND INVITATIONS

1   In the beginning,
before time, before people,
before the world began,
God was.

Here and now
among us, beside us,
enlisting the people of earth
for the purposes of heaven,
God is.

In the future,
when we have turned to dust
and all we know has found fulfilment,
God will be.

Not denying the world, but delighting in it,
not condemning the world, but redeeming it,
through Jesus Christ,
by the power of the Holy Spirit,
God was,
God is,
God will be.

2   This is the place
and this is the time;
here and now,
God waits
to break into our experience:
to change our minds,
to change our lives,
to change our ways;
to make us see the world
and the whole of life
in a new light:
to fill us with hope,
joy and certainty
for the future.

This is the place
as are all places;
this is the time
as are all times.
Here and now
let us praise God.

3   I will light a light
     in the name of the Maker,
     who lit the world
     and breathed the breath of life for me.

A first candle is lit.

     I will light a light
     in the name of the Son,
     who saved the world
     and stretched out his hand to me.

A second candle is lit.

     I will light a light
     in the name of the Spirit
     who encompasses the world
     and blessed my soul with yearning.

A third candle is lit.

**We will light three lights
for the trinity of love:
God above us,
God beside us,
God beneath us.
The beginning,
the end,
the everlasting one.**

4   Among the poor,
     among the proud,
     among the persecuted,
     among the privileged,
     Christ is coming to make all things new.

     In the private house,
     in the public place,
     in the wedding feast,
     in the judgement hall,
     Christ is coming to make all things new.

     With a gentle touch,
     with an angry word,
     with a clear conscience,
     with burning love,
     Christ is coming to make all things new.

That the kingdom might come,
that the world might believe,
that the powerful might stumble,
that the hidden might be seen,
Christ is coming to make all things new.

Within us, without us,
behind us, before us,
in this place, in every place,
for this time, for all time,
Christ is coming to make all things new.

Many scripture verses are suitable as a call to worship or as a statement concerning God which invites the response of worship. This is just a small selection of suitable verses. The psalms in particular offer many declarations and invitations to worship.

5   The Lord is my light and salvation;
    whom shall I fear?
    The Lord is the stronghold of my life;
    of whom shall I be afraid?   *Psalm 27.1*

6   O God, you are my God, I seek you,
    my soul thirsts for you;
    my flesh faints for you,
    as in a dry and weary land where there is no water.

    So I have looked upon you in the sanctuary,
    beholding your power and glory.

    Because your steadfast love is better than life,
    my lips will praise you.
    So I will bless you as long as I live;
    I will lift up my hands and call on your name.

    My soul is satisfied as with a rich feast,
    and my mouth praises you with joyful lips   *Psalm 63.1–5*

7   I will sing of your steadfast love, O Lord, for ever;
    with my mouth I will proclaim your faithfulness to all generations.
    I declare that your steadfast love is established for ever;
    your faithfulness is as firm as the heavens.   *Psalm 89.1f.*

8   O come, let us sing to the Lord;
    let us make a joyful noise to the rock of our salvation!
    Let us come into his presence with thanksgiving;
    let us make a joyful noise to him with songs of praise!

    For he is our God,
    and we are the people of his pasture,
    and the sheep of his hand.

Psalm 95.1f., 7

9   Enter his gates with thanksgiving,
    and his courts with praise.
    Give thanks to him, bless his name.
    For the Lord is good;
    his steadfast love endures forever,
    and his faithfulness to all generations.

Psalm 100.4f.

10   The Lord is gracious and merciful,
    slow to anger and abounding in steadfast love.
    The Lord is good to all,
    and his compassion is over all that he has made.

    All your works shall give thanks to you, O Lord,
    and all your faithful shall bless you.
    They shall speak of the glory of your kingdom,
    and tell of your power.

Psalm 145.8–11

11   Holy, holy, holy is the Lord of hosts;
    the whole earth is full of his glory.

    Holy, holy, holy,
    the Lord God the Almighty,
    who was and is and is to come.

Isaiah 6.3; Revelation 4.8

12   Have you not known? Have you not heard?
The Lord is the everlasting God,
the Creator of the ends of the earth.
He does not faint or grow weary;
his understanding is unsearchable.

He gives power to the faint,
and strengthens the powerless.
Even youths will faint and be weary,
and the young will fall exhausted;
but those who wait for the Lord shall renew their strength,
they shall mount up with wings like eagles,
they shall run and not be weary,
they shall walk and not faint.

Isaiah 40.28–31

13   Seek the Lord while he may be found,
call upon him while he is near;

let the wicked forsake their way,
and the unrighteous their thoughts;
let them return to the Lord,
that he may have mercy on them,
and to our God, for he will abundantly pardon.

Isaiah 55.6f.

14   The steadfast love of the Lord never ceases,
his mercies never come to an end;
they are new every morning;
great is your faithfulness.

Lamentations 3.22f.

15   Let us test and examine our ways,
and return to the Lord.
Let us lift up our hearts as well as our hands
to God in heaven.

Lamentations 3.40f.

16   Come to me,
all you that are weary and are carrying heavy burdens,
and I will give you rest.
Take my yoke upon you, and learn from me;
for I am gentle and humble in heart,
and you will find rest for your souls.
For my yoke is easy, and my burden is light.

Matthew 11.28–30

17   Where two or three are gathered in my name,
      I am there among them.

Matthew 18.20

18   The Word became flesh;
      he made his home among us,
      and we saw his glory,
      such glory as befits the Father's only Son,
      full of grace and truth.

John 1.14 REB

19   God so loved the world that he gave his only Son,
      so that everyone who believes in him
      may not perish but may have eternal life.

John 3.16

20   We proclaim Jesus Christ as Lord.
      For it is the God who said,
      'Let light shine out of darkness,'
      who has shone in our hearts
      to give the light of the knowledge of the glory of God
      in the face of Jesus Christ.

2 Corinthians 4.5f.

21   Rejoice in the Lord always;
      again I will say, Rejoice.
      Do not worry about anything,
      but in everything by prayer and supplication with thanksgiving
      let your requests be made known to God.
      And the peace of God, which surpasses all understanding,
      will guard your hearts and your minds in Christ Jesus.

Philippians 4.4, 6f.

22   Then I heard every creature
      in heaven and on earth and under the earth and in the sea,
      and all that is in them, singing,
              'To the one seated on the throne and to the Lamb
              be blessing and honour and glory and might
              for ever and ever!'

Revelation 5.13

OPENINGS: PRAYERS

23   Living God, we pray
      that as the Holy Spirit came in wind and fire to the apostles,
      so your Spirit may come to us,
      breathing new life into our lives,
      and setting our hearts
      aflame with love;
      through Jesus Christ our Lord.

24   Lord Jesus Christ, you declared yourself
      the way, the truth, and the life.
      Reveal to us your truth, and inspire us with your life,
      that now and at all times
      we may find in you the way to the Father.

25   Living God:
      in this building,
      used to the sound of singing,
      where there have been baptisms and funerals,
      where people have come to be married,
      or to celebrate the birth of a child;
      this building,
      where some have wept, and some been filled with joy,
      where people have struggled with the deep things of life,
      have prayed urgently,
      been stirred and changed;
      in this building
      where you have so often been with your people,
      be with us now.

26   Your glory fills the whole earth
      and your power is beyond measuring.
      Your gifts are good and perfect,
      your love is more than we can know
      and your grace is enough for everything.
      Eternal God, we come to you.

27   Walk softly as you come here
      for this is holy ground.
      God dwells in this place.
      God the Lord of time and space
      was here before us,
      and is here now.

      Tread carefully as you come here
      for this is holy ground.
      By God's life-giving word
      every creature was spoken into existence,
      and is loved into eternity.
      God the Lord of abundant life
      was here before us
      and is here now,

      Walk quietly as you come here
      For this is holy ground.
      Now is the time
      and here is the place:
      to listen intently to God's Spirit within us;
      to see, as for the first time,
      the hidden depths
      of Christ's suffering for us;
      to look expectantly
      for the signs of God's Kingdom around us.

      Holy God:
      softly, carefully, quietly,
      we come here,
      celebrating your presence
      within us
      and between us,
      this day and always.

28   Worship is the doorstep of heaven
      where the children speak to their Father,
      the poor sit at table with their Saviour
      and the weak are empowered by God's Spirit.
      This is where love and mercy meet,
      love and obedience hold hands,
      and where love bids us welcome:
      for this is the doorstep of heaven.
      Loving God,
      let it be this and more for us today,
      for Jesus' sake.

29   Lord God,
        whether we have rushed or taken our time
        in coming to church,
        we have come ill-prepared.

        You have invited us to meet with you;
        you have created space for time together
        that will affect all the other moments of the week.
        You have called us to take time
        to recall your love and mercy.
        Yet we have come in heedlessly
        as if we were going shopping.
        We may even have lists in our minds
        of things we want you to sort out:
        of feelings and emotions that we want to gain
        and which will last us
        without too much effort.
        We have not prepared ourselves to worship.

        Stop us now, and help us,
        as we wonder at the scope of your love.
        You care for each of us
        as if you care for each one alone.
        Help us face you today,
        to receive what you want to give
        and wonder at your love.

30   True God, living Spirit,
        you move like the wind
        and in quiet ways you refresh us.

        Like the wind, you will not be stopped:
        and if we build against you
        our constructions of mind and matter crumble.

        Ever present Spirit,
        breathe on us.

        Let us breathe-in thankfulness and joy;
        let us find our strength for living
        in your clean air.
        purify our lives,
        restore our polluted world.

31   Come Lord Jesus,
      you blessed the children and dined with outcasts,
      spared the sinner and forgave the offender:
      speak to us again of love.
      We long to be sure of your welcome.

      Come, Lord Jesus,
      you humbled the proud and exalted the humble,
      proclaimed good news to the poor
      and release to the captives:
      speak to us again of justice.
      We long for our world to be changed.

      Come Lord Jesus,
      you felt terror at the future,
      begged your disciples' prayers
      and needed another to shoulder your cross:
      speak to us again of humility.
      We long to know you in our frailty.

      Come Lord Jesus,
      You faced the torture of oppressors,
      and died abandoned on the cross:
      speak to us again of suffering.
      We long to meet you in our pain.

      Come Lord Jesus,
      you left the tomb empty,
      and promised us the Spirit:
      speak to us again of new life.
      We long to trust you for the future.

      Lord Jesus Christ,
      so deep is your love
      that nowhere are we excluded from it.
      Help us to know you
      in our doubt as well as our faith,
      our weakness as well as our strength,
      that meeting you in our depths
      you may lift us to your heights.

32   Let us praise God.
      From before the world began
      and after the end of eternity,
      You are God.

      From the sea bursting out of its womb
      to the wind ceasing from its chase,
      You are God.

      In the constancy of created things
      and in their fickleness,
      You are God.

      In the vastness of the universe
      and the forgotten corner of our hearts
      You are God.
      You are our God
      and we bless you.

ADORATION AND PRAISE

33   Now to him who by the power at work within us
is able to accomplish abundantly
far more than all we can ask or imagine,
to him be glory in the church and in Christ Jesus
to all generations, forever and ever. Amen.   *Ephesians 3.20f.*

34   Worthy is the Lamb that was slain,
to receive power and wealth and wisdom and might
and honour and glory and blessing!

To the one seated on the throne and to the Lamb
be blessing and honour and glory and might
forever and ever!   *Revelation 5.12, 13b*

35   Blessed are you, Lord God of our father Israel,
from of old and for ever.
Yours, Lord, is the greatness and the power, the glory,
the splendour, and the majesty;
for everything in heaven and on earth is yours;
yours, Lord, is the sovereignty,
and you are exalted over all as head.
Now, our God, we give you thanks
and praise your glorious name.   *1 Chronicles 29.10b 11, 13 REB*

36   Glory to God in the highest,
and peace to God's people on earth.

Lord God, heavenly King,
almighty God and Father,
      we worship you, we give you thanks,
      we praise you for your glory.

Lord Jesus Christ, only Son of the Father,
Lord God, Lamb of God,
you take away the sin of the world;
      have mercy on us;
you are seated at the right hand of the Father:
      receive our prayer.

For you alone are the Holy One,
you alone are the Lord,
you alone are the Most High,
      Jesus Christ,
      with the Holy Spirit,
      in the glory of God the Father.

37   From the rising of the sun
     till its setting in the west,
     God's holy name be praised.

     On the lips of children,
     by babies at the breast,
     God's holy name be praised.

     In the visions of the old
     and the dreaming of the young,
     God's holy name be praised.

     In the banquet hall of heaven
     and the forgotten corners of our hearts,
     God's holy name be praised.

     Let all that has life and breath
     praise the Lord.
     Amen. We praise the Lord!

38   My rock, my redeemer, my rescuer,
     I adore you.
     I adore you

     My hope, my help, my heart,
     I adore you.
     I adore you.

     My friend, my future, my faithful one,
     I adore you.
     I adore you.

     My light, my life, my love:
     I adore you.
     I adore you.

39 Great God beyond all words:
    help us to shape our words
    to do you justice.

    In you, there is no conflict
    between power and tenderness.
    The birth-pangs of creation
    are the way of your wisdom;
    your love suffers crucifixion
    and is not defeated:
    restoring the world
    to life and hope.

    We do not deserve that hope
    which you have prepared for us.
    Measured by your ways,
    we get lost in the paths we choose.
    But you are ready to guide us
    and lead us onwards.

    Over-awed by the vastness of the universe,
    perplexed and battered
    by the events of our lives,
    we turn to you
    and find you waiting to meet us
    in the smallness of each day:
    eternity in each present moment.

    Great God
    we worship you
    through Jesus
    and your Spirit's gift.

40   Glory to you, Almighty God!
You spoke, and light came out of darkness,
order rose from confusion.

You breathed into the dust of the earth
and we were formed in your image.

You looked on the work of your hands,
and declared that it was all good.

And still you speak, breathe life and look for us:
we praise you.

Glory to you, Jesus Christ!
You met us as a refugee, a threatened child,
the word made flesh, born in a forgotten place.

You called us by name, to leave what was comfortable,
to be your disciples, companions and friends.

You saved us by kneeling at our feet,
stretching your arms wide to take away our sins,
walking through death to life again.

And still you meet, call and save us:
we praise you.

Glory to you, Holy Spirit!
You brooded over chaos,
mothering and shaping God's new creation.

You inspired prophets and evangelists
to discover the right word for the right season.

You liberated the early church for mission,
claiming all of life for the Lord of all.

And still you brood over, inspire and liberate us:
we praise you.

41   Lord God, our ways are not your ways,
and your love is not like ours.

Our love judges by appearance
but yours looks deep in the heart.

Our love coldly counts the cost
but yours is freely given.

Our love cannot bear much pain
but yours is ready to suffer.

Our love wants instant results
but yours keeps waiting and hoping.

Holy God, in Christ
we celebrate
the warmth of your welcome,
the strength of your goodness,
and the folly of your faith in us.
Glory to God!

42   Living God,
we give you thanks and praise,
for you have made us and given us life,
you have redeemed us and set us free.

Loving God,
we give you thanks and praise,
for you have found us and made us your own,
named us and called us 'Beloved'.

Accompanying God,
we give you thanks and praise,
for you have promised to be with us always
and nothing can separate us from your love.

God, our God,
we love you and adore you.

43   Lord God,
early in the morning,
when the world was young,
you made life in all its beauty and terror,
you gave birth to all that we know.

Hallowed be your name.
Hallowed be your name.

Early in the morning,
when the world least expected it,
a newborn child crying in a cradle
announced that you had come among us,
that you were one of us.

Hallowed be your name.
Hallowed be your name.

Early in the morning,
surrounded by respectable liars,
religious leaders, anxious politicians
and silent friends,
you accepted the penalty for doing good,
for being God:
you shouldered and suffered the cross.

Hallowed be your name.
Hallowed be your name.

Early in the morning,
a voice in a guarded graveyard
and footsteps in the dew
proved that you had risen,
that you had come back
to those and for those
who had forgotten, denied and destroyed you.

Hallowed be your name.
Hallowed be your name.

Early in the morning,
in the multicoloured company of your church,
on earth and in heaven,
we celebrate your creation,
your life,
your death and resurrection,
your interest in us
now and always.

CONFESSION

44   Create in me a clean heart, O God,
and put a new and right spirit within me.
Do not cast me away from your presence,
and do not take your holy spirit from me.

Restore to me the joy of your salvation,
and sustain in me a willing spirit.
Then I will teach transgressors your ways,
and sinners will return to you.

O Lord, open my lips,
and my mouth will declare your praise.

Psalm 51.10–13, 15

45   This is the message we have heard from him and proclaim to you,
that God is light and in him there is no darkness at all.
If we say that we have fellowship with him
while we are walking in darkness,
we lie and do not do what is true;
but if we walk in the light as he himself is in the light,
we have fellowship with one another,
and the blood of Jesus his Son cleanses us from all sin.

1 John 1.5–7

46   We confess that we have lived superficially.
We have pushed to the back of our minds
the questions that trouble us.
We have not found time to face the emotions that disturb us.
We have hidden from life
behind habit, activity, and entertainments.
We have avoided you, God, even as you came after us.

In our relationships we have given less than our whole selves
and we have not received from others
what they wished to give us of their selves.
We have countered the sharp demands of justice
with hardened hearts.
We have allowed imagination and sympathy to wither.
Routine has been our ally and honesty our dread.

Lord God, we have shut ourselves up.
Come after us again, knock once more,
that we may open up to meet others,
rediscover ourselves, know your love, and live again.

47 Merciful God, we confess to you now that we have sinned.
    We confess the sins that no one knows
    and the sins that everyone knows:
    the sins that are a burden to us
    and the sins that do not bother us
    because we have got used to them.

    We confess our sins as a church:
    we have not loved one another as Christ loved us
    and we have not given ourselves in love and service for the world
    as Christ gave himself for us.

    Father forgive us.
    Send your Holy Spirit to us,
    to give us power
    to live as, by your mercy, you have called us to live;
    through Jesus Christ our Lord.

48 Most merciful God,
    Father of our Lord Jesus Christ,
    we confess that we have sinned
    in thought, word and deed.
    We have not loved you with our whole heart.
    We have not loved our neighbours as ourselves.
    In your mercy
    forgive what we have been,
    help us to amend what we are,
    and direct what we shall be;
    that we may do justly,
    love mercy,
    and walk humbly with you, our God.

49 Almighty God, our heavenly Father,
    we have sinned against you
    and against our neighbour
    in thought and word and deed,
    through negligence, through weakness,
    through our own deliberate fault.
    We are truly sorry
    and repent of all our sins.
    For the sake of your Son, Jesus Christ,
    who died for us,
    forgive us all that is past
    and grant that we may serve you in newness of life
    to the glory of your name.

50   Learn to do good;
      seek justice,
      rescue the oppressed,
      defend the orphan,
      plead for the widow.

      Come now, let us argue it out, says the Lord:
      though your sins are like scarlet, they shall be like snow;
      though they are red like crimson, they shall become like wool.

Isaiah 1.17f.

      Lord, we have got it wrong.
      We thought you just wanted our worship:
      songs of praise and prayers of passion.
      But you want the whole of our lives:
      a worldly worship of acting justly and living compassionately.
      You look inside and ask us who we are and what we want.

      Forgive us our sins, we pray
      challenge us where we are unjust,
      disturb us when we don't care
      and transform our selfishness
      through the love of your Son
      and the life-giving power of your Spirit.

51   Lord Jesus, you wept over the sins of your city.
      On our city: Lord, have mercy.
      Lord, have mercy.

      Lord Jesus, you heal the wounds
      of sin and division, jealously and bitterness.
      On us: Christ have mercy.
      Christ, have mercy.

      Lord Jesus, you bring pardon and peace to the sinner.
      Grant us peace: Lord, have mercy.
      Lord, have mercy.

52   Loving God,
you are faithful and forgiving:
help us now to grasp the greatness of your love.

Help us to pray honestly
as we make our confession and seek your forgiveness.

Silent Reflection

Where we have failed to love, and have loved to hurt:
Forgive us, and heal us.

Where we have scorned difference
and have been indifferent to those in need:
Forgive us, and heal us.

Where we have spoken harsh words to others,
and have been quick to take offence ourselves:
Forgive us, and heal us.

Where we have prayed and sung about injustice,
and have ignored the injustice around us:
Forgive us, and heal us.

Merciful God, unlike us, you are true to your word.
When we cry to you in sorrow and repentance,
you hear our cries and are swift to forgive.
For your faithful love we praise you.

53   *Each section of this prayer may be answered by the congregation saying 'Lord, have mercy' or by singing a Taizé (or other) setting of Kyrie eleison.*

Eternal God,
your love is from everlasting to everlasting.
Through your Son Jesus,
you call us to love you,
to love our neighbour,
to love our enemy.
Lord have mercy:
Kyrie eleison ...

Eternal God,
your word is truth,
it stands as ageless as the hills.
You have called us
to speak and live the truth.
Lord have mercy:
Kyrie eleison ...

Eternal God,
where your Spirit is there is freedom.
You call us to live
as your sons and daughters,
freed from all slavery,
delivered from all tyranny.
Lord have mercy:
Kyrie eleison ...

Eternal God,
your kingdom is justice and peace,
you call us to be its citizens,
men and women of hope,
and generous integrity.
Lord have mercy:
Kyrie eleison ...

Eternal God,
you made us in your image,
you make us anew in the image
of your Son, Jesus Christ.
Lord have mercy:
Kyrie eleison ...

Eternal God,
in Jesus you show us that to be holy
is to sit with the outcast,
to embrace the unclean,
to welcome the unloved,
to love with heart and mind,
with all our strength.
You call us to be holy
as you are holy.
Lord have mercy:
Kyrie eleison …

54 Lord, your ways are not our ways,
your thoughts are not our thoughts:
what to us seems like eternity
is only a moment to you.
In the face of eternity,
help us to be humble.

If we have been singing praise with our voices
and kept the joy our of our hearts;

if we have prayed only for what is possible
and hoped only for what we could see;

if we have taken your grace for granted
and expected instant answers to instant requests;

if we have allowed waiting on your Spirit to slip into laziness
and waiting on the Kingdom to be replaced by apathy;

if we have only thought of us waiting on you
and never pondered how you wait on us:

Lord have mercy,
Christ have mercy,
Lord have mercy.

Silence

To all and to each,
where regret is real,
God pronounces pardon
and grants us the right
to begin again.

Thanks be to God. Amen.

55   We confess to you, Lord,
      what we are:

      we are not the people
      we like others to think we are;

      we are afraid to admit even to ourselves
      what lies in the depths of our souls.

      But we do not want to hide
      our true selves from you.

      We believe that you know us as we are,
      and yet you love us.

      Help us not to shrink
      from self-knowledge;

      teach us to respect ourselves
      and affirm our uniqueness and worth;

      give us the courage to put our trust
      in your guiding and power.

      We also confess to you, Lord,
      the unrest of the world,

      to which we contribute
      and in which we share.

      Forgive our reliance
      on weapons of terror,

      our cold indifference
      to the needs of others,

      our discrimination
      against people of different race

      our preoccupation
      with material standards.

      Forgive our being unsure
      of the good news about you and from you,

      and so unready to tell it,
      share it and live it.

Raise us out of the paralysis of guilt
into the freedom and energy
of forgiven people.

And for those who through long habit
find forgiveness hard to accept
we ask you to break their bondage
and set them free.

Through Jesus Christ our Lord.

56   Lord, we find it so easy to talk about forgiveness
but so difficult to accept it for ourselves.
We know our need, Lord.
We know our need for newness of life;
confession comes readily to us
and yet so little changes.

Lord, we are afraid.
We want your forgiveness, but we fear being known.
There are those things within us which we prefer to hide,
deep shadows vaguely sensed.
There are those things we know too well about ourselves,
and things we dare not know.
Without our being known there is no forgiveness for us,
and so we are afraid.

Lord give us the courage to accept your forgiveness for us,
and so to grow into our promised newness.
Lord forgive us.

Lord, we would be free:
free from bondage to our own past,
and free from the past of our community.
Take us into your future, O God,
with the power that comes with freedom;
renew us as creatures and as creators
that we may face our world with hope
in the power of your forgiving love,
through Jesus Christ our Saviour.

ASSURANCE OF PARDON

The assurance of forgiveness after a prayer of confession offers pastoral help to those struggling with their sins and at the same time proclaims the gospel of Jesus Christ.

57 If we say we have no sin,
    we deceive ourselves, and the truth is not in us.
    If we confess our sins,
    he who is faithful and just will forgive us our sins
    and cleanse us from all unrighteousness.

1 John 1.8f.

58 The Lord is merciful and gracious,
    slow to anger and abounding in steadfast love.
    He does not deal with us according to our sins,
    nor repay us according to our iniquities.
    For as the heavens are high above the earth,
    so great is his steadfast love toward those who fear him;
    as far as the east is from the west:
    so far he removes our transgressions from us.

Psalm 108.8, 10–12

59 The Lord is near to all who call on him,
    to all who call on him in truth.
    He fulfils the desire of all who fear him;
    he hears their cry, and saves them.

Psalm 145.18f.

60 Listen:
    here is good news:
    'Christ Jesus came into the world to save sinners'

    O depth of wealth, wisdom, and knowledge in God!
    How unsearchable his judgements, how untraceable his ways!
    Source, Guide, and Goal of all that is –
    to him be glory for ever! Amen.

Romans 11.33, 36 REB

61 God, the Father of mercies,
    has reconciled the world to himself
    through the death and resurrection of his Son, Jesus Christ,
    not counting our trespasses against us,
    but sending his Holy Spirit
    to shed abroad his love among us.
    Receive his pardon and peace
    to stand before him in his strength alone,
    this day and evermore.

62   The saying is sure and worthy of full acceptance,
      that Christ Jesus came into the world to save sinners.

      To the King of the ages,
      immortal, invisible, the only God,
      be honour and glory forever and ever. Amen.

1 Timothy 1.15, 17

63   Almighty God,
      who forgives all who truly repent,
      have mercy upon *you*,
      pardon and deliver *you* from all *your* sins,
      confirm and strengthen *you* in all goodness,
      and keep *you* in life in life eternal;
      through Jesus Christ our Lord.

64   The saying is sure and worthy of full acceptance,
      that Christ Jesus came into the world to save sinners:
      of whom I am the foremost.

      To all who confess their sins
      and resolve to lead a new life,
      he says:
      Your sins are forgiven,

      and he also says:
      Follow me.

      To the King of the ages,
      immortal, invisible, the only God,
      be honour and glory forever and ever. Amen.

incorporating 1 Timothy 1.15, 17

LAMENT

65 My God, my God, why have you forsaken me?
Why are you so far from helping me,
from the words of my groaning?
O my God, I cry by day, but you do not answer;
and by night, but find no rest.

Yet you are holy,
enthroned on the praises of Israel.
In you our ancestors trusted;
they trusted, and you delivered them.

Psalm 22.1—4

66 Out of the depths I cry to you, O Lord.
Lord, hear my voice!
Let your ears be attentive
to the voice of my supplications!

If you, O Lord, should mark iniquities,
Lord, who could stand?
But there is forgiveness with you,
so that you may be revered.

I wait for the Lord, my soul waits,
and in his word I hope;
my soul waits for the Lord
more than those who watch for the morning,
more than those who watch for the morning.

O Israel, hope in the Lord!
For with the Lord there is steadfast love,
and with him is great power to redeem.
It is he who will redeem Israel
from all its iniquities.

Psalm 130

67   Our God, you know that the night has been deep and long,
chill shadows have fallen upon our hearts,
and we have seen the darkness creep across the face of our land.

**We have felt helpless against the growing darkness, O God,
and so have stood silent and numbed,
concerned only for our own loss of light,
and our seeming powerlessness to change the season.**

We know that despair is ever seeking a home,
that love grows cold through fear and bitterness.
We too can retreat into indifference,
let tears fall unnoticed,
and harden ourselves to the pain of others.

**But still, O God, there is within us
that longing for the light of dawn,
for the ending of night,
and the rising of your sun.**

And so we ask you now,
not for the patience of passivity,
but for the endurance and love that gains its strength
from the crucified and risen one
who has pierced the darkness,
who knows the way,
and is with us still.

68   I believe, although everything
hides you from my faith.
I believe, although everything shouts No! to me.
I believe, although everything may seem to die.
I believe, although I no longer would wish to live,
because I have founded my life
on a sincere word,
on the word of a friend,
on the word of God.

I believe, although I feel alone in pain.
I believe, although I see people hating.
I believe, although I see children weep,
because I have learnt with certainty
that he comes to meet us
in the hardest hours,
with his love and his light.
I believe, but increase my faith.

69   Compassionate God
       we come to you in our need
       confessing to you
       what we often dare not admit to ourselves:

       it is hard to celebrate life
       when faced with the mystery of death.

       It is hard to look to the future
       when surrounded by the uncertainty of the present;
       it is hard to embrace the day
       when hope is eclipsed by despair.

       Help us this day
       to know you and find you
       in the whole of life:
       its beginnings and its endings,
       to discover you
       in our pain as well as our joy,
       in our doubts
       as well as our believing,

       to receive this day,
       and in the days to come.
       comfort from your word
       and light for our darkness.

70   Why, God? Why? When our need
       is desperate, when all other help is vain,
       do you turn away from us?

       Why? Why, when the darkness is deepest
       and our midnight is starless
       do you hide yourself from us?

       Why? In times of grief and distress,
       when there is no light in the window,
       do we find a door slammed in our face,
       and a sound of bolting and
       double bolting from within?

       Why forsake us when we need you most?
       Why are you present when the skies are clear,
       our help in our days of prosperity,
       but so absent in our time of trouble?

We know that faith does not exempt us from sorrow
or shield us from evil;
we know that; we know, too,
that the earth is wet with the blood of the innocent
but why this? Why now? Why?

Know this, God, know this:
if faith were dependent on feelings,
if our trust in you were no more than
a matter of the mind, we would be done with you,
done with you now, done with you forever.

And hear this, God, hear this:
if it were not for that man
who was a friend of the poor and the damned
for that man who healed the sick
and gave sight to the blind;
if it were not for that man
whom we cursed and crucified,
and who is crucified still,
for that man who bore our griefs and carried ours sorrows,
and who carries them still;

God, God eternal, God of Jesus,
God who said Yes to his life,
his love, his suffering, his death,
God of the cross, crucified God,
sharing our pain, bearing our sin,
if it were not, O God, for you,
for you our lover, you our judge,
you our hope, you our friend,
we would indeed be lost.

God of Christ,
God who raised him from the dead,
God with whom life can begin again,
come to us now, hold us, help us, heal us,
for you and you alone are our salvation.

71   Almighty God,
      Great sorrow has come over me;
      My cares would overpower me;
      I know of no way out.

      God be gracious and help me;
      Give strength to bear what you have sent;
      Let me not be overcome by fear;
      Give fatherly care for my loved ones.

      Merciful God, forgive my sins
      against you and those whom I have hurt.
      I trust your grace, and give my life
      Entirely into your hands;

      Do with me as it pleases you,
      and as it is good for me.
      Whether I live or die, I am with you
      and you are with me, my God

      Lord I look for your salvation
      and your kingdom.

72   Eternal God who desires our wholeness
      because life is difficult and love is not easy,
      and doubt and struggle, suffering and failure,
      are inevitable for each and every one of us,
      help us to respect the darkness of our pain and grief
      and make a bold place for them in our lives.

      Help us to recognise that without them
      we can have no true sense of life's great depth,
      and that within them lies our capacity
      to love, to create and to make meaning.

      Help us also to welcome our yearnings for joy
      and release, for flowers and the sun,
      spaces to dream and the need to be loved.

      May our joy and despair, loneliness and longings,
      not remain hidden or divided from one another;
      but help us to build each other up in mutual friendship,
      that we may be enlivened and made strong.

      God our life, our wholeness, our friend,
      lead us to that place within us
      where darkness and light, the mornings and evenings of the heart,
      may meet one another, know one another, and embrace.

THANKSGIVING

73   Creator God, we praise and thank you
for the earth and the wonder of its life:
the beauty of landscape, sky and seasons;
the variety of animals and plants;
with their intricate interdependence;
for making us to be part of it all,
shaping landscape, affected by seasons,
partners in creation.

Redeemer God, we praise you
for Jesus Christ and the glory of your work in him:
his life in all its fullness of doing and being;
his following through of your way to the end;
for your raising of him and all who follow him.

Inspirer God, we praise and thank you
for human history and the richness of our inheritance:
the heights of human artistry
and the depths of human understanding.
You come to us by your Spirit
and perform your work of new creation.

Generous and bountiful God
all good things come from you
and now we give you thanks.

74   All powerful God,
you have created all things:
the vast reaches of space and the intricacies of life
are the work of your hands
and we give you praise.

Loving God you have redeemed us:
in Jesus Christ, you have shared our humanity and given us hope.
In his befriending, his teaching and healing,
you have come close to those in need.
In his death on the cross you have dealt with our sin
and shown us that nothing can separate us from your love.
In his resurrection you have demonstrated
that death cannot have the last word
and you have shown us the hope of glory.
We give you thanks.

75   God our creator, parent and friend,
we thank you

> for the wonderful gift of life,
> with all its joys and responsibilities,
> its experiences and opportunities.

We praise you

> for good health and daily food,
> for the shelter and care of our homes,
> the love and loyalty of our friends.

We thank you

> for work honestly done,
> for games well played,
> for all the truth we have learned
> and the good that has been achieved.

We thank you

> for the teaching and example of Jesus Christ,
> for forgiveness and salvation,
> for his presence with us always
> and for the service into which he has called us.

Help us to thank you

> not only with our lips, in praise and prayer,
> but in our lives of hope and love;
> through Jesus Christ our Lord.

76   For all the saints
who went before us
who have spoken to our hearts
and have touched us with your fire,
we praise you, O God.

For all the saints
who live beside us
whose weaknesses and strengths
are woven with our own,
we praise you, O God.

For all the saints
who live beyond us
who challenge us
to change the world with them,
we praise you, O God.

77   Creator God
     maker of all that is:
     in creation we see
     the glorious outworking
     of your imagination.
     Every creature,
     through your life-giving Spirit,
     is spoken into existence
     and loved into eternity.

     For the gift of life
     we praise and thank you.

     Generous God
     giver of all good things;
     in your Son we see
     the wonder and the cost of love.
     In his living and dying
     we feel your compassion
     and see your purpose.
     In his glorious resurrection
     we know death
     not only as ending
     but as beginnings.

     For the promise of life eternal
     we praise and thank you.

78   Life-giving God,
     by your Spirit you brought creation out of chaos
     and gave life to the world.
     Now you sustain all things
     and still you give life to the lifeless.
     You have found us and changed us,
     awoken us and inspired us.
     You have given us new life in Jesus Christ:
     you have wooed us in love
     and created love within us.

     God our creator, redeemer and sustainer,
     we give you thanks and praise.

79 My rock, my redeemer, my rescuer,
I adore you.
I adore you.

My hope, my help, my heart,
I adore you.
I adore you.

My friend, my future, my faithful one,
I adore you.
I adore you.

My light, my life, my love:
I adore you.
I adore you.

INTERCESSION

Prayers of intercession and petition follow. They are offered as a guide to the different styles and approaches which can be developed for this area of prayer.

These prayers take different forms but normally include all or most of the following

- *Prayers for ourselves (perhaps in the light of the theme of the service).*
- *Prayers for our fellowship (maybe naming those in special need where this is appropriate), and for neighbouring churches.*
- *Prayers for the local community of the church, especially areas of tension or joy, or where national issues come to some sort of focus.*
- *Prayers for our country, perhaps picking up on items from the news in the week.*
- *Prayer for the world: perhaps this may include prayers for BMS or similar agencies but should not be confined to such 'churchy' causes.*

80   Loving and Holy Spirit of God
we pray:

that we and all people
may increasingly work together
to establish on earth
the rule of the Kingdom of heaven;
that the resources of the world
may be gathered,
distributed and used
with unselfish motives and scientific skill
for the greatest benefit of all;

that beauty may be given
to our towns and cities,
and left untarnished in the countryside;
that children may grow up strong in body,
sound in mind and trained in spirit;

that there may be open ways,
and peace and freedom,
from end to end of the earth;

and that people everywhere may learn to live in love
through keeping the company
of Jesus Christ our Lord,
in whose great name we pray.

81 Gracious God
rejoicing in your blessings,
trusting in your loving care for all,
we bring you our prayers for the world.

We pray for the created world:
for those who rebuild where things have been destroyed;
for those who fight hunger poverty and disease;
for those who have power
to bring change for the better and to renew hope.

Silence

In the life of our world
Your kingdom come, O Lord,
Your will be done.

We pray for our country:
for those in leadership;
who frame our laws
and shape our common life;
who keep the peace
and administer justice;
for those who teach
and those who heal
for all who serve the community

Silence

In the life of our land
Your kingdom come, O Lord,
Your will be done.

We pray for people in need:
those for whom life is a bitter struggle;
those whose lives are clouded
by death or loss,
by pain or disability,
by discouragement or fear,
by shame or rejection.

Silence

In the lives of those in need
Your kingdom come, O Lord,
Your will be done.

We pray for those
in the circle of friendship and love around us:
children and parents;
sisters and brothers;
friends and neighbours;
and for those especially in our thoughts today ...

Silence

In the lives of those we love,
your kingdom come, O Lord,
your will be done.

We pray for the church
in its stand with the poor,
in its love for the outcast and the ashamed,
in its service to the sick and the neglected,
in its proclamation of the Gospel,
in this land and in this place.

Silence

In the life of your church,
your kingdom come, O Lord,
your will be done.

Eternal God:
hear these our prayers,
the spoken and the silent,
through Jesus Christ our Lord,
to whom with you and the Holy Spirit,
be all praise and glory for ever.

82 Lord, as you hear our hymns and rejoice in our friendship,
so hear our prayers:

Guide me O thou great Jehovah

for all facing tough choices at work or in personal life
for leaders of the nations ...
**Lead them all their journeys through
and use us – if not in our wisdom then in our humanity –
to show a way to the One who is the Way, the Truth, the Life**

I am weak but thou art mighty

for all who feel vulnerable, abused or at risk
for the community of ...
for those near to us ...
**Hold them with your powerful hand
and show us how we may be your hands,
how even our weakness might be a conduit for your strength**

Bread of heaven – feed me now and evermore

for those who live today in real hunger
because their crops have failed
or their land is bad
or because they have no reward for their labour
or because no one wants their labour
or they are too unfit to work
**Feed them now and evermore:
prosper the work of the Red Cross, the UNHCR
and all those working for short-term relief
and long-term quality of life**

Bread of heaven – feed me now and evermore

for those who have a hunger for meaning and purpose
for those asking themselves today:
God where are you?
Jesus who are you?
**Feed them now and evermore
that they might find God in Jesus Christ**

When I tread the verge of Jordan

for those facing death or serious illness
for those anxiously awaiting tests or surgery
for those who care for them and watch with them

**Bid their anxious fears subside
and make us agents of your loving care
so that whatever side we are landed**

we and all your people may know your care and love
to be stronger than death.

So then with
Songs of praises, songs of praises
we will ever sing to thee, sing to thee,
we will ever sing to thee
through Jesus Christ our Lord.

83   God of kindness,
you gave your only Son,
because you loved the world so much.
We pray for the peace of the world.
Move among us by your Spirit,
break down barriers
of fear, suspicion, and hatred.
Heal the human family of its divisions
and unite it in the bonds of justice and peace.

We pray for our country.
Enrich our common life;
strengthen the forces of truth and goodness;
teach us to share prosperity,
that those whose lives are impoverished
may pass from need and despair
to dignity and joy.

We pray for those who suffer.
Surround them with your love,
support them with your strength,
console them with your comfort,
and give them hope
and courage beyond themselves.

We pray for our families,
for those whom we love.
Protect them at home;
support them in times of difficulty and anxiety,
that they may grow together
in mutual love and understanding,
and rest content in one another

We pray for the Church.
Keep her true to the Gospel
and responsive to the gifts and needs of all.
Make known your saving power in Jesus Christ
by the witness of her faith,
her worship
and her life.

84   Almighty God,
we pray for those
locked in circumstances beyond their control,
restrained by oppressors,
and seeing no end to their captivity.
May they discover hope
buried in deepest suffering;
through Jesus Christ,
who shared the weakness and despair of human life,
yet gave even death a new outcome
and brought resurrection from a closed tomb.

Lord in your mercy
Hear our prayer

We pray for the church
set in the world
to show how people belong together
and how your gifts are given to be shared.
Grant that, as we feel
for the rejection and voicelessness of others,
we may meet Christ in them
and bear witness to his transforming love.

Lord in your mercy
Hear our prayer

We pray for the communities
in which we live and work;
for people under stress
and unable to deal with their difficulties;
for those who seek comfort
in ways which bring no help;
for all who are fearful.
Give us grace to show by our concern and actions
how each is loved and valued by you.

Lord in your mercy,
Hear our prayer.

We remember those now hidden from us
but at home with you.
We give thanks especially
for those who have strengthened our weak faith,
built up our trust in you,
and by their life have drawn us
into the life of Christ
who died in weakness and reigns in glory.

85   Holy God,
though this world depends on your grace,
it is governed and tended by mortals.

So we pray for those
who walk the corridors of power
in the parliaments of this and other lands,
whose judgements we value or fear.

Names may be said aloud.

May they always consider those they represent,
make decisions with courage and integrity,
and resist and temptation
to abuse the trust placed in them.

Lord hear us,
Lord graciously hear us.

We pray for those who hold the key positions
in the world's of finance, business and industry
whose decisions may profit some
or impoverish many.

Names may be said aloud.

May they always value people higher than profit;
may they never impose burdens on the poor
which they would not carry themselves;
and may they never divorce money from morality
or ownership from stewardship.

Lord hear us,
Lord graciously hear us.

We pray for those in the caring professions,
who look after and listen to
kind, cruel and cantankerous folk,
and for those who make decisions
regarding the nation's health and welfare.

Names may be said aloud.

May they always sense the sanctity of life
and every person's uniqueness;
may they help and heal
by their interest as well as their skill;
and may they be saved from tiredness
and an excess of demands.

Lord hear us,
Lord graciously hear us.

And let us remember
those for whom we are responsible
and to whom we are accountable
in what we do today.

Names may be said aloud.

May we show to them
the thoughtfulness, tolerance
and kindness of Jesus.

Lord hear us,
Lord graciously hear us.

Lord hear our prayers,
and if today we might be the means
by which you answer the prayers of others,
then may you find us
neither deaf nor defiant,
but keen to fulfil your purpose,
for Jesus' sake.

86   Father we thank you this morning that we are here in church at all.
        Someone first helped us to understand
            what the Christian faith was all about
        Someone first helped us to know your love.
        Someone first took the risk of sharing their own faith
            by what they did or said.
We thank you for that person, or those people,
through whom we first made contact with a living faith.
We thank you for them now, in the silence of our hearts.

Lord, in your mercy,
Hear our prayer.

Father, we know that the Church will die in this generation
unless people go on doing what was done for us —
sharing their faith in action or explanation.
We pray for those who have a special gift
for making the gospel relevant and attractive *[particularly ...]*.
We pray for those who have a special way of living
that draws others to Christ.
We pray for those who have a special opportunity for mission
coming up soon *[particularly ...]*.

Lord, in your mercy,
Hear our prayer.

Father, we acknowledge our own diffidence in sharing our faith —
the fear of embarrassment,
of seeming manipulative,
of losing the trust of friends.
Give us instead hearts full of love, and lives centred on Jesus Christ,
so that our words and actions are all of a piece and always Christian.
So may we find ourselves naturally talking of Christian things,
or talking of other things Christianly:
> in the way we respond to stories in the news;
> in the way we handle issues in the workplace;
> in the way we defend the weak;
> in the way we care for the wounded;
even in the way we answer the question 'What did you do on Sunday?'

Lord, in your mercy,
Hear our prayer.

Father, we pray that this week we shall not be ashamed of being Christians:
> that we shall not disown you or your standards;
> that we shall not ignore the honest question.
We pray that this week we shall be glad to know you as Lord:
> that we shall relax in the sheer normality of belonging to you;
> that we shall speak of you and act for you with courtesy and integrity.
Give us we pray the dignity that was in Christ Jesus
as he spoke of his Father's love.

Merciful Father,
**Accept these prayers
for the sake of your Son,
our Saviour Jesus Christ.
Amen.**

87   Let us come to God today with a concern for mission and social action, remembering that he is interested not simply in collecting Christians, but in renewing creation.

Lord, give to your Church we pray a profound concern for the well-being of the world you made.
Guide our church leaders into judgements that are just and compassionate. Give them words which are wise and incisive.
They have to speak for the Church at the moment about so many different issues *[such as ...]*.
May they have time to ponder, experts to give them good advice, and the insight which comes from you alone.

Lord, in your mercy,
Hear our prayer.

Lord, give to us also we pray, here in this church, a full and rounded gospel, so that we engage properly with our locality rather than seeming to shout at it.
Give us a concern for the well-being of our schools and teachers, for the quality of our community life and local councillors, for the treatment of our weak and marginalized members.
[And here we pray in particular for ... *issue in the community*.]

Lord, in your mercy,
Hear our prayer.

Lord, we know that it is so much easier to relate our faith to our interior life, and our home and church life. But your vision is so much bigger.
What use is a cosy church if society around us is in despair? Open our minds and hearts to confront the darkness with justice, and to embrace the broken with love.
Here in our imagination are many people:

     a black family who dare not leave the house at night:
         we pray for them ...
     a gay Christian whose inner conflict nearly drives him to despair:
         we pray for him ...
     a young woman whose childhood abuse
     has ruined her relationships with men:
         we pray for her ...
     an old lady who only got two cards at Christmas,
     still on her mantelpiece in June:
         we pray for her ...

Lord, we pray that you will give to the gospel we proclaim the radical edge that we see in the words and actions of Jesus, who came not to be served but to serve, and not to save his life but to give it up in the cause of the Kingdom.

Merciful Father,
**Accept these prayers
for the sake of your Son,
our Saviour Jesus Christ.**

88   Our minds are so often full of words, and what is worse our hearts are often clogged up with thoughts and ideas as well, which leaves little room for meeting God in simplicity and stillness. So this morning we are going to have space to pray ourselves, guided with leads and prompts.

So first, let us take a little time to notice how many good things surround us, how much there is that we take for granted, and how much our lives have been blessed this last week with good people and enjoyable experiences.

Silence

We pray now for some of those people and places in the new, things we will read in the Sunday papers when we get home, or maybe have seen on our TV screens during the week. We hold them now within God's love.

Silence

We turn now to pray for the Church, for any of the big issues facing it at present *[such as ...]*, and we pray for our own church, particularly with many opportunities and some problems before us *[for example ...]*. We ask for guidance and grace for the Church.

Silence

Between us all, we know many people who are struggling today with illness, crises, big decisions and major changes in life. God's care for them is even greater than ours, but let us show our own love and concern for them as we pray, naming our own people in quiet trust before God.

Silence

Each of us has things on our mind, perhaps things we hesitate to mention to anyone else. But our heavenly Father understands us totally, and wants only the very best outcome for us. Let us pray to him in the honesty of our own hearts.

Silence

These, Lord, are the prayers of your people this morning. We ask you to take each one of these prayers and answer them in your own time and in your own way. And in the meantime give us expectant and trustful hearts. For Jesus' sake.

SPECIFIC INTERCESSIONS

89   Almighty God,
your son had nowhere to lay his head.
Have compassion on those who are homeless
or who live in overcrowded conditions.
Give them strength and hope,
and keep them close to you.
Help us to work and pray
for the day when all your children
are housed and healthy
and free to live full and happy lives;
through Jesus Christ our Lord.

90   God our Father
in the name of him
who gave bread to the hungry,
we remember all
who through our human ignorance, folly, and sin
are condemned to live in want.
show us who have so much,
what we can do
to help those who have so little;
and bless the efforts of those
who work to overcome poverty and hunger,
that sufficient food may be found for all;
through Jesus Christ our Lord

91   God of grace and comfort,
hear our prayer for those who are unhappy,
who are lonely or neglected,
who are damaged or abused,
or whose life is darkened
by fear or pain or sorrow.
Give us grace to help them when we can.
Give them faith
to look beyond their troubles to you,
their heavenly father and unfailing friend,
that they may take up the threads of life again
and go on their way with fresh courage
and renewed hope;
through Jesus Christ our Lord.

PETITION

92   Eternal God,
conceiver and shaper,
ruler and saviour of the world,
we bless you that, awake and aware,
we are free to praise you.
Bound in the family of Christ
to worshippers in every land,
we worship you in our mother tongue
as others do in theirs.
Deepen our resolve and strengthen our hands
that we might be part of your pattern and purpose.

93   From the cowardice
that does not face new truths,
from the laziness
that is content with half truths,
from the arrogance
that thinks it knows all the truth:
deliver us today, good Lord.

94   Show us, good Lord
the peace we should seek,
the peace we must give,
the peace we can keep,
the peace we must forgo,
and the peace you have given in Jesus Christ our Lord.

95   O Lord,
go before us,
look favourably on us
and be our constant help.
In all our actions
begun,
continued,
and ended in you,
may we glorify your holy name,
until, by your mercy,
we enter at last
into the joy of your eternal light.

96   Almighty and merciful God,
you are more ready to hear than we to pray,
and you give more
than either we desire or deserve.
Pour down upon us
the abundance of your mercy.

Forgive those things
of which our conscience is afraid,
and give us those good things
which we are not worthy to ask,
save through the merits and mediation
of Jesus Christ, your Son, our Lord.

97   God of unfailing power,
you give vigour to the weary,
fresh hope to the exhausted.
We look to you to win new strength,
that we may soar as on eagles' wings,
run and not feel faint,
march on and not grow weary.
Keep us aglow with your Spirit,
that with unflagging zeal
we may serve the Lord.

DEDICATION AND COMMITMENT

98   This is my command:
be strong, be resolute;
do not be fearful or discouraged,
for wherever you go
the Lord your God is with you.

Joshua 1.9 REB

99   How can I repay the Lord
for all his benefits to me?
I shall lift up the cup of salvation
and call on the Lord by name.
I shall pay my vows to the Lord
in the presence of all his people.

Psalm 116.12—14 REB

100   Whoever wishes to become great among you
must be your servant,
and whoever wishes to be first among you
must be slave of all.

Mark 10.43f.

101   So we are to use our different gifts
in accordance with the grace that God has given us.
If our gift is to speak God's message,
we should do it according to the faith that we have;
if it is to serve, we should serve;
if it is to teach, we should teach.
Serve the Lord with a heart full of devotion.

Romans 12.6f., 11 GNB

102   Lord, make time our gift and not our captor.
Save us from the folly of yearning for past time
or counting upon future time,
but teach us true thankfulness for the present,
the gift of now, which you fill and gladden
and will use for your purpose.

103   For each new venture, give us new heart
for each new step, give us new strength
for each new problem, give us new wisdom
for all things new,
give us the word that is old, yet ever new.

104   Eternal God
        because of what you have done in Jesus Christ
        we know that in spite of all that is wrong in it,
        this world belongs to you.
        Help us, and all Christ's people,
        to live and speak the Good news of your love,
        so that all human life,
        can be an offering to you.
        We ask this in Jesus' name. **Amen.**

105   I am no longer my own but yours,
        your goodness helps my faith grow stronger,
        you give us all you have, and all you are.
        All that we have and are, you take and bless.
        And so, my God, I offer you my life
        I freely give all to you,
        for everything comes from you. **Amen.**

106   Christ has many services to be done;
        some are easy, some are difficult;
        some bring sorrow, others bring reproach;
        some are suited to our natural inclinations
        and materialist interests,
        others are contrary to both.
        In some we please Christ and please ourselves,
        in others we cannot please Christ
        except by denying ourselves.

        The power to do all things
        is given us in Christ who strengthens us.

107   Lord God, we thank you
        for calling us into the company
        of those who trust in Christ
        and seek to obey his will.
        May your Spirit guide and strengthen us
        in mission and service to the world;
        for we are strangers no longer,
        but pilgrims together on the way to your kingdom. **Amen.**

108   For each new venture give us new heart,
        for each new step give us new strength,
        for each new problem give us new wisdom,
        for all things new, give us the word that is old, yet ever new. **Amen.**

109　Lord Jesus,
　　　we thank you for loving us so much
　　　that you endured the cross.
　　　We thank you that amidst the pain and humiliation of Golgotha
　　　you forgave your persecutors and prayed for them.

　　　Fill us with such wonder at your suffering love,
　　　that we might long to be transformed by it.
　　　Woo us with your costly compassion,
　　　that we might become compassionate people
　　　open to others, and responsive to their need.
　　　For Christ's sake. Amen.

110　Almighty God,
　　　in whom we live and move and have our being,
　　　you have made us for yourself,
　　　so that our hearts are restless till they rest in you;
　　　grant us purity of heart and strength of purpose,
　　　that no selfish pattern may hinder us
　　　from knowing your will, nor any weakness from doing it;
　　　but that in your light we may see the light clearly,
　　　and in your service find perfect freedom:
　　　through Jesus Christ our Lord.

111　*Prayer of Dedication after Communion*

　　　In gratitude
　　　for this moment
　　　this meal
　　　these people,
　　　we give ourselves to you.

　　　Take us out
　　　to live as changed people
　　　because we have shared the living bread
　　　and cannot remain the same.
　　　Ask much of us,
　　　enable much by us,
　　　encourage many through us.

　　　So Lord, may we live to your glory,
　　　both as inhabitants of earth
　　　and citizens of the commonwealth of heaven.
　　　Amen.

OFFERING

112   In glad thanksgiving for your goodness,
we offer you our gifts,
and pray for the power
to offer and present our very selves to you,
a living sacrifice
dedicated and fit for your acceptance,
through Jesus Christ our Lord. **Amen.**

113   Lord God
we acknowledge that
you are our Father,
we are your children,
and our neighbours are our brothers and sisters in Christ.
To their service and to your glory,
we dedicate ourselves,
our hearts and minds,
our wills and our works.
Strengthen our resolve
to stand fast in your faith
to seek the help of your Holy Spirit,
and to work willingly for your perfect kingdom,
in the name of Jesus Christ our Lord. **Amen.**

114   Lord Jesus Christ, you were rich,
but for our sake you became poor,
so that through your poverty we might become rich.
Accept this gift as a sign of our gratitude for all you have done. **Amen.**

115   Everything in heaven and earth comes from you , Lord.
We give you only what is yours.
May you be praised for ever and ever. **Amen.**

116   Creator God,
all we have comes from you.
Now we bring these gifts
as a sign of all we have and all we are.
Accept this offering:
the life of this fellowship
and our witness to the Gospel;
our day to day living,
the things we pray for and the things we hope for;
accept all these things
bless them and weave them into your purposes,
through Jesus Christ our Lord. **Amen.**

RESPONSES

117   From where we are
to where you need us,
Christ be beside us.

From what we are
to what you can make of us,
Christ be before us.

From the mouthing of generalities
to making signs of your kingdom,
Christ be beneath us.

Through the streets of this world
to the gates of heaven,
Christ be above us.

Surround us with your presence,
inspire us with your purpose,
confirm us in your love.

118   From where we are
to where you need us,
Jesus, now lead on.

From the security of what we know
to the adventure of what you will reveal,
Jesus, now lead on.

To refashion the fabric of this world
until it resembles the shape of your kingdom,
Jesus, now lead on.

Because good things have been prepared
for those who love God,
Jesus, now lead on.

119   For all that God can do within us,
for all that God can do without us,
Thanks be to God.

For all in whom Christ lived before us,
for all in whom Christ lives beside us,
Thanks be to God.

For all the Spirit wants to bring us,
for where the Spirit wants to send us,
Thanks be to God.

Listen,
Christ has promised to be with us
in the world as in our worship.
Amen.
We go to serve him.

BLESSINGS

120 Go forth into the world in peace:
be of good courage;
hold fast that which is good;
render to no one evil for evil;
strengthen the faint-hearted;
support the weak;
help the afflicted;
honour all people;
love and serve the Lord
rejoicing in the power of the Holy Spirit.

121 To thy name, Lord Jesus, help me
to bow the knee
and all its worshipping
to bow the head
and all its thinking
to bow the will
and all its choosing
to bow the heart
and all its loving.

122 May God bless us
in our sleep with rest,
in our dreams with vision,
in our waking with a calm mind,
in our soul with the friendship of the Holy Spirit
this night and every night.

123 On our heads and our houses,
the blessing of God.

In our coming and going,
the peace of God.

In our life and believing,
the love of God.

At our end and new beginning,
**the arms of God to welcome us
and bring us home.**

124   Now may the Spirit of God,
who brooded over the waters
and brought order out of chaos,
find a home in our hearts
and settle our minds as we sleep
that tomorrow we may wake
and live to God's glory.

125   The grace of the Lord Jesus Christ
and the love of God
and the partnership of the Holy Spirit
be with all of you.

126   The blessing of God almighty,
the Father, the Son, and the Holy Spirit,
be among you, and remain with you always.

127   The blessing of God,
life-giver, pain-bearer, love-maker,
be with us all, now and always.

128   May you be strong to grasp, with all God's people,
what is the breadth and length and height and depth of the love of Christ,
and to know it, though it is beyond knowledge.
So may you attain to fullness of being,
the fullness of God himself.

Ephesians 3.18f.

DISCIPLES ON THE WAY: WORSHIP THROUGH THE YEAR

DISCIPLES ON THE WAY:
WORSHIP THROUGH THE YEAR

God's word should shape our worship and, whether or not a lectionary of readings is followed, there are certain times in the year when it is important to lead a congregation in worship relevant to the season. In this way we can journey through the story of salvation and God's redeeming way with humanity: from the advent hope, through God's coming to us in Jesus, with his birth and ministry, cross and resurrection, to the coming of the Holy Spirit and new life in Christ. Here we can be exposed to the full counsels of God, as God's story shapes our story.

What follows attempts to show both the variety of subject matter and the way in which themes may be explored. If the cycle of the year is not followed, then themes may still be used on appropriate occasions.

Each section includes brief suggestions on how the main theme might be developed through various kinds of prayers. The scripture references are offered as calls to worship of varying length, but they may be expanded to provide suitable readings, and in some cases are expanded here. Further readings may be found in a lectionary such as The Revised Common Lectionary which offers a three-year table of readings and has gained wide acceptance across Christian denominations.

The prayers themselves are not comprehensive but, as well as providing material for use in worship, they offer examples and starting points for exploration by those leading worship. The sections follow the classic pattern of the Christian year, but have been given thematic titles.

ADVENT 1: THE GOD WHO COMES

God comes to us in redemption and judgement. Themes of hope, yearning, preparation and confession.

Psalms 24.7–8; 96.11–13; Isaiah 40.3–5; 52.?–10; Luke 12.35–37a, 40; Romans 13.11–12, 14a.

PRAISE AND GREETING

129   Advent God, we worship you: the God who comes.
You are not remote from the world you have made,
but each day you come to us,
blessing us with your presence.

You came in creation itself,
as your Spirit moved over the waters of chaos.
You came in Jesus Christ,
made flesh in our world of weakness and need.
You came in power to raise him from death,
a mighty promise for all creation.
Each day you come, by your Spirit,
gently and powerfully working
in the lives of men and women.
At the end of time you will come,
in power and righteousness,
in mercy and redeeming love.

Grant us the grace to welcome your coming.
Inflame our love to yearn for your presence.
Enlarge our vision to recognize your coming day by day.
We greet you, Advent God.

ADORATION

130   Lord God,
we adore you
because you have come to us in the past:
you have spoken to us in the law of Israel
you have challenged us in the words of the prophets,
you have shown us in Jesus what you are really like.

Lord God,
we adore you
because you still come to us now:
you come to us through other people
        in their love and concern for us,
you come to us through those who need our help,
you come to us now, even as we worship you.

Lord God,
we adore you
because you will come to us at the end:
you will be with us at the hour of death,
you will reign supreme when all institutions fall,
you will still be our God when our history has run its course.

We welcome you, the God who comes.
Come to us now in the power of Jesus Christ our Lord.

PRAYER OF LONGING

131   Lord Jesus Christ
       your world awaits you.
       In the longing of the persecuted for justice;
       in the longing of the poor for prosperity;
       in the longing of the privileged
       for riches greater than wealth;
       in the longing of our hearts for a better life;
       and in the song of your Church,
       expectation is ever present.

       O come, Lord, desire behind our greatest needs.
       O come, Lord, Liberator of humanity.
       O come, Lord, O come, Immanuel.

COLLECT

132   O Lord our God,
       make us watchful and keep us faithful
       as we await the coming of your Son our Lord;
       that, when he shall appear,
       he may not find us sleeping in sin
       but active in his service
       and joyful in his praise;
       through Jesus Christ our Lord.

ADVENT 2: THE GOD WHO SPEAKS

God's revelation in the scripture. Thanksgiving for the Bible and confession for taking it for granted. Prayers for scholars, translators, preachers, and publishers.

Deuteronomy 6.4—7; 30.11—15; Psalms 119.97—98, 103—105; Isaiah 40.6—8; 55.6, 9—11; John 1.1—5; 2 Timothy 3.16—17; Hebrews 4.12—13.

INTERCESSION

133   God of revelation,
       we thank you that you are not a silent God,
       isolated from humanity,
       leaving us to guess and speculate
       about the things that matter.

       We pray for those who serve you
       by studying manuscripts and clarifying texts;
       for scholars and preachers
       who wrestle with the words of life
       for the building up of your Church;
       for linguists, translators, and publishers
       who continue to serve the cause of your gospel
       by making the Bible available to more
       and more people.

       Lord, create in us a hunger for your word,
       a thankfulness for your gospel,
       and a faithfulness to your commands;
       through Jesus Christ our Lord.

A PRAYER FOR HELP

134   God of eternity,
       when the voice of the prophet was silent
       and the faith of your people low;
       when darkness had obscured light
       and indifference displaced zeal:
       you saw that the time was right,
       and prepared to send your Son.
       Set us free from fear and faithlessness
       that we may be ready to welcome him
       who comes as Saviour and Lord.

ADVENT 3: THE FORERUNNER

John the Baptist as a servant of God's preparation and call. Thanksgiving for ministry and for those involved in ministerial formation. Prayers for those engaged in prophetic witness and its dangers.

Isaiah 6.8–9a; 40.35; 40.9; Jeremiah 1.4–10; Malachi 3.13; Matthew 3.1–3; 3.11; Romans 10.11–15; 1Corinthians 1.26–31.

INTERCESSION AND PETITION

135   God of love and truth,
        you call men and women to full-time service
        for the building up of your Church
        and the proclamation of your gospel.
        We pray for local churches and associations
        that they might be responsive to the leading of your Spirit,
        able to discern the gifts of ministry and the signs of your call.
        We pray for regional ministers and those who serve our Union
        as they lead and encourage the churches in ministry and mission,
        caring for the pastors, and encouraging the people.

        God of grace, you call us and you equip us for our calling.
        Open our ears to hear your call.
        Open our eyes to read your word
        and to see your world as Christ sees it.
        Open our hands to give what we have and what we are
        back to you for your service.
        Open our hearts to the wonder and the glory of your love,
        that we might all minister in the way of Christ;
        in whose name we pray.

PRAYER FOR RENEWAL

136   God of faithfulness and truth,
        you sent your servant John the Baptist
        to preach in the desert
        and summon the people to repentance.
        Make us and all things new,
        that in the wilderness of our hearts
        we too may prepare a way
        over which your Son may walk.

KINGDOM PRAYER

137   God our deliverer,
       whose approaching birth
       still shakes the foundations of our world:
       may we so wait for your coming
       with eagerness and hope
       that we embrace without terror
       the labour pangs of the new age,
       through Jesus Christ.

COLLECT

138   Living God,
       as we remember John the Baptist
       who by his integrity prepared the way for Jesus,
       and every other faithful witness
       who has stood by your truth
       whatever the cost,
       make us faithful
       to the truth we know,
       so that by our integrity
       we may prepare the way for Jesus
       into many lives,
       to the honour of your name.

ADVENT 4: MARY'S FAITH

Mary as a model of faith, as one who responds to God's call. Women and God's valuing of those regarded by the world as lowly.

Isaiah 7.14; 9.2–7; Zechariah 2.10–11; Matthew 1.21–23; Luke 1.28–33; 1.35, 38; 1.46–49; 1.52–53; 1 Corinthians 1.26–27.

THANKSGIVING AND DEDICATION

139   Life-giving God,
       we thank you for calling Mary
       to be the mother of Jesus.
       In a world where men were in control,
       you chose a young girl
       to nurture the Saviour of the world.
       In a world where power is sought,
       you turned our values upside-down
       by inviting Mary to share in the great work of redemption.

       We thank you
       that still you call women and men
       to share in your saving actions.
       You call us to live and serve in the way of Christ,
       uncertain of the future but trusting in your faithfulness.
       Sometimes your choice surprises us,
       the way you seem to point daunts us,
       and your faith in our possibilities awes us.

       Help us to say 'Yes' when you call.
       Enlarge our vision,
       strengthen our resolve
       and increase our sense of your all-sufficient grace,
       that we might be used mightily
       for your glory and for the serving of your world;
       through Jesus Christ our Lord.

INTERCESSION

140 Lord, prepare us for your Advent coming.
In our prayers today
we try to come to you,
sure that you will come the rest of the way.

Lord, prepare us for your coming – in the church.
Clean out the unnecessary clutter of our church life,
the piles of dead habits,
the cupboards full of prejudice,
the cobwebs of compromise
and the sad rotas of forgotten dreams.
Open our church to the free flow of your refreshing Spirit.
Give to this church a new vision and hope.
We want to belong to you again.
[In particular, Lord, we pray for ... *a special local plan or project*]

Lord in your mercy,
hear our prayer.

Lord, prepare us for your coming – in the world.
Come, drive away despair from our politics;
revive our dreams of justice;
restore our passion for what is good, right and true.
Establish your just and gentle rule [in places like ...]
where peace has been powerless
and violent people have had their day.
Set a flame to the fuse of justice [in places like ...]
where arrogant people have defied the moral order year after year.
Guard well the new springtime of hope [in ...]
where peace has come like a gift,
wrapped in reconciliation and gladness.
[In particular, Lord, we long for this ... *a particular world need*]

Lord in your mercy,
hear our prayer

Lord, prepare us for your coming – in our community.
In the problems of our locality
help us never to forget the supremacy of love.
May love motivate our care for this neighbourhood.
May love heal the social ills which drag us into despair.
May love inspire our citizenship to rise beyond mediocrity.
We name in our minds the problems locally of which we are aware
[particularly ... *local issue*]
and pray that love, gracious and practical, will find a way.

Lord in your mercy,
hear our prayer.

Lord prepare us for your coming – in those in need.
Give us eyes to search the face of the stranger
and there to see the face of the saviour.
Give us sensitivity to hear the doubt and hesitation,
and there, with that person, to share the confusion and futility.
There are those we know who are ill now,
struggling this *morning* to handle the pain.
Let us pray for them, for you come to us in them,
and you ask for our love.
We give that now, as we name them and love them, in our hearts.
What we have promised in love and prayer,
let us never forget to do.

Lord in your mercy,
hear our prayer.

Advent Lord, come ever nearer.
Come to rejuvenate our faith.
Come to fortify our social conscience.
Come to open wide our eyes of wonder.
So that when the Saviour comes,
he may steal into our heart – and find them ready.
Even so come, Lord Jesus.

BENEDICTION

141   Look forward in hope
to the coming of your Saviour,
prepare the way for Christ your Lord;
welcome him with love and faith
when he comes in glory.
And the blessing of God almighty,
the Father, the Son, and the Holy Spirit,
be among us and remain with us always.

CHRISTMAS: INCARNATION

The birth of Jesus as Immanuel, God with us. The wonder of the divine word made human flesh. Praise and thanksgiving for God alongside us in Christ and for the opportunities for proclamation which the season brings. Prayers for peace.

Isaiah 9.6f.; Luke 2.6f.; 2.10f.; John 1.10–14; 2 Corinthians 4.5f.; Hebrews 1.1f.; 1 John 1.1f.

FOR A CAROL SERVICE

142 Loving God,
  we come to hear again the familiar story
  and to sing the familiar songs.
  Break through our cosy celebration,
  that we might recognize your voice
  and heed your call.

CHRISTMAS EVE

143 God of light and hope,
  of stars and surprises:
  open our eyes to your glory
  and our hearts to your presence,
  that we may respond with joy to the angel song;
  through Jesus Christ our Lord.

INVOCATION

144   Immanuel, God with us,
show us where you may be found today:
in each human birth,
in family joy,
in relentless tragedy,
in treasured babes
and homeless families.

Immanuel,
we rejoice that you are with us
in everything,
through everything.
Lord Christ, be born in us today.
Word of God become flesh in us
that we might live your gospel.
Light of the world, shine
in us and through us
for the sake of your world.

Loving God,
help us to see your grace,
hear your voice,
and follow in your way;
through Jesus Christ our Saviour.

CHRISTMAS PRAYER

145   Living God,
may the worship we have shared this Christmas
lead to acts of service which transform people's lives;

may the carols we have sung this Christmas
help others to sing, even in their sadness;

may the gifts we have exchanged this Christmas
deepen our spirit of giving throughout the year;

may the candles we have lit this Christmas
remind us that you intend no one to live in darkness;

may the new people we have met this Christmas
remind us that we meet you in our neighbours;

may the gathering together of family and friends this Christmas
make us appreciate anew the gift of loved ones;

may the stories we have told again this Christmas
be good news of great joy to us and all people
on our lips and in our lives;

may the ways you have come close to us this Christmas
not be forgotten
but, hidden in our memories,
be a rich resource
to lift us when times are painful
and humble us when things go well,
for you are our life, our light and our salvation
this season and always,
because of Jesus Christ our Lord.

AN ENCIRCLING PRAYER

For those for whom Christmas is a difficult time of year.

146   God of the past, present and future
encircle in your love and care
those for whom we pray:

For the housebound:
keep warmth in heart and home
and cold and loneliness at bay.

For the homeless:
give shelter and hope,
and save from despair and addiction.

For those facing violence in the home:
affirm their worth and dignity,
protect from blows and shield from scorn.

For those missing a loved one:
may memories be precious,
not morbid nor morose.

God of the past, present and future
encircle in your love and care
those for whom we pray.

NEW YEAR: NEW BEGINNINGS

Prayers of praise and trust to the eternal God. Confession for the past and hope for the future. Prayers for the leaders of the nations. New beginnings.

Deuteronomy 8.11–14, 17f.; Joshua 1.9; Psalm 90.1–4; Isaiah 55.6–11; Luke 12.35–37; Philippians 3.13b–14.

THANKSGIVING AND TRUST

147   Lord of the ages,
        you are our beginning and our end.

        Everlasting God,
        we place our days within your care.
        We trust you and praise you
        for your faithfulness in the past,
        and for your constant care.
        We put ourselves into your keeping,
        to guard and guide us this day and every day;
        and we offer our lives for your service,
        through Jesus Christ,
        your eternal Son, our Saviour.

COLLECT

148   Lord of history,
        to whom a thousand years are as a day:
        renew us by your Holy Spirit,
        that, while we have life and breath,
        we may serve you with courage and hope;
        through the grace of your son,
        our Saviour Jesus Christ.

BLESSING

149   May the blessing of the God of Eternity,
        the God who calls time into being and marks its passing;
        the God who enters human history in Jesus;
        the God who gives the gift of his Spirit to all, for all time;
        be upon us this night
        empowering us to live our time in faithfulness to the gospel,
        now and always.

EPIPHANY: CHRIST FOR ALL THE NATIONS

The coming of wise men from the east is a sign that all the nations can find their hope in Jesus Christ and that all human wisdom finds fulfilment in the babe of Bethlehem. Pray for the mission of the church in proclaiming the gospel of Christ and for scholars and teachers, that their learning may be for good and not evil.

Psalm 27.1; Isaiah 9.2,6; 60.1–3; Matthew 2.10f.; John 8.12; 2 Corinthians 4.6; Psalms 67.1–3; 96.7–10a; Isaiah 6.8; Matthew 9.36–38; 28.18–20; Luke 10.8f.; John 10.16; Romans 10.13–15.

THANKSGIVING

150   Eternal God,
        creator of all, saviour of all, Lord of all,
        your love and power
        encompass all things and all people.
        There is no one
        beyond the reach of your redeeming love.

        We thank you that in all countries
        there are witnesses to your gospel,
        bearing testimony through their words and actions
        to the good news of Jesus Christ.

        We thank you for your Church in each place,
        for your Spirit equipping it with gifts
        and empowering your people to proclaim
        the good news of Jesus Christ.

        We thank you for Christian partnership
        across continents and national boundaries,
        for those who have responded to your call
        to serve the Church in a land that is not their own.
        Grant that we may be worthy of this great company of saints,
        ready to witness and serve in the name of Jesus Christ,
        the light of the world.

PETITION

151 Lord Jesus, shed your light in the darkness of our hearts.
Lord, have mercy,
Christ, have mercy.

Lord Jesus, open our ears to your saving love.
Lord, have mercy,
Christ, have mercy.

Lord Jesus, open our ears to hear your living word.
Lord, have mercy,
Christ, have mercy.

DEVOTION AND PRAISE

152 Star child,
wanted and welcomed by the humble,
hated and hounded by power-seekers;
refuge and refugee,
we love you!

Apple of God's eye,
cherished and chosen by Kingdom-travellers,
rejected and ridiculed by the earth-bound:
sacred and scarred,
we honour you!

Light of the world,
tended and treasured by the pure in heart,
shadowed and shunned by the deceitful:
peerless and pierced,
we exalt you!

PRAYER FOR HELP

153   Journeying God, who beckons us to join you on the road,
be with all your peoples as we set out into this new year.

Give courage to the cautious,
strength to the weary,
vision to the short-sighted,
hope to those who are broken in spirit.

When we are unsure of where you are leading
and cannot chart our path or progress,
give us trust and a toleration of not knowing.

When we are certain about the pattern of your mission,
give us humility – and the grace
to listen and learn from each new situation.

As the wise men brought gifts to the Christ-child,
so may we bring gifts to one another in the world:

GOLD
May we share material resources justly;
practise fair trade; respect the earth;
and exercise mutual deference.

FRANKINCENSE
May we promote freedom of thought, speech and worship;
find opportunities for all to grow in grace and stature;
take quietness with us wherever we go;
and exercise mutual encouragement.

MYRRH
May we stand in solidarity with the oppressed and suffering;
weep with those who weep; lament the atrocities of history;
bring balm for tomorrow
and exercise mutual love.

Journeying God, help us to follow you,
however risky it seems,
for in you lies our ultimate security, our greatest freedom.

FOR HELP AND HOPE

154 Beckoning God,
who called the rich to travel towards poverty,
the wise to embrace your folly,
the powerful to know their frailty;
who gave to strangers
a sense of home-coming in an alien land;
and to star-gazers
true light and vision as they bowed to earth;
we lay ourselves open to your signs for us.

Stir us with holy discontent over a world
which gives its gifts to those
who have plenty already,
whose talents are obvious,
whose power is recognized;
and help us
both to share our resources with those who have little
and to receive with humility the gifts they bring to us.

Rise with us like a star
and make us restless
till we journey forth
to seek our rest in you.

BAPTISM OF JESUS:
SOLIDARITY AND COMMISSIONING

The one who was without sin underwent the baptism of repentance: the baptism of Jesus by John is a sign of God's solidarity with sinners. It is a story of assurance and commissioning as Jesus is equipped by the Spirit for ministry. It is also a biblical scene in which Father, Son and Spirit all participate and which can lead to reflections on the Triune nature of the God of grace.

Matthew 3.1–17; Mark 1.1–11; Luke 3.15–22; Romans 11.33–36; 1 Corinthians 12.4–6, 12f.; Hebrews 4.14–16.

DEDICATION

155   Lord Jesus,
you did not need to repent,
but still you came to be baptized,
immersed in the Jordan
and showing us the way.
Help us to be penitent
and, by your grace, to walk the new path life.

Lord Jesus Christ,
you are the anointed one, God's messiah,
commissioned for service
and empowered by the Holy Spirit.
Fill us with your Spirit
that we might live to serve and praise you,
proclaiming your love
in word and deed.

Saviour Christ,
you call us through the waters of baptism
and promise that, as we are united with you in death,
so we shall be united with you in resurrection life.
Help us to keep saying 'yes' to your call,
that in trusting your faithfulness
we might live faithful lives.
In your name we ask it.

LIVING OUR BAPTISM

156   Almighty God,
who anointed Jesus at his baptism with the Holy Spirit
and revealed him as your beloved Son:
inspire us, your children,
who are born of water and the Spirit,
to surrender our lives to your service,
that we may rejoice to be called
the sons and daughters of God;
through Jesus Christ our Lord.

DISCIPLESHIP

157   Almighty God,
we give you thanks for your Son, Jesus Christ,
who was baptized in the river Jordan
and passed through
the deep waters of death.
We praise you that you raised him to life and exalted him.

Help us to follow in his way
as disciples and faithful servants of his gospel.
By your grace, help us,
that being united with him,
we may continually die to sin
and live to your praise an glory,
though Jesus Christ our Saviour.

THE WEEK OF PRAYER FOR CHRISTIAN UNITY
RECONCILIATION (SEE ALSO PENTECOST)

The God of unity and confession for divisions in the Church. Prayers for healing, and the increasing of love and understanding. Prayers for those people and organizations who are striving for unity and working for reconciliation. Commitment to shared mission.

Matthew 5.23—24; Mark 12.29—31; John 13.34—35; 17.20—21; 1 Corinthians 10.16—17; 12.12—13; 2 Corinthians 5.14—15, 17; 8.7—9; Galatians 3.26—28; Ephesians 2.13—16; 2.17—22; 4.1—3; Colossians 1.18—20; 1 John 4.7 —8, 19—21.

CONFESSION

158   Go-between God, bridge-builder, community-maker:

You call us, your Church,
to be a laboratory of peace:
accept our sorrow for the hostilities we harbour
and the walls we continue to build.

You call us, your Church,
to be a parable of your kingdom:
accept our sorrow for telling a very different story:
a story of attachment to worldly values.

You call us, your Church,
to be a sign of contradiction:
accept our sorrow for being content with the way things are
and fearful of speaking the prophetic word.

You call us, your Church,
to be a place of welcome and warmth:
accept our sorrow for sour faces, cold hands,
judgemental attitudes and lack of compassion.

You call us, your Church,
to be a community of praise:
accept our sorrow for allowing anxiety about human failures
to muzzle confidence in your power to transform the world.

INTERCESSION

159 God of peace,
   you have shown us that your will for the world
   is that all people should live in justice and peace.
   You have given us a vision of hope
   where all humanity lives
   in that wholeness of life
   for which we have been created.
   We pray for your world,
   torn apart by conflict and fear:
   nations divided one from another
   by suspicion, aggression, and greed,
   nations divided within themselves
   by injustice, oppression, and powerlessness.
   We pray especially for …

   You have called your Church to be a sign of hope
   in a world without hope,
   a healing community in a broken world,
   a people of peace in a world at war with itself.
   Forgive our failures of the past
   and create in us a vision of unity and hope, of love and sharing,
   that we might indeed be a light for the nations;
   through Jesus Christ our peace.

COMMITMENT

160 Lord God,
   we thank you
   for calling us into the company
   of those who trust in Christ
   and seek to obey his will.

   May your Spirit guide and strengthen us
   in mission and service to your world;
   for we are strangers no longer
   but pilgrims together
   on the way to your kingdom.

LENT: FOLLOWING JESUS

The period of Lent has traditionally been a period of self-examination, penitence and preparation for Holy Week and Easter. In many churches, worship will follow the story of Jesus and the approach to Jerusalem and offer a continuing engagement with the promise and challenge of discipleship. In prayer we can follow Jesus' story and pledge our commitment, seeing the church as a community of disciples.

Deuteronomy 30.19—20; Psalms 51.1—4; 51.10—11; 103.8, 10—12; Isaiah 1.18; 30.15; 55.6—7; Joel 2.13; Micah 6.6, 8; Matthew 16.24—26; Romans 5.6—8; Ephesians 6.18; Philippians 4.6—7, Colossians 1.24—27; Hebrews 10.19—22; 1 John 1.8—9.

CONFESSION

161   Lord, we remember the depth of your love for us,
and we repent of our half-hearted discipleship.

We have been called to deny ourselves:
forgive us for putting self-interest
before the interests of your kingdom;
forgive us that Christ's Lordship in our hearts
has been challenged by our ambition, our appetites,
our desires, and our needs;
forgive us for the times when self-interest
hindered our care for others.

Lord, we have been called to carry a cross:
forgive us for complaining when it has weighed heavily upon us;
forgive us that, having received so much,
we have sacrificed so little;
forgive us for the limits we have set to Christian love;
forgive us that we have settled for mediocrity,
resisting the fire and passion of Christ's love upon the cross.

DEVOTION

162   Lord Jesus Christ
you have walked where we walk
and now you help us in our weakness:
blessed be your name.

Lord Jesus Christ,
you have been tempted as we have
and now you come to help us in our danger:
blessed be your name.

Lord Jesus Christ,
you have suffered for us
and now you help us when we reach our wit's end:
blessed be your name.

Lord Jesus Christ,
you were deserted and betrayed,
and now you are with us when all others have gone:
blessed be your name.

Lord Jesus Christ,
companion Christ,
friend and saviour,
we adore you,
we love you,
we need you:
help us to follow.

INTERCESSION

163   Lord of Lent, come to your Church
and ask us your hard questions.
Are we faithfully proclaiming your gospel?
Are we demonstrating in our life together
the justice of your kingdom?
Have we welcomed the weak
and given prominence to the poor?

Come to your Church
to spring-clean our ways of life,
our structures and priorities.
Point out to us the cobwebs,
the dirt, the extravagance and the waste.
Create in us a clean heart, O God,
and renew a right spirit within us.

Lord of Lent,
renew our lives.

Lord of Lent, come to the nations and challenge our idolatries.
Spring-clean the sordid cupboard of this world's false gods.
Sweep out the false pride,
the self-seeking, the deceit, corruption and lies.
May the kingdoms of this earth
seek justice, peace and the integrity of creation.
May we look beyond immediate advantage
to seek the common good,
and be drawn to it, as a lark to the dawn.
Especially we ask for your cleansing hand in …

Lord of Lent,
renew our lives.

Lord of Lent, look with compassion
on those whose minds are full of anxiety and bewilderment.
We remember people who are lonely,
imprisoned, despairing and humiliated.
Clear away from them all unnecessary feelings
of fear, guilt and self-hatred.
Assure them that when you spring-clean our hearts and minds
you know what you are doing,
for you have been there, one of us,
and you are to be trusted.

Lord of Lent,
renew our lives.

For ourselves, Lord,
we pray that your spring-cleaning
would be thorough and true this Lent.
Show us clearly these effortless sins
we no longer even notice,
and help us to address the sins
which sit on our shoulders every day,
our constant companions.
Give us both discipline in dealing with some faults
and gentleness in dealing with others,
and help us to know the difference.
Create in us a clean heart, O God,
and renew a right spirit within us.

Lord of Lent,
renew our lives,
through Jesus Christ our Lord.

TEACH US TO PRAY

164   Lord, lead us into the wilderness
that we may meet you
in the flame that burns but does not destroy.
Help us to put aside our business and stress
and to rediscover silence.
Help us to shut out the clamouring voices
that are around us and inside us,
and listen only for your voice.

Lord, teach us to pray.
Through prayer,
lead us into a deeper communion with you
and nurture within us
a greater concern for your world.

In silence and prayer,
help us to find you
and to be found by you,
that we might be remade
in the likeness of Jesus Christ,
in whose name we pray.

MOTHERING SUNDAY: FAMILY LIFE

Prayers for families under stress and the supporting services. Thanksgiving for the love of God which comes through the love of those who care for us. See also Mary the mother of Jesus (Fourth Sunday in Advent).

Genesis 17.15—17; 1 Samuel 2.1—3; Luke 1.46—49; 2.6—7; 2.51—52; John 19.25—27.

PRAYER OF ST ANSELM

165   And you, Jesus, sweet Lord,
        are you not also a mother?
        Truly, you are a mother,
        the mother of all mothers,
        who tasted death
        in your desire to give life
        to your children.

FOR FAMILIES

166   God, father and mother of us all,
        we pray for families in their joy.
        Where parents are loving and children are lively;
        where home is comfortable and jobs are secure,
        we pray that our joy may be hallowed by thanksgiving
        and our happiness increased by sharing it.
        Amid the blessings you send,
        keep us mindful of you,
        the one who sends them.

        Son of God, Saviour of all, joy and sword for Mary's heart,
        we pray for families in their sorrow.
        Where grief has come for a loved one,
        or where love is no more;
        where jobs or home are lost or health has failed;
        where neighbours or relatives make trouble
        and children are wayward;
        where one or another is left coping
        with more than they bargained for,
        and nobody laughs, or sings.
        Lord Jesus, in our desert and our Gethsemane,
        give us your grace of strength and peace.

Holy Spirit of unity, wisdom and love,
we pray for families in their growing.
Reconcile us with change in one another,
and in ourselves.
Teach us that love need not be unaltering
in order to be constant.
Show us joy as a baby's trust
becomes an adolescent's questioning,
the beauty of strong hands grown waxen-veined in age.
Strengthen our relationships by contradiction and temper,
as well as by acquiescence and peace.
Creator Spirit, help us grow towards mature humanity
measured by nothing less than the full stature of Christ.

Father, Son and Holy Spirit,
providence, grace and love:
fit our families for the life of the heavenly household,
and for the service of humanity.
O Lord our God, make your way in our hearts
and be glorified
in the manner of our life together.

PRAYER FOR HELP

167   God of compassion,
       whose Son Jesus Christ, the child of Mary,
       shared the life of a home in Nazareth,
       and on the cross drew the whole human family to himself:
       strengthen us in our daily living
       that in joy and in sorrow
       we may know the power of your presence
       to bind together and to heal;
       through Jesus Christ our Lord,
       who is alive and reigns with you,
       in the unity of the Holy Spirit,
       one God, now and for ever.

PASSION SUNDAY: SUFFERING LOVE

The cross and the costliness of our redemption. Thanksgiving for the gospel and God's costly love. Our response in devotion and service.

Isaiah 53.2–4; 53.5–7; Luke 23.33–34; Hebrews 4.14–15; Revelation 5.12.

ADORATION

168   Lord Jesus,
your love is more than I can understand
but in that love I praise you.

Lord Jesus,
your love is more than I can ever know
but I rejoice that you know me and love me.

Lord Jesus Christ,
the costliness of your love takes my breath away
but in faltering love I give myself to you.

Lord Jesus Christ,
in love you have found me
by your cross you have saved me
and though your Spirit you have changed.
I love you and adore you.

CONFESSION

169   Lord Jesus Christ,
we confess we have failed you as did your disciples.
We ask for your mercy and help.

When we take our ease
rather than watch with you:
Lord, forgive us.
Christ, forgive us.

When we bestow a kiss of peace
yet nurse enmity in our hearts:
Lord, forgive us.
Christ, forgive us.

When we strike at those who hurt us
rather than stretch out our hands to bless:
Lord, forgive us.
Christ, forgive us.

When we deny that we know you
for fear of the world and its scorn:
Lord, forgive us.
Christ, forgive us.

CONFESSION

170 O Christ,
   on whose body was visited
   all the violence of the world,
   and in whose memory is contained
   our profoundest grief,

   we lay open to you:
   the violence done to us in time before memory;
   the unremembered wounds that have misshapen our lies;
   the injuries we cannot forget and have not forgiven.

   The remembrance of them is grievous to us:
   the burden of them is intolerable.

   We lay open to you:
   the violence done in our name in time before memory;
   the unremembered wounds we have inflicted;
   the injuries we cannot forget
   and for which we have not been forgiven.

   The remembrance of them is grievous to us:
   the burden of them is intolerable.

   We lay open to you:
   those who have pursued a violent knowledge
   the world cannot forget;
   those caught up in violence they have refused to name;
   those who have enacted violence which they have not repented.

   The remembrance of them is grievous to us:
   the burden of them is intolerable.

   We lay open to you:
   the victims of violence whose only memorial is our anger;
   those whose suffering was sustained on our behalf;

those whose continued oppression
provides the ground we stand on.

The remembrance of them is grievous to us:
the burden of them is intolerable.

Hear what comfortable words
our Saviour Christ says to all who truly turn to God:

Come to me all who labour and are heavy-laden,
and I will give you rest.
Take my yoke upon you, and learn of me,
for I am gentle and lowly in heart,
and you will find rest for your souls.
For my yoke is easy, and my burden is light.

We wholeheartedly repent
of the evil we have done,
and of the evil done on your behalf;
and we look for grace to offer forgiveness,
and to know ourselves forgiven.

THANKSGIVING AND DEDICATION

171   Lord Jesus,
we thank you for loving us so much
that you endured the cross for our salvation.
We thank you that amidst the pain and humiliation of Golgotha
you forgave your persecutors and prayed for them.

Fill us with such wonder at your suffering love,
that we might long to be transformed by it.
Woo us with your costly compassion,
that we might become compassionate people,
open to others in their need.

Living Lord,
we celebrate your resurrection:
for the way of your cross
is shown to be the way of our salvation,
your love and forgiveness are displayed
as the keys of our redemption,
and your sacrificial love is offered
as the foundation of our hope.
Lord Jesus, help us to follow.

PALM SUNDAY: GREETING JESUS ON THE WAY

The servant Messiah. Prayers of greeting. Confession that our hosannas turn to 'crucify'. Commitment to following Jesus and anticipation of the events of Holy Week.

Isaiah 50.4–9; Zechariah 9.9; Luke 19.37–38; 1 Corinthians 1.20b–21; Philippians 2.5–11.

INVITATION

172   Lord, with joy we greet your coming today:
we lay before you our love and faith,
rejoicing that you came in peace to be our king.

Come, Lord, and teach us the ways of peace
that we may know the strength of love
and the power of forgiveness.

Come, Lord, and teach us humble ways
that we may be free of arrogance
and without pretence.

Let our songs fill this place with hosannas,
for now the day of our redemption draws near:
Blessed is he who come in the name of the Lord,
to whose kingdom there is not end.

DEDICATION

173   Lord Jesus, we greet your coming,
pilgrim messiah, servant king, rejected saviour.

You trod the way of a pilgrim
and ascended the hill of the Lord;
you followed the path of your calling
even though Mount Zion gave way to the hill of Calvary.
Lord Jesus,
help us to follow.

You rode into Jerusalem on a donkey,
symbol of humility and lowliness,
mocking our dream of pomp and glory,
demonstrating the foolishness of God before the eyes of the world.
You have shown us the way of humble service,
the way of true greatness.
Lord Jesus,
help us to follow.

The cries of 'Hosanna' soon turned to 'Crucify'.
The acclamation of the crowds gave way to fear and contempt.
You have shown us the cost of love
and you have called us to follow in your way:
pilgrims of the kingdom,
living out the foolishness of God,
and trusting only in your forgiving faithfulness.
Lord Jesus,
help us to follow.

COLLECT

174   Living God,
your light has risen over us
in the person of Jesus Christ,
who was greeted as king
and crucified as slave
because he came in your name;
help us, who continue to greet his coming,
to welcome him into our lives with humility,
so that we may not desert him,
betray him, or turn against him,
but may follow him faithfully to the end,
serving each other and all our neighbours,
for his name's sake.

GOOD FRIDAY: THE CROSS

Confession for our sin and the sins of the world. Quiet reflection and wonder at God's love, the work of redemption and the appeal of the crucified saviour.

Psalms 22.1–4; 40.4–5, 10f.; 42.8–11; 43.5; Isaiah 42.1–4; Romans 5.6–8; 6.5–11; 1 Corinthians 1.22–25; 2 Corinthians 5.14–17; Galatians 6.14–16; Revelation 5.12–13.

APPROACH AND ADORATION

175   Loving God,
       today, in remembrance and awe,
       we tread the holy ground of Calvary:
       this place of abandonment
       that has become the scene of our adoration,
       this place of suffering
       that has become the source of our peace,
       this place of violence
       that has become the battlefield
       on which love is victorious.

       Merciful God,
       as we relive the events of this day,
       it is with awe
       that we count again the cost of our salvation.
       Words cannot be found to utter our thanksgiving.
       Accept our adoration;
       in Jesus' name.

LAMENT BEFORE THE CROSS

176   Lord, we want to come back.
You have torn,
but we know you will heal;
you have struck down,
but we know you will bind us up.
Bring us out of the prison,
so that we shall praise you again.

We feel as though you have deserted us,
but we know we have deserted you:
Do not leave us here, O Lord.
Do not let this be the end.

Loving God,
even now, even here, your love is real,
your mercy is sure.
Have mercy on us,
and forgive us all our sins.

Silence

For Christ also suffered for sins once for all,
the righteous for the unrighteous,
in order to bring you to God.
He was put to death in the flesh, but made alive in the spirit,
in which also he went and made
a proclamation to the spirits in prison.

1 Peter 3.18—19

EASTER DAY: RESURRECTION

Easter day is a celebration of victory, a rejoicing at the wonder, power, and surprise of the resurrection. Prayers of adoration and thanksgiving.

1 Samuel 2.6—8a; Psalms 16.9—11; 30.10—12; 73.23—28; 118.22—24; Hosea 6.1—3; Matthew 12.39—40; 28.5—7; 28.8—10; Mark 16.6—7; Luke 24.5—9; 24.36, 45—47; John 20.19—20; Acts 2.22—24; 1 Corinthians 15.3—4.

TRADITIONAL SENTENCES

177   Christ is risen!
Alleluia!

The Lord is risen!
He is risen indeed!

It is fitting that the heavens should rejoice:
and that the earth should be glad,
and that the whole world, both visible and invisible,
should keep the feast.
For Christ is risen, the everlasting joy.
Now all things are filled with light,
heaven, and earth, and all places under the earth.
All creation celebrates the resurrection of Christ.

It is the day of resurrection,
Let us be glorious in splendour for the celebration,
and let us embrace one another.
Let us speak also, brothers and sisters,
to those that hate us,
and in the resurrection let us forgive all things.
So let us cry:
Christ has risen from the dead,
by death trampling on death,
and has bestowed life to those who were dead.

ADORATION

178   Living God,
we worship you today with joy in our hearts
and thanksgiving on our lips.
When the powers of evil had done their worst,
crucifying your son, and burying him in death,
you raised him to life again:
an act of power giving hope to the world.

Lord Jesus,
we rejoice that death could not keep you in its grip;
that you were raised to life, alive for evermore.
You greeted your friends
and now you stand amongst us in your risen power.

Spirit of God,
you are always giving life to the people of God,
giving birth to children of God.
Remodel us in the image of Jesus,
fill us with his love
and enable us with his risen power,
that we might be faithful to his way,
used by you in the redeeming of your world.

PETITION

179   When we are despairing;
when the world is full of grief;
when we see no way ahead,
and hope has gone away:
Roll back the stone.

Although we fear change;
although we are not ready;
although we'd rather weep
and run away:
Roll back the stone.

Because we're coming with the women;
because we hope where hope is vain:
because you call us from the grave
and show the way:
Roll back the stone.

EASTER PRAYER WITH CHILDREN

180   Dear Father,
this is the best day of the year —
the best day of all time.
For on Easter Day we find that Jesus, who was dead,
is alive again:
and we see his promise that those who put their trust in him
will not be swept away by death,
but shall have eternal life.

O this day of light and gladness,
help us to put darkness out of our lives.

Make us willing and able to change our ways
of thinking and speaking and doing
into Easter ways:
so that how we behave
may bear out what we believe,
and so that Christ's new creation
may become in us not just a hope but a fact;
through Jesus Christ our Lord.

EASTER: ETERNAL LIFE

The weeks following Easter Day provide opportunity for the themes of life and death, hope and joy to be explored. This may lead to prayers of praise, a confidence in God's love and a commitment to life-enhancing, rather than life-denying, actions.

Luke 24.29—32; John 11.25—26; 20.27—29; 21.15—17; Romans 6.3—4; 1 Corinthians 15.19—20; 15.54—58; 2 Corinthians 4.16—18; Philippians 3.8—11; Colossians 2.6—7, 12; Revelation 21.3—6.

CONFESSION

181   God of life,
        forgive our denial of life,
        our destruction of its hopes,
        our denial of its needs,
        our distorting of its possibilities.

        Fill us with your Spirit of life,
        that we might be people of life,
        servants of life, encouragers of life,
        signs of Christ, the life of the world;
        in his name we pray.

THE BREAKING OF BREAD

182   Risen Christ,
        you walked with friends
        and explained the scriptures.
        Warm our hearts
        with your living word.

        Lord Jesus Christ,
        be known to us in the breaking of bread.

        Risen Christ,
        you were a guest in the home of disciples,
        In this fellowship, be our guest,
        and transform our life together
        with you living presence.

        Lord Jesus Christ,
        be known to us in the breaking of bread.

You blessed bread and broke it,
recognised by those who knew you.
Feed us with your living bread
that we might live as witnesses to your risen life.

Lord Jesus Christ,
be known to us in the breaking of bread.

THE WAY, THE TRUTH AND THE LIFE

183   God, so near and far,
journey's beginning, journey's end:
our way to you is Jesus Christ.
He is the truth
which guarantees our integrity;
he is the life,
calling us through death to resurrection.
Help us, then, through him,
to trust you
and, with quiet minds,
to take the way,
proclaim the truth
and live your life
for the sake of all the world.

LIVING RESURRECTION LIFE

184   Almighty God,
through the raising of your Son from the grave,
you broke the power of death
and condemned death itself to die.
As we celebrate this great triumph
may we also make it a model for our living.

Help us to identify in our lives
all that should rightly die –
redundant relationships,
tired habits,
fruitless longings.
Resurrect in our lives faith, hope and love,
as surely as you raised Jesus Christ
from the grave.

ASCENSION: THE EXALTATION OF CHRIST

Praise for the enthronement of Christ and the uplifting of humanity into the life of the triune God. Prayers of dedication in following Christ the pioneer of our faith. The hope of glory.

Psalms 24.7, 10; 47.5—7; Matthew 28.18—20; Luke 24.50—51; Acts 1.11; Ephesians 1.7—10; Philippians 2.7b—11; Colossians 1.18—20; Hebrews 4.14—16; 12.1f.

CONFESSION

185   Forgive us, Lord,
       when we are rooted to the earth,
       unable to see beyond the present,
       blind to the glory of your presence.
       We become engrossed in what is happening now
       and forget all that you yet have in store for us.

       We are so concerned with what is
       immediate, temporary, and short-lived
       that we leave ourselves no time
       for the things that are eternal and full of your love.

       Lift up our heads,
       that we may see Christ in all his glory
       and all things in their true perspective.
       We ask this with the forgiveness of our sins,
       in your name.

PETITION

186   When we stand gazing upwards,
       bring us down to earth:
       with the love of a friend,
       through the songs of the sorrowing,
       in the faces of the hungry.

       When we look to you for action,
       demand some work from us:
       by your touch of fire,
       your glance of reproof,
       your fearful longing.

As ruler over all,
love us into action,
fire us with your zeal,
enrich us with your grace,
to make us willing subjects of your rule.

THANKSGIVING

187 Risen and ascended Lord,
we would have lingered on Transfiguration Mount,
clung to you in the Easter garden,
been saddened by your Emmaus departure,
and begged the Ascension skies never to close.
But you have taught us deeper truth:
you are not absent,
even in departure.

We give thanks
that mountain-top resources
lie waiting in the valley,
that you are as near in the busy streets
as in the quiet garden,
that you are the guest at every meal,
and heaven has come down to earth,
as one day earth may be as heaven.

Risen and ascended Lord,
travel with us.

MISSION

188 Almighty and everlasting God
you raised our Lord Jesus Christ
to your right hand on high.
As we rejoice in his exaltation,
fill us with his Spirit,
that we may go into all the world
and faithfully proclaim the gospel.
This we ask through Jesus Christ our Lord,
who is alive and reigns with you,
in the unity of the Holy Spirit,
one God, for ever and ever.

PENTECOST: THE GIFT OF THE SPIRIT

The gift of the Holy Spirit and the birth of the Church. The Spirit empowering the people of God for mission, unifying people across barriers of race, gender and class. The gifts of prophecy. Prayers of praise and thanksgiving, as well as confession for our lack of anticipation in what God can do. Prayers for the Church, its fellowship and its mission.

Genesis 1.1–2; Isaiah 11.1f.; 32.15f.; 61.1–3; Ezekiel 37.9f.; Joel 2.28; Mark 1.9–13; John 4.23–24; 14.15–17; 16.13–14; Acts 2.1–4; 1 Corinthians 12.4 –7; 14.12; Ephesians 6.18; 1 Peter 2.9.

INVOCATION

189   Come, Holy Spirit:
breath into our prayers
your breath of life.

Come, Holy Spirit:
fan the flame of love within us,
and draw us into the life of God:
Father, Son and Spirit.

Come Holy Spirit:
renew us and revive us,
that in our worship
and in our living,
we may live a life of love
for the praise and glory of God.

CONFESSION

190   Spirit of God,
you are the breath of creation,
the wind of change that blows through our lives,
opening us up to new dreams, and new hopes,
new life in Jesus Christ.
Forgive us our closed minds
which barricade themselves against new ideas,
preferring the past
to what you might want to do through us tomorrow.
Forgive us our closed eyes
which fail to see the needs of your world,
blind to opportunities of service and love.

Forgive us our closed hands
which clutch our gifts and our wealth
for our own use alone.
Forgive us our closed hearts
which limit our affections to ourselves and our own.

Spirit of new life, forgive us
and break down the prison walls of our selfishness,
that we might be open to your love
and open for the service of your world;
through Jesus Christ our Lord.

INTERCESSION

191 Missionary God,
the followers of Jesus waited behind locked doors,
yet your Spirit came to them in power,
changing them from a bewildered band
into a proclaiming people.
We pray for ourselves and for your whole Church,
that we might be
open to the empowering presence of your Spirit,
open to the gracious gifting of your Spirit,
and open to the adventurous leading of your Spirit.

Holy Spirit,
as you filled those first Christians
with an enthusiasm for the gospel of Christ,
so enthuse us,
that we may go out into the streets and market places of our world,
preaching the good news of Jesus Christ.

Holy Spirit,
all who heard the apostles' preaching
understood in their own language.
Fill us with a vision of the whole earth
filled with your glory.
Send us out to all people of every race and colour,
rich and poor, powerful and oppressed,
that we may be messengers of the gospel
and servants of your kingdom.

Holy Spirit,
that first Christian community
began a life of sharing in worship and in living.
Fill us with a generous spirit,
ready to share what we are and what we have with others.

Break down our pride
that we might have the grace to receive from the riches of others.

Holy Spirit, God with us,
fill your people with power and love,
vision and purpose,
that we might be agents of your gospel
for the whole world; through Jesus Christ our Lord.

INVOCATION

192   Holy Spirit of God,
who brooded over the waters long before we were born,
who inspired the people of God to praise and trust,
who lit the fire of the prophets
and sustained their faith among unbelief;
who took possession of our brother Jesus
so that he became transparent with your promise
and reliable in all his dealings.

Holy Spirit of God,
fill us with confidence
and make us available for your work.
Teach us to pray
and to hear the moanings of those in distress;
help us interpret the signs of the times
and prepare us for the kingdom of God,
each day and for ever.

PETITION

193   Loving God,
open our hearts
so that we may feel the breath and play of your Spirit.
Unclench our hands
so that we may reach out to one another,
and touch and be healed.
Open our lips
that we may drink in the delight and wonder of life.
Unstop our ears
to hear your agony in our inhumanity.
Open our eyes,
so that we may see Christ in friend and stranger.
Breathe your Spirit into us,
and touch our lives with the life of Christ.

TRINITY SUNDAY: THE RICHES OF GOD

The wonder and mystery of God. Life in the Spirit as participating in the fellowship in God. Prayers of praise, wonder and offering. Prayers for unity and the healing of divisions.

Matthew 28.19; John 14.17—11; 14.26—27; 16.12—15; 17.1—5; Romans 1.2—4; 2 Corinthians 13.14; Ephesians 4.4—6; 1 Peter 1.1a, 2; Jude 20b—21.

ADORATION

194   Living Love,
        beginning and end,
        giver of food and drink,
        clothing and warmth,
        love and hope:
        life in all its goodness —
        we praise and adore you.

        Jesus, Wisdom and Word;
        lover of outcasts,
        friend of the poor;
        one of us, yet one with God;
        crucified and risen:
        life in the midst of death —
        we praise and adore you.

        Holy Spirit, storm and breath of love;
        bridge-builder, eye-opener,
        unseen and unexpected,
        untameable energy of life —
        we praise and adore you.

        Holy Trinity, forever one,
        whose nature is community;
        source of all sharing,
        in whom we love, and meet, and know our neighbour:
        life in all its fullness, making all things new —
        we praise and adore you.

BLESSING

195   Holy, holy, holy – let angels cry
who see and know you face to face.

Blessed are you, Maker of all from nothing.
Blessed are you, Saviour of all from sin.
Blessed are you, Spirit of all,
in all, and through all.
Blessed are you,
God alone, yet God in community.

Bless, O God, your Church on earth
with the harmony and diversity of heaven,
that we may be one, as you are one.

PETITION

196   Holy God,
faithful and unchanging:
enlarge our minds with the knowledge of your truth,
and draw us more deeply into the mystery of your love,
that we may truly worship you,
Father, Son and Holy Spirit,
one God, now and for ever.

FOR UNITY AND PEACE

197   Lord Jesus Christ,
      you said that you were one with the Father
      and you gave your Spirit to the disciples,
      offering them your peace;
      we pray for the unity of your Church
      and the peace of your world.

      Lord God, forgive us the fears and suspicions,
      the half truths and ignorance which reinforce our divisions.
      We pray that your Spirit of truth will open our minds
      so that we might learn from one another.
      We pray that your Spirit of love will fill our hearts
      that we might forgive and encourage one another.
      We pray that your Spirit of unity will work in our lives,
      binding us together in you,
      our only God, Father, Son, and Holy Spirit.
      We pray for your world, broken into hostile camps by fear,
      hatred, suspicion, greed, and the pursuit of power.

      We pray for all those who are working for peace,
      the reconciling of conflicts, and the healing of divisions.
      We pray for those who are caring for the casualties of conflict,
      used by your love in caring for the downtrodden and oppressed.
      We pray for those who are leaders in communities,
      that they might lead with wisdom and in a spirit of service.
      We pray that the search for unity in your Church
      might serve the search for unity in our divided world,
      for there is one God and Father of all,
      who is over all, and through all, and in all.

PRAISE AND INTERCESSION

198   Ever One, Sacred Three,
      Holy God, the Trinity.

      God beyond us, lead us forward to pray.
      God beside us, teach us gently to pray.
      God within us, still our hearts to pray … *pause.*

      Holy God beyond us,
      you create and sustain all things,
      but only by the power of self-giving love.
      We celebrate your creativity,
      the risk and imagination you demonstrated
      in making such wild diversity in the world:

rhinoceros and dragonfly,
the mountain range and spider's web,
earthworm and human brain.
There is mystery and joy at the heart of creation.
Holy God beyond us,
we celebrate the mystery and the joy
which is found even in us ... *pause*.

Son of God beside us,
you never leave us comfortless.
Always you walk with us,
neither too far ahead nor a step behind.
And you teach us the love songs of the kingdom.
Bless, we pray, those who have not noticed
that you are there beside them,
or who have chosen to ignore you.
Bless those who are dying of loneliness
and those who need you so desperately.
In the quiet,
we name such people before you,
and pray that they will raise their eyes to see you,
Son of God beside us ... *pause*.

Holy Spirit within us,
always you are seeking to infiltrate our lives
with peace and strength;
always you are trying to give us more of yourself.
And yet we often feel empty and afraid,
and so does the community of nations.
Fill, we pray, all those dark, dank places of this world
with your warm life:
... where violence terrorizes people;
... where hunger stalks the land.
And where there are people we know
in whom hope is running low,
be for them a summer breeze
and a spring of fresh water.
Holy Spirit within us ... *pause*.

God beyond us, give us faith.
Christ beside us, give us peace.
Spirit within us, give us life.

Ever One, Sacred Three,
Holy God, the Trinity.

HARVEST: THE GENEROSITY OF GOD

A celebration of creation. Confession for the misuse of the planet and the unjust distribution of wealth. Prayers for those who grow food and produce wealth. Thanksgiving and commitment to good stewardship.

Genesis 1.11f.; 1.26—31; 8.22; Deuteronomy 8.11—15, 17f.; 16.16b—17; Psalms 24.1; 65.9—13; 104.24, 27 f.; 107.8f.; 145.14—16; Hosea 6.1—3; Joel 2.23—24; Amos 5.10—15; Micah 6.8; 6.9—12; Mark 4.26—29; Luke 12.15; 2 Corinthians 8.1f., 8f.; 9.6—9.

PRAISE AND CONFESSION

199   God of creation,
we praise you.
Once there was nothing,
but now the world teems with life
and the cup of your provision overflows.
Once there was dark emptiness
but now there is sound and colour,
majestic mountains and intricate petals.
Beasts and birds gain their food from you,
and all humankind depends
on the fruitfulness of the earth you have made.
We praise you, faithful provider,
generous and gracious God.

You have made more than enough
and your love and care are prodigal;
but now we confess
that we have been blind to the beauty,
selfish in our stewardship
and arrogant in our taking and using of what is not ours.
Our hands have been closed
when they should have be open in sharing,
our hearts have been cold
when they should have been warm with your love,
and all we have created is chaos and distress.
Forgive us, that our brothers and sisters are hungry;
forgive us, that we have exploited your world
when we should have cared for it.
Send your Spirit to move over amongst us
to make a new creation in Jesus Christ,
in whose name we pray.

COLLECT

200 God of faithfulness,
　　your generous love supplies us
　　with the fruits of the earth in their seasons.
　　Give us grace to be thankful for your gifts,
　　to use them wisely,
　　and to share our plenty with others;
　　through Jesus Christ our Lord.

THANKSGIVING AND DEDICATION

201 Creator God,
　　We thank you today
　　for the splendour and beauty of creation;
　　for the ordered succession of seasons;
　　for your love which made the world.
　　We thank you for the good and fertile earth;
　　for the fruits of the earth in their seasons;
　　for the life that sustains our life;
　　for the food that we daily enjoy.
　　We thank you for those whose labour supplies our physical needs;
　　for those who harvest our crops, those who transport them,
　　those who process them, those who sell them.

　　Loving God,
　　we thank you for the gift of yourself
　　in Jesus, our Saviour and Lord;
　　for his living, dying, and rising again
　　in your loving redemption of the world.

　　Life-giving God,
　　we thank you for your Holy Spirit, the giver of life;
　　for the Church, a foretaste of your new creation,
　　and for our privilege in being part of it.

　　Redeeming God,
　　we thank you for your mighty acts
　　in creating and saving your world.
　　We offer ourselves to you in gratitude,
　　that we may serve you
　　and our fellow men and women
　　joyfully and faithfully throughout our lives;
　　in the name of Jesus Christ our Lord.

INTERCESSION

202   Loving Lord, we pray for those who have no harvest to celebrate,
no crops to gather, or labour to pursue.
We pray for those who live on land that is hard to farm,
scratching out a living in a hostile soil,
amidst rocky ground and scorching earth.
We pray for those who scratch no living from the earth,
where the whole world seems to squeeze the life from their bodies.
We pray for those who have left their homes,
driven by war or want,
to become refugees, aliens dependent on others.
We pray for those without work:
women and men made redundant by changing needs,
children living off their wits in the streets of sprawling cities.
We pray for those with no energy for praise,
whose bread is bitterness and whose water is tears.

We confess our part in the sin of the world
and pray that you might grant us a vision of justice as well as charity
and strengthen our readiness to change as well as to help;
through Jesus Christ our Lord.

OFFERTORY PRAYER

203   Generous God,
we know that all we have is yours:
save us from the delusion
of believing it is ours;
save us from our possessiveness,
that your grace may abound
in all things at all times;
through Jesus Christ our Saviour.

ONE WORLD WEEK: COMMON HUMANITY

All the earth is the Lord's and all people are his children. The unity of humanity within the purposes of God. Thanksgiving for the variety of cultures and traditions. Prayers for the World Council of Churches, for aid agencies, for peace, reconciliation, and the healing of the nations.

Genesis 1.26–28; 2.7 f.; 9.12–16; Exodus 3.7–8a, 10; Psalms 24.1f.; 100; Isaiah 60.1–3; Micah 4.1–4; Matthew 25.37–40; Luke 4.18f.; John 12.31f.; Acts 10.34–36; Galatians 3.14; Ephesians 3.14–19; 1 John 4.19–21.

GATHERING PRAYER

204   All-embracing God,
      you love all people as your children.
      Here we are:
      different people from different homes and different backgrounds
      but united in faith.
      Join us with our brothers and sisters around the world
      in worship to the glory of your name.

INTERCESSION

205   God of hope,
      you have given the rainbow as a symbol of your faithfulness:
      in its colours, you have shown us the variety of human life
      and your call to unity;
      its span between heaven and earth reminds us
      that our hopes for the future are founded on your grace;
      that you have turned your face from judgement to redemption
      and have called us to be peacemakers;

      We pray for people whose humanity is denied by others;
      for those persecuted or imprisoned
      because of their religion or their politics;
      for those who try to oppress and manipulate others
      and in so doing lose sight of their own humanity;
      for those who work for peace and justice, whatever the cost.

      Lord God,
      make us your rainbow people,
      glorying in our God-given variety,
      passionate for peace, trusting in your grace;
      in the name of Jesus Christ, the hope of the world.

BLESSING

206   Deep peace of the running wave to you;
    deep peace of the flowing air to you;
    deep peace of the quiet earth to you;
    deep peace of the shining stars to you;
    deep peace of the Son of Peace to you.

REMEMBRANCE: THE HEALING OF THE NATIONS

Remembrance of those who have served and died in war. Prayers for peace and for those who work for peace, for the victims of war: civilians, refugees, and all brutalized by violence.

Deuteronomy 7.9; 2 Samuel 1.21, 27; Psalms 46.1—3; 46.10f.; 67.1f.; 90.1—4, 12—14; Isaiah 25.4—5; 25.6—8; John 12.24; 12.31—32; Romans 8.38—39; Hebrews 12.1f.; Revelation 7.9—12.

PRAISE

207   Gracious God,
        we heard you even in the sea of disorder
        and the darkness of the void,
        crying, 'Light and life become!
        and all creation was begun.
        We gather to praise.

        Redeeming God,
        we heard you even in the sins of destruction
        and the night-time of sadness,
        crying, 'Enough! Here is my Son:
        love and hope for the future!'
        We gather to praise.

        Inspiring God,
        we heard you even in the silence of sorrow
        and the anguish of pain,
        crying, 'If God be for us,
        who can be against us!'
        We gather to praise.

SENTENCES

208 The righteous though they die early, will be at rest.
For old age is not honoured for length of time,
or measured by number of years;
but understanding is grey hair for anyone,
and a blameless life is ripe old age.

The righteous live for ever
and their reward is with the Lord;
the Most High takes care of them.
Therefore they will receive a glorious crown
and a beautiful diadem from the hand of the Lord,
because with his right hand he will cover them,
and with his arm he will shield them.

Wisdom 4.7–9, 5.15f.

COMMEMORATION

209 Friends, let us remember in silence before God,
all those who have died in war.

The two minutes' silence.

They shall grow not old, as we that are left grow old.
Age shall not weary them, nor the years condemn.
At the going down of the sun and in the morning
we will remember them.
We will remember them.

INTERCESSION

210 Father of mercies and God of all comfort,
we pray this day for all those
who continue to suffer because of war:
widows, orphans, and all who are bereaved;
the wounded, crippled, deaf, dumb, and blinded;
the shell-shocked and the traumatized;
refugees without home, work, or country.
Grant to them all your healing and strength,
your help and consolation,
and use us in this service, we pray;
for Jesus Christ's sake.

FOR PEACE

211   God of hosts,
        yours is the battle against evil,
        yours is the victory over death.
        We come to you
        with memories of war and death,
        with scars of victory and defeat.
        By your Son Jesus,
        who bears the scars of his victory
        won not for himself but for others,
        grant us this day healing for the past,
        and resolution for the future.
        So may your world discover and know that peace
        which is your purpose for us all;
        through Jesus Christ our Lord.

COLLECT

212   Almighty Father,
        you call your children
        to live as brothers and sisters in love and harmony,
        and have given your Son to be our Saviour, the Prince of Peace;
        grant that we, who are called by his name,
        may yield our lives to your service,
        and strive for reconciliation, understanding, and peace
        in all our relationships;
        for the sake of Jesus Christ our Lord.

COLLECT

213   Eternal God,
        in whose perfect realm
        no sword is drawn but the sword of justice,
        and no strength known but the power of love:
        guide and inspire all you seek your kingdom,
        that peoples and nations may find their security
        in the love which casts out fear;
        through Jesus Christ our Saviour.

INTERCESSION

214   Gracious God,
      we pray for peace in your world:
      for all national leaders,
      that they may have wisdom to know
      and courage to do what is right;
      for all men and women,
      that their hearts may be turned to yourself
      in the search for righteousness and truth;
      for those who are working
      to improve international relationships,
      that they may find the true way of reconciliation;
      for those who suffer as a result of war:
      the injured and disabled,
      the mentally distressed,
      the homeless and hungry,
      those who mourn their dead,
      and especially for those who are without hope or friend
      to sustain them in their grief.
      God of grace, here our prayer,
      through Jesus Christ the Prince of Peace
      and the Saviour of the World.

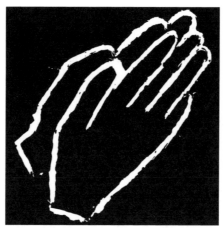

DEVOTIONAL PRAYERS
FOR DISCIPLES

215 Christ be with me, Christ within me,
Christ behind me, Christ before me,
Christ beside me, Christ to win me,
Christ to comfort and restore me,
Christ beneath me, Christ above me,
Christ in quiet, Christ in danger,
Christ in hearts of all that love me,
Christ in mouth of friend and stranger.

St Patrick's Breastplate

216 O Lord our God,
grant us grace to desire you with our whole heart;
that so desiring, we make seek and find you;
and so finding, may love you;
and so loving, may hate those sins
from which you have delivered us;
through Jesus Christ our Lord.

Anselm

217 O gracious and holy Father,
give us wisdom to perceive you,
diligence to seek you,
patience to wait for you,
eyes to behold you,
a heart to meditate upon you,
and a life to proclaim you,
through the power of the Spirit
of Jesus Christ our Lord.

Benedict of Nursia

218   Lord Jesus Christ, we thank you
      for all the benefits you have won for us,
      for all the pains and insults you have borne for us.
      Most merciful redeemer,
      friend and brother,
      may we know you more clearly
      love you more dearly
      and follow you more nearly,
      day by day.

after Richard of Chichester

219   God be in my head, and in my understanding;
      God be in my eyes and in my looking;
      God be in my mouth, and in my speaking;
      God be in my heart, and in my thinking;
      God be at mine end, and at my departing.

Sarum Primer

220   Eternal God,
      the light of the minds that know you,
      the joys of the hearts that love you,
      and the strength of the wills that serve you;
      grant us so to know you, that we may truly love you,
      and so to love you, that we may fully serve you,
      whom to serve is perfect freedom,
      in Jesus Christ our Lord.

Gelasian Sacramentary

221   Lord, make me an instrument of your peace.
      Where there is hatred, let me sow love,
      where there is injury, pardon;
      where there is doubt, faith;
      where there is despair, hope;
      where there is darkness, light;
      where there is sadness, joy.

      O divine master, grant that I may not so much seek
      to be consoled, as to console,
      to be understood, as to understand,
      to be loved, as to love.
      For it is in giving that we receive;
      it is in pardoning that we are pardoned;
      it is in dying that we are born to eternal life.

Francis of Assisi

222   Teach us, good Lord,
     to serve you as you deserve:
     to give and not to count the cost,
     to fight and not to heed the wounds,
     to toil and not to seek for rest,
     to labour and not to ask for any reward
     except our knowing that we do your will,
     through Jesus Christ our Lord.

Ignatius of Loyola

223   O Christ, the Master Carpenter,
     who at the last, through wood and nails,
     purchased our whole salvation,
     wield well your tools
     in the workshop of your world,
     so that we who come rough-hewn to your bench
     may be fashioned
     to a truer beauty of your hand.
     We ask it for your own name's sake.

Common Order

224   Lord, the house of my soul is narrow:
     enlarge it, that you may enter in.
     It is ruined:
     O repair it!
     It displeases you:
     I confess it, I know.
     But who shall cleanse it,
     to whom shall I cry but to you?
     Lord, cleanse me from my secret faults
     and spare your servant from strange sins.

Augustine of Hippo

225   If only I possessed the grace, good Jesus,
to be utterly at one with you!
Amidst all the variety of world things around me,
Lord, the only thing I crave is you.
You are all my soul needs.
Unite, dear friend of my heart,
this unique little soul of mine to your perfect goodness.
You are all mine;
when shall I be yours?
Lord Jesus, my beloved,
be the magnet of my heart;
clasp, press, unite me for ever to your sacred heart.
You have made me for yourself;
make me one with you.
Absorb this tiny drop of life
into the ocean of goodness from whence it came.

Francis de Sales

226   Grant us, Lord,
to know that which is worth knowing,
to love that which is worth loving,
to praise that which can bear with praise,
to hate that which in your sight is unworthy,
to prize what to you is precious,
and, above all,
to search out and to do what is pleasing to you,
though Jesus Christ our Lord.

Thomas à Kempis

227   Tender God,
gentle protector in time of trouble:
pierce the gloom of despair
and give us, with all your people,
the song of freedom and the shout of praise,
in Jesus Christ our Lord.

Michael Vasey

ACKNOWLEDGEMENTS

Every effort has been made to trace the owners of copyrights and obtain permission. But, as with other denominational worship books, material has often been drafted and revised by a number of people and sometimes the identity of original sources may have been lost. If we have infringed at any point we are sorry and will readily make amends in any future edition once our attention is drawn to it.

We readily express our thanks to all those copyright holders who have allowed us to use their work.

PART ONE
WORSHIP IN THE COMMUNITY OF DISCIPLES

GATHERING AND SENDING

GATHERING FOR CELEBRATION: THE LORD'S SUPPER

The Lord's Supper: a Simple Pattern
Invitation to the Table: 'Come to this table ...' W Barclay, *The Lord's Supper* SCM 1967.

Prayer: 'Almighty God ...' *Common Worship: Services and Prayers for the Church of England* is copyright © The Archbishops' Council, 2000 and extracts are reproduced by permission.

Words of Acclamation and Prayer: 'Your death, O Lord ...' *Common Worship: Services and Prayers for the Church of England* © The Archbishops' Council, 2000.

The Lord's Supper: an Ecumenical Pattern
Invitation to the Table: 'Come to this table ...' W Barclay, *The Lord's Supper* SCM 1967.

Confession: 'Almighty God ...' *Common Worship: Services and Prayers for the Church of England* © The Archbishops' Council, 2000.

The Lord's Supper: Hungering for Justice
Closing Responses: 'From where we are ...' *A Wee Worship Book*, Wild Goose Publications 1999, © WGRG, Iona Community, G2 3DH.

Additional Material
Prayers of Thanksgiving: 'Loving God ...' *Common Worship: Services and Prayers for the Church of England* © The Archbishops' Council, 2000.

WALKING TOGETHER

PRESENTING INFANTS AND CHILDREN

Presenting, Blessing and Dedicating
Promises: 'A, the Lord bless you and guard you …' *Common Order* © Panel on Worship, Church of Scotland.

Presenting and Blessing
Prayers: 'Faithful God …' Alec Gilmore in *Praise God* by Alec Gilmore, Edward Smalley and Michael Walker, Baptist Union of Great Britain 1980.

Additional Material
Prayers for the Child and Family: 'Loving God, you are father and mother …' A Gilmore, *Praise God*, as above;
'God of love, we rejoice in your faithfulness …' *Common Order* © Panel on Worship, Church of Scotland.

WELCOMING DISCIPLES

Baptizing Disciples
Declaration of Faith: 'Do you renounce …' Adapted from *Book of Occasional Services* © 1999 Presbyterian Church (USA) a Corporation for Congregational Ministries Division, Office of Theology and Worship. Used by permission of Geneva Press.

Baptism: 'I believe in God …' English translation of the Apostles' Creed copyright © 1988, by the English Language Liturgical Consultation.

Nurturing New Faith
'As we follow …' and 'Almighty God …' *Common Worship: Services and Prayers for the Church of England* © The Archbishops' Council, 2000.

Reaffirming Baptismal Vows
Declaration of Faith: 'I believe in God …' English translation of the Apostles' Creed copyright © 1988, by the English Language Liturgical Consultation; 'Do you believe …' The creed [CW p. 143] as it appears in *Common Worship: Services and Prayers for the Church of England* (Church House Publishing, 2000) is copyright © The English Language Liturgical Consultation and is reproduced by permission of the publisher.

Recognizing and Giving Thanks for Faithful Service
Based on a service in *Book of Occasional Services* © 1999 Presbyterian Church (USA), as above.

COVENANTING TOGETHER

Making and Renewing Covenant

We Believe: 'I believe in God …' English translation of the Apostles' Creed (amended) copyright © 1988, by the English Language Liturgical Consultation.

CALLING AND SERVING

ORDAINING FOR ACCREDITED MINISTRY

Ordination Prayer with the Laying on of Hands: 'Generous God …' Adapted from *Book of Occasional Services* © 1999 Presbyterian Church (USA), as above.

COMMISSION FOR SECTOR MINISTRY

Induction of a Chaplain into a Chaplaincy Team

Declaration and Blessing: 'The everlasting God …' © Iona Community, from *The Iona Community Worship Book*, 1998 (out of print) ISBN 0 94798 828 9, Wild Goose Publications, Glasgow G2 3DH www.ionabooks.com

LIVING AND CARING

ENTERING AND CELEBRATING CHRISTIAN MARRIAGE

First Pattern for Christian Marriage

Statement of Purpose: 'We are gathered …' *Common Order* © Panel on Worship, Church of Scotland;
'We gather in …' *Common Worship: Services and Prayers for the Church of England* © The Archbishops' Council, 2000.

Prayer: 'Gracious God …' *Common Order* © Panel on Worship, Church of Scotland.

Giving of Rings: 'God of steadfast love …' *Common Order* © Panel on Worship, Church of Scotland.

Marriage Blessing: 'Blessed be God the Father …' *Common Order* © Panel on Worship, Church of Scotland.

Prayers: 'By your grace …' Taken from *The Methodist Worship Book* © 1999 Trustees for Methodist Church Purposes used by permission of Methodist Publishing House;
'Gracious God …' *Common Order* © Panel on Worship, Church of Scotland.

Closing Worship and Blessing: 'The grace of Christ ...' *Book of Common Worship* © 1993 Westminster John Knox Press.

Second Pattern for Christian Marriage
Statement of Purpose: 'We have come together ...' *Common Order* © Panel on Worship, Church of Scotland.

Presentation for Marriage: 'Will you, the families ...' Taken from *The Methodist Worship Book* © 1999 Trustees for Methodist Church Purposes, as above.

Blessing a Civil Marriage
Statement of Purpose: 'We rejoice in the marriage ...' *Common Order* © Panel on Worship, Church of Scotland;
'A and C, you have already ...' Taken from *The Methodist Worship Book* © 1999 Trustees for Methodist Church Purposes, as above.

Prayer: 'Living God ...' *Common Worship: Services and Prayers for the Church of England* © The Archbishops' Council, 2000.

Reaffirmation of Marriage Vows: 'C, you are my wife ...' *Book of Common Worship* © 1993 Westminster John Knox Press.

Marriage Blessing: 'Blessed be God ...' *Common Order* © Panel on Worship, Church of Scotland.

CONFRONTING DEATH – CELEBRATING RESURRECTION

This chapter has drawn freely on *In Sure and Certain Hope*, © Paul Sheppy 2003, SCM-Canterbury Press.

First Funeral Pattern
Opening Prayer: 'Loving God ...' *Common Order* © Panel on Worship, Church of Scotland.

A Prayer Trilogy: 'To your loving care ...' *Common Order* © Panel on Worship, Church of Scotland.

Pattern for the Burial or Scattering of Ashes
Scripture Reading: 'The Lord is full ...' *Common Worship: Services and Prayers for the Church of England* © The Archbishops' Council, 2000.

Prayer: 'God our maker ...' *Common Worship: Services and Prayers for the Church of England* © The Archbishops' Council, 2000.

GATHERING AND PRAYING FOR HEALING

Notes: Adapted from *The Methodist Worship Book* © 1999 Trustees for Methodist Church Purposes, as above.

A Pattern for a Healing Service
Adapted from *The Methodist Worship Book* © 1999 Trustees for Methodist Church Purposes, as above.

Confession: 'Our Lord Jesus Christ …' Taken from *The Methodist Worship Book* © 1999 Trustees for Methodist Church Purposes, as above;
'Father eternal …' *Common Worship: Services and Prayers for the Church of England* © The Archbishops' Council, 2000;
'God is love …' Taken from *The Methodist Worship Book* © 1999 Trustees for Methodist Church Purposes, as above;
'Almighty God …' *Common Worship: Services and Prayers for the Church of England* © The Archbishops' Council, 2000.

Laying on of Hands: 'May the Spirit …' Taken from *The Methodist Worship Book* © 1999 Trustees for Methodist Church Purposes, as above.

A Pattern of Prayer for Healing in People and Places, in Church and World
Confession: 'We confess to …' © Iona Community, from *The Iona Community Worship Book* 1998, as above.

Additional Material
Confession: 'Lord Jesus …' Taken from *The Methodist Worship Book* © 1999 Trustees for Methodist Church Purposes, as above.

Blessing: 'I bless you …' from *Carmina Gadelica* by Alexander Carmichael (1899), by permission of Flora Books;
'May the Father …' *Celtic Daily Prayer* © 2000 The Northumbria Community Trust Ltd.

PART TWO
PRAYERS IN THE COMMUNITY OF DISCIPLES

COMMUNITY IN PRAYER

2   'This is the place …' *New Prayers for Worship* Alan Gaunt © 1973.

36   'Glory to God …' © 1990 English Language Liturgical Consultation.

47   'Merciful God …' Adapted from *Contemporary Prayers for Public Worship* SCM Press 1967.

48 'Most merciful God …' *Common Worship: Services and Prayers for the Church of England* © The Archbishops' Council, 2000.

49 'Almighty God …' *Common Worship: Services and Prayers for the Church of England* © The Archbishops' Council, 2000.

55 'We confess …' from *Be Our Freedom Lord* prepared and edited by Terry C Falla, Openbook Publishers, Adelaide, Australia, second edition © 1994 p.139, which was originally based on material from Caryl Micklem *Contemporary Prayers for Public Worship* © SCM Press 1967.

61 'God, the Father …' *Common Worship: Services and Prayers for the Church of England* © The Archbishops' Council, 2000.

63 'Almighty God …' *Common Worship: Services and Prayers for the Church of England* © The Archbishops' Council, 2000.

67 'Our God …' Adapted from material by Terry C Falla and Mike Riddell in *Be Our Freedom Lord* prepared and edited by Terry C Falla, Openbook Publishers, Adelaide, Australia, second edition © 1994.

70 'Why, God …' *Be Our Freedom Lord* prepared and edited by Terry C Falla, Openbook Publishers, Adelaide, Australia, second edition © 1994.

71 'Almighty God …' from *Be Our Freedom Lord* prepared and edited by Terry C Falla, Openbook Publishers, Adelaide, Australia, second edition © 1994 p.112, which was originally adapted from Dietrich Bonhoeffer in *Congremur* edited by the Youth Department of the World Council of Churches, Geneva, revised © 1967.

72 'Eternal God …' *Be Our Freedom Lord* prepared and edited by Terry C Falla, Openbook Publishers, Adelaide, Australia, second edition © 1994. Material by Terry C Falla based on a theme and phrases from Michael Leunig Collins Dove Publishers, Blackburn, Victoria, Australia, © 1991.

76 'For all the saints …' Janet Morley in *Bread of Tomorrow*, Christian Aid 1992.

83 'God of kindness …' *Common Order* © Panel on Worship, Church of Scotland.

85 'Holy God …' From *A Wee Worship Book*, Wild Goose Publications 1999, © 1999, WGRG, as above.

86 'Father we thank you …' John Pritchard, *The Intercessions Handbook* © SPCK 1997.

87 'Let us come …' John Pritchard, *The Intercessions Handbook* © SPCK 1997.

88 'Our minds are …' John Pritchard, *The Intercessions Handbook* © SPCK 1997.

89   'Almighty God …' *Common Order* © Panel on Worship, Church of Scotland.

91   'God of grace …' *Common Order* © Panel on Worship, Church of Scotland.

94   'Show us …' *Contemporary Prayers for Public Worship* SCM Press 1967.

97   'God of unfailing …' Adapted from *Common Order* © Panel on Worship, Church of Scotland.

102   'Lord, make time …' *Danger! People at Prayer!* Congregational Prayer Fellowship Handbook 1972.

103   'For each new …' *Danger! People at Prayer!* Congregational Prayer Fellowship Handbook 1972.

117   'From where we are …' *A Wee Worship Book*, Wild Goose Publications 1999, © 1999, WGRG, as above.

118   'From where we are …' *A Wee Worship Book*, Wild Goose Publications 1999, © 1999, WGRG, as above.

119   'For all that God …' *A Wee Worship Book*, Wild Goose Publications 1999, © 1999, WGRG, as above.

122   'May God bless …' *A Wee Worship Book*, Wild Goose Publications 1999, © 1999, WGRG, Iona Community, G2 3DH.

123   'On our heads …' *A Wee Worship Book*, Wild Goose Publications 1999, © 1999, WGRG, as above.

124   'Now may the …' *A Wee Worship Book*, Wild Goose Publications 1999, © 1999, WGRG, as above.

DISCIPLES ON THE WAY: WORSHIP THROUGH THE YEAR

130   'Lord God …' *Contemporary Prayers for Public Worship* SCM Press 1967.

131   'Lord Jesus Christ …' *Common Order* © Panel on Worship, Church of Scotland.

134   'God of eternity …' *Common Order* © Panel on Worship, Church of Scotland.

136   'God of faithfulness …' *Common Order* © Panel on Worship, Church of Scotland.

137 'God our Deliverer ...' Janet Morley in *All Desires Known*, 1992, by permission of SPCK.

138 'Living God ...' *New Prayers for Worship*, Alan Gaunt © 1973.

140 'Lord, prepare us ...' John Pritchard, *The Intercessions Handbook* © SPCK 1997.

141 'Look forward ...' *Common Order* © Panel on Worship, Church of Scotland.

143 'God of light ...' based on a prayer by Gordon Nodwell in *Worship for All Seasons 1*, volume 1, Thomas Harding, ed., The United Church Publishing House, 1993. Used with permission.

145 'Living God ...' David Jenkins in *Seasons and Celebrations* compiled by Donald Hilton, National Christian Education Council, 1996, 1998. Reproduced with permission.

148 'Lord of history ...' from *The Methodist Worship Book* © 1999 Trustees for Methodist Church Purposes, as above.

152 'Star child ...' Kate Compston in *Seasons and Celebrations* compiled by Donald Hilton, National Christian Education Council, 1996, 1998. Reproduced with permission.

153 'Journeying God ...' Kate Compston in *Seasons and Celebrations* compiled by Donald Hilton, National Christian Education Council, 1996, 1998. Reproduced with permission.

154 'Beckoning God ...' Kate Compston in *Seasons and Celebrations* compiled by Donald Hilton, National Christian Education Council, 1996, 1998. Reproduced with permission.

156 'Almighty God ...' from *The Alternative Service Book 1980* © The Central Board of Finance of the Church of England, 1980; the Archbishops' Council, 1999. Reproduced by permission.

161 'Lord, we remember ...' Michael Walker in *Praise God*, as above. Used by permission of Mrs A M Walker.

163 'Lord of Lent ...' John Pritchard, *The Intercessions Handbook* © SPCK 1997.

164 'Lord, lead us ...' Michael Walker in *Praise God*, as above. Used by permission of Mrs A M Walker.

166 'God, father and mother ...' Jamie Wallace, *There's a Time and Place* in *Praise God*, as above. Used by permission of Mrs R Wallace.

167 'God of compassion ...' *Common Worship: Services and Prayers for the Church of England* © The Archbishops' Council, 2000.

170 'O Christ ...' Janet Morley in *Bread of Tomorrow*, Christian Aid 1992

172 'Lord, with joy ...' Michael Walker in *Praise God*, as above. Used by permission of Mrs A M Walker.

174 'Living God ...' *New Prayers for Worship* Alan Gaunt © 1973.

177 'Christ is risen ...' © Fellowship of St Alban and St Sergius.

179 'When we are ...' Janet Morley in *Bread of Tomorrow*, Christian Aid 1992.

180 'Dear Father ...' *Contemporary Prayers for Public Worship*, SCM Press 1967.

183 'God, so near ...' *New Prayers for Worship*, Alan Gaunt © 1973.

184 'Almighty God ...' *Common Order* © Panel on Worship, Church of Scotland.

185 'Forgive us ...' Michael Walker in *Praise God*, as above. Used by permission of Mrs A M Walker.

186 'When we stand ...' *Bread of Tomorrow*, Christian Aid 1992.

194 'Living Love ...' *Book of Christian Prayer*, SPCK 1995.

195 'Holy, holy ...' *Common Order* © Panel on Worship, Church of Scotland.

196 'Holy God ...' *Common Worship: Services and Prayers for the Church of England* © The Archbishops' Council, 2000.

198 'Ever One ...' John Pritchard, *The Intercessions Handbook* © SPCK 1997.

200 'God of faithfulness ...' *Common Order* © Panel on Worship, Church of Scotland.

213 'Eternal God ...' *Celebrating Common Prayer* (Mowbray), © Society of St Francis, 1992. Used with permission.

214 'Gracious God ...' *Book of Christian Prayer*, SPCK 1995.

DEVOTIONAL PRAYERS FOR DISCIPLES

223   'O Christ …' *Common Order* © Panel on Worship, Church of Scotland.

224   'Lord, the house …' *Book of Christian Prayer*, SPCK 1995.

225   'If only I …' *Book of Christian Prayer*, SPCK 1995.

226   'Grant us, Lord …' *Book of Christian Prayer*, SPCK 1995.

227   'Tender God …' *Book of Christian Prayer*, SPCK 1995.